Best Loved Poems

GEOFFREY CHAUCER

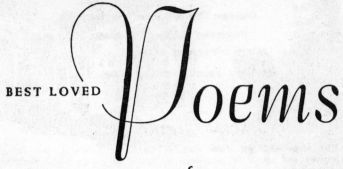

BEST LOVED *Poems*

of

Best Loved Poets

With

SEVENTEEN ORIGINAL ILLUSTRATIONS BY

Chauncey Maltman

The Spencer Press, Inc.

CHICAGO

ACKNOWLEDGMENTS

The editor and publishers wish to thank the following publishers, authors, and agents for permission to reprint the poems in the modern poetry supplement of this book.

BRANDT & BRANDT—for "God's World" by Edna St. Vincent Millay from RENASCENCE AND OTHER POEMS, published by Harper & Brothers, copyright 1913, 1941 by Edna St. Vincent Millay.

E. P. DUTTON & COMPANY, INC.—for the first and last stanzas of "America the Beautiful" by Katharine Lee Bates, from POEMS, published by E. P. Dutton & Co., Inc.

HARCOURT, BRACE AND COMPANY, INC.—for "Evening Waterfall" by Carl Sandburg, from SMOKE AND STEEL by Carl Sandburg, copyright 1920, by Harcourt, Brace and Company, Inc.; renewed by Carl Sandburg.

HENRY HOLT AND COMPANY, INC.—for "The Listeners" from COLLECTED POEMS by Walter de la Mare, copyright 1920, by Henry Holt and Company, Inc., copyright 1948 by Walter de la Mare; "Mending Wall" from COMPLETE POEMS OF ROBERT FROST, copyright 1930, 1949 by Henry Holt and Company, Inc., "Loveliest of Trees" from A SHROPSHIRE LAD by A. E. Housman.

J. B. LIPPINCOTT COMPANY—for "The Barrel-Organ" by Alfred Noyes from COLLECTED POEMS, Vol. 1, by Alfred Noyes, copyright 1913, 1941, by Alfred Noyes, published by the J. B. Lippincott Company.

THE MACMILLAN COMPANY—for "West Wind" by John Masefield from COLLECTED POEMS; "The Master" by Edwin Arlington Robinson from COLLECTED POEMS; "Spring Night" by Sara Teasdale from COLLECTED POEMS; "Lake Isle of Innisfree" by William Butler Yeats from COLLECTED POEMS.

Juanita Miller—for permission to reprint the poem "Columbus" by Joaquin Miller.

G. P. PUTNAM'S SONS—for "To a Wanderer" by Jake Falstaff from BULLS of SPRING.

Foreword

THIS excellent collection of familiar verse includes not only the time-less lyrics of such Olympian bards as Shakespeare and Shelley, but the works of the "humbler poets"—minor masterpieces which we have all known from childhood, though the names of the poets have all but faded from our memory.

Here are Elizabeth Barrett Browning's immortal "Sonnets from the Portuguese," with their tender enumeration of the ways of love; and here, too, is her husband Robert's haunting tale, "The Pied Piper of Hamelin." Here is the entire text of Coleridge's enchanting "Rime of the Ancient Mariner" and of Fitzgerald's matchless translation of the *Rubaiyat* of Omar. Here is Gray's stately, somber "Elegy" and Shelley's mighty lament on the death of Keats. And, among more than a hundred lesser pieces, the stirring ballads of Kipling, Scott, and Macaulay; the irresistible jingles of Edward Lear and William Schwenck Gilbert; Tennyson's grim memorial of Balaclava, "The Charge of the Light Brigade"; Clement Moore's "Visit from St. Nicholas" ("The Night Before Christmas"), a unique contribution to our literary folklore; and gemlike lyrics by Spenser, Shakespeare, Swinburne, Poe, and many others.

Mingled with these classics is a rich assortment of sentimental lyrics and ballads; the lilting love songs of Tom Moore, Stephen Foster's old plantation ballads, George Pope Morris' plea to the woodman, and Samuel Woodworth's nostalgic recollection of the "moss-cover'd bucket, which hung in the well."

These are the poems which people like to clip out of magazines and newspapers and which they cherish for years in scrapbooks and albums. These are the poems we read and commit to memory; poems we quote at the fireside or even on the battlefield. These are poems which have become part of our everyday living.

Authors

Contents

[ALPHABETICALLY ARRANGED]

Contents

Contents

Contents

Portraits

Contents

ANONYMOUS

ATTAINMENT

With every rising of the sun,
Think of your life as just begun,
The past has cancelled and buried deep
All yesterdays: there let them sleep.
Concern yourself with but today;
Grasp it and teach it to obey
Your will and plan.
Since time began, today has been
The friend of man.
You and today: a soul sublime
And the great heritage of time.
With God himself to bid the twain,
"Go forth, brave heart; attain! Attain!

NAVAJO SONG
WALK ON THE RAINBOW TRAIL

Walk on a Rainbow Trail;
Walk on a Trail of Song,
And all about you will be beauty.
There is a way
Out of every dark mist—
    Over a Rainbow Trail!

JOSEPH ADDISON

THE SPACIOUS FIRMAMENT ON HIGH

The spacious firmament on high,
With all the blue ethereal sky,
And spangled heavens, a shining frame,
Their great Original proclaim.

The unwearied sun, from day to day,
Does his Creator's power display,
And publishes to every land
The work of an Almighty hand.

Soon as the evening shades prevail,
The moon takes up the wondrous tale,
And nightly to the listening earth
Repeats the story of her birth;
Whilst all the stars that round her burn,
And all the planets in their turn,
Confirm the tidings as they roll,
And spread the truth from pole to pole.

What though, in solemn silence, all
Move round this dark terrestrial ball?
What though no real voice nor sound
Amid their radiant orbs be found?
In Reason's ear they all rejoice,
And utter forth a glorious voice,
Forever singing, as they shine,
"The hand that made us is divine!"

ELIZABETH BARRETT BROWNING

A MUSICAL INSTRUMENT

What was he doing, the great god Pan,
  Down in the reeds by the river?
Spreading ruin and scattering ban,
Splashing and paddling with hoofs of a goat,
And breaking the golden lilies afloat
  With the dragon-fly on the river?

He tore out a reed, the great god Pan,
  From the deep cool bed of the river.
The limpid water turbidly ran,

And the broken lilies a-dying lay,
And the dragon-fly had fled away,
  Ere he brought it out of the river.

High on the shore sate the great god Pan,
  While turbidly flowed the river,
And hacked and hewed as a great god can,
With his hard bleak steel at the patient reed,
Till there was not a sign of a leaf indeed
  To prove it fresh from the river.

He cut it short, did the great god Pan,
  (How tall it stood in the river!),
Then drew the pith, like the heart of a man,
Steadily from the outside ring,
Then notched the poor dry empty thing
  In holes as he sate by the river.

"This is the way," laughed the great god Pan,
  (Laughed while he sate by the river!)
"The only way since gods began
To make sweet music they could succeed."
Then, dropping his mouth to a hole in the reed,
  He blew in power by the river.

Sweet, sweet, sweet, O Pan,
  Piercing sweet by the river!
Blinding sweet, O great god Pan!
The sun on the hill forgot to die,
And the lilies revived, and the dragon-fly
  Came back to dream on the river.

Yet half a beast is the great god Pan
  To laugh, as he sits by the river,
Making a poet out of a man.
The true gods sigh for the cost and pain—
For the reed that grows nevermore again
  As a reed with the reeds in the river.

SONNETS FROM THE PORTUGUESE

I

I THOUGHT once how Theocritus had sung
Of the sweet years, the dear and wished-for years,
Who each one in a gracious hand appears
To bear a gift for mortals, old or young;
And, as I mused it in his antique tongue,
I saw, in gradual vision through my tears,
The sweet, sad years, the melancholy years,
Those of my own life, who by turns had flung
A shadow across me. Straightway I was 'ware,
So weeping, how a mystic Shape did move
Behind me, and drew me backward by the hair;
And a voice said in mastery, while I strove,—
"Guess now who holds thee?"—"Death," I said. But, there,
The silver answer rang,—"Not Death, but Love."

II

BUT only three in all God's universe
Have heard this word thou has said,—Himself, beside
Thee speaking, and me listening! and replied
One of us . . . *that* was God, . . . and laid the curse
So darkly on my eyelids, as to amerce
My sight from seeing thee,—that if I had died,
The deathweights, placed there, would have signified
Less absolute exclusion. "Nay" is worse
From God than from all others, O my friend!
Men could not part us with their worldly jars,
Nor the seas change us, nor the tempests bend;
Our hands would touch for all the mountain-bars:
And, heaven being rolled between us at the end,
We should but vow the faster for the stars.

III

UNLIKE are we, unlike, O princely Heart!
Unlike our uses and our destinies.
Our ministering two angels look surprise
On one another, as they strike athwart

Their wings in passing. Thou, bethink thee, art
A guest for queens to social pageantries,
With gages from a hundred brighter eyes
Than tears even can make mine, to play thy part
Of chief musician. What hast *thou* to do
With looking from the lattice-lights at me,
A poor, tired, wandering singer, singing through
The dark, and leaning up a cypress tree?
The chrism is on thine head,—on mine, the dew,—
And Death must dig the level where these agree.

IV

THOU hast thy calling to some palace-floor,
Most gracious singer of high poems! where
The dancers will break footing, from the care
Of watching up thy pregnant lips for more.
And dost thou lift this house's latch too poor
For hand of thine? and canst thou think and bear
To let thy music drop here unaware
In folds of golden fulness at my door?
Look up and see the casement broken in,
The bats and owlets builders in the roof!
My cricket chirps against thy mandolin.
Hush, call no echo up in further proof
Of desolation! there's a voice within
That weeps ... as thou must sing ... alone, aloof.

V

I LIFT my heavy heart up solemnly,
As once Electra her sepulchral urn,
And, looking in thine eyes, I overturn
The ashes at thy feet. Behold and see
What a great heap of grief lay hid in me,
And how the red wild sparkles dimly burn
Through the ashen greyness. If thy foot in scorn
Could tread them out to darkness utterly,
It might be well perhaps. But if instead
Thou wait beside me for the wind to blow
The grey dust up, ... those laurels on thine head,

O my Belovëd, will not shield thee so,
That none of all the fires shall scorch and shred
The hair beneath. Stand farther off then! go.

VI

Go from me. Yet I feel that I shall stand
Henceforward in thy shadow. Nevermore
Alone upon the threshold of my door
Of individual life, I shall command
The uses of my soul, nor lift my hand
Serenely in the sunshine as before,
Without the sense of that which I forbore—
Thy touch upon the palm. The widest land
Doom takes to part us, leaves thy heart in mine
With pulses that beat double. What I do
And what I dream include thee, as the wine
Must taste of its own grapes. And when I sue
God for myself, He hears that name of thine,
And sees within my eyes the tears of two.

VII

The face of all the world is changed, I think,
Since first I heard the footsteps of thy soul
Move still, oh, still, beside me, as they stole
Betwixt me and the dreadful outer brink
Of obvious death, where I, who thought to sink,
Was caught up into love, and taught the whole
Of life in a new rhythm. The cup of dole
God gave for baptism, I am fain to drink,
And praise its sweetness, Sweet, with thee anear.
The names of country, heaven, are changed away
For where thou art or shalt be, there or here;
And this . . . this lute and song . . . loved yesterday,
(The singing angels know) are only dear
Because thy name moves right in what they say.

VIII

What can I give thee back, O liberal
And princely giver, who hast brought the gold

And purple of thine heart, unstained, untold,
And laid them on the outside of the wall
For such as I to take or leave withal,
In unexpected largesse? am I cold,
Ungrateful, that for these most manifold
High gifts, I render nothing back at all?
Not so; not cold,—but very poor instead.
Ask God who knows. For frequent tears have run
The colours from my life, and left so dead
And pale a stuff, it were not fitly done
To give the same as pillow to thy head.
Go farther! let it serve to trample on.

IX

CAN it be right to give what I can give?
To let thee sit beneath the fall of tears
As salt as mine, and hear the sighing years
Re-sighing on my lips renunciative
Through those infrequent smiles which fail to live
For all thy adjurations? O my fears,
That this can scarce be right! We are not peers,
So to be lovers; and I own, and grieve,
That givers of such gifts as mine are, must
Be counted with the ungenerous. Out, alas!
I will not soil thy purple with my dust,
Nor breathe my poison on thy Venice-glass,
Nor give thee any love—which were unjust.
Beloved, I only love thee! let it pass.

X

YET, love, mere love, is beautiful indeed
And worthy of acceptation. Fire is bright,
Let temple burn, or flax; an equal light
Leaps in the flame from cedar-plank or weed:
And love is fire. And when I say at need
I love thee ... mark! ... *I love thee*—in thy sight
I stand transfigured, glorified aright,
With conscience of the new rays that proceed
Out of my face toward thine. There's nothing low

In love, when love the lowest: meanest creatures
Who love God, God accepts while loving so.
And what I *feel,* across the inferior features
Of what I *am,* doth flash itself, and show
How that great work of Love enhances Nature's.

XI

And therefore if to love can be desert,
I am not all unworthy. Cheeks as pale
As these you see, and trembling knees that fail
To bear the burden of a heavy heart,—
This weary minstrel-life that once was girt
To climb Aornus, and can scarce avail
To pipe now 'gainst the valley nightingale
A melancholy music,—why advert
To these things? O Belovëd, it is plain
I am not of thy worth nor for thy place!
And yet, because I love thee, I obtain
From that same love this vindicating grace,
To live on still in love, and yet in vain,—
To bless thee, yet renounce thee to thy face.

XII

Indeed this very love which is my boast,
And which, when rising up from breast to brow,
Doth crown me with a ruby large enow
To draw men's eyes and prove the inner cost,—
This love even, all my worth, to the uttermost,
I should not love withal, unless that thou
Hadst set me an example, shown me how,
When first thine earnest eyes with mine were crossed,
And love called love. And thus, I cannot speak
Of love even, as a good thing of my own:
Thy soul hath snatched up mine all faint and weak,
And placed it by thee on a golden throne,—
And that I love (O soul, we must be meek!)
Is by thee only, whom I love alone.

XIII

AND wilt thou have me fashion into speech
The love I bear thee, finding words enough,
And hold the torch out, while the winds are **rough**,
Between our faces, to cast light on each?—
I drop at thy feet. I cannot teach
My hand to hold my spirit so far off
From myself—me—that I should bring thee **proof**
In words, of love hid in me out of reach.
Nay, let the silence of my womanhood
Commend my woman-love to thy belief,—
Seeing that I stand unwon, however wooed,
And rend the garment of my life, in brief,
By a most dauntless, voiceless fortitude,
Lest one touch of this heart convey its grief.

XIV

IF thou must love me, let it be for nought
Except for love's sake only. Do not say
"I love her for her smile—her look—her way
Of speaking gently,—for a trick of thought
That falls in well with mine, and certes brought
A sense of pleasant ease on such a day"—
For these things in themselves, Belovëd, may
Be changed, or change for thee,—and love, so **wrought**,
May be unwrought so. Neither love me for
Thine own dear pity's wiping my cheeks dry,—
A creature might forget to weep, who bore
Thy comfort long, and lose thy love thereby!
But love me for love's sake, that evermore
Thou may'st love on, through love's eternity.

XV

ACCUSE me not, beseech thee, that I wear
Too calm and sad a face in front of thine;
For we two look two ways, and cannot shine
With the same sunlight on our brow and hair.
On me thou lookest with no doubting care,

As on a bee shut in a crystalline;
Since sorrow hath shut me safe in love's divine,
And to spread wing and fly in the outer air
Were most impossible failure, if I strove
To fail so. But I look on thee—on thee—
Beholding, besides love, the end of love,
Hearing oblivion beyond memory;
As one who sits and gazes from above,
Over the rivers to the bitter sea.

XVI

AND yet, because thou overcomest so,
Because thou art more noble and like a king,
Thou canst prevail against my fears and fling
Thy purple round me, till my heart shall grow
Too close against thine heart henceforth to know
How it shook when alone. Why, conquering
May prove as lordly and complete a thing
In lifting upward, as in crushing low!
And as a vanquished soldier yields his sword
To one who lifts him from the bloody earth;
Even so, Belovëd, I at last record,
Here ends my strife. If *thou* invite me forth,
I rise above abasement at the word.
Make thy love larger to enlarge my worth.

XVII

MY poet, thou canst touch on all the notes
God set between His After and Before,
And strike up and strike off the general roar
Of the rushing worlds a melody that floats
In a serene air purely. Antidotes
Of medicated music, answering for
Mankind's forlornest uses, thou canst pour
From thence into their ears. God's will devotes
Thine to such ends, and mine to wait on thine.
How, Dearest, wilt thou have me for most use?
A hope, to sing by gladly? or a fine

Sad memory, with thy songs to interfuse?
A shade, in which to sing—of palm or pine?
A grave, on which to rest from singing? Choose.

XVIII

I NEVER gave a lock of hair away
To a man, Dearest, except this to thee,
Which now upon my fingers thoughtfully,
I ring out to the full brown length and say
"Take it." My day of youth went yesterday;
My hair no longer bounds to my foot's glee,
Nor plant I it from rose or myrtle-tree,
As girls do, any more: it only may
Now shade on two pale cheeks the mark of tears,
Taught drooping from the head that hangs aside
Through sorrow's trick. I thought the funeral-shears
Would take this first, but Love is justified,—
Take it thou,—finding pure, from all those years,
The kiss my mother left here when she died.

XIX

THE soul's Rialto hath its merchandise;
I barter curl for curl upon that mart,
And from my poet's forehead to my heart
Receive this lock which outweighs argosies,—
As purply black, as erst to Pindar's eyes
The dim purpureal tresses gloomed athwart
The nine white Muse-brows. For this counterpart, . . .
The bay-crown's shade, Belovèd, I surmise,
Still lingers on thy curl, it so black!
Thus, with a fillet of smooth-kissing breath,
I tie the shadows safe from gliding back,
And lay the gift where nothing hindereth;
Here on my heart, as on thy brow, to lack
No natural heat till mine grows cold in death.

XX

BELOVÈD, my Belovèd, when I think
That thou wast in the world a year ago,

What time I sat alone here in the snow
And saw no footprint, heard the silence sink
No moment at thy voice, but, link by link,
Went counting all my chains as if that so
They never could fall off at any blow
Struck by thy possible hand,—why, thus I drink
Of life's great cup of wonder! Wonderful,
Never to feel thee thrill the day or night
With personal act or speech,—nor ever cull
Some prescience of thee with the blossoms white
Thou sawest growing! Atheists are as dull
Who cannot guess God's presence out of sight.

XXI

SAY over again, and yet once over again,
That thou dost love me. Though the word repeated
Should seem "a cuckoo-song," as thou dost treat it,
Remember, never to the hill or plain,
Valley and wood, without her cuckoo-strain
Comes the fresh Spring in all her green completed,
Belovèd, I, amid the darkness greeted
By a doubtful spirit-voice, in that doubt's pain
Cry, "Speak once more—thou lovest!" Who can fear
Too many stars, though each in heaven shall roll,
Too many flowers, though each shall crown the year?
Say thou dost love me, love me, love me—toll
The silver iterance!—only minding, Dear,
To love me also in silence with thy soul.

XXII

WHEN our two souls stand up erect and strong,
Face to face, silent, drawing nigh and nigher,
Until the lengthening wings break into fire
At either curvèd point,—what bitter wrong
Can the earth do to us, that we should not long
Be here contented? Think. In mounting higher,
The angels would press on us and aspire
To drop some golden orb of perfect song

Into our deep, dear silence. Let us stay
Rather on earth, Belovëd,—where the unfit
Contrarious moods of men recoil away
And isolate pure spirits, and permit
A place to stand and love in for a day,
With darkness and the death-hour rounding it.

XXIII

Is it indeed so? If I lay here dead,
Wouldst thou miss any life in losing mine?
And would the sun for thee more coldly shine
Because of grave-damps falling round my head?
I marvelled, my Belovëd, when I read
Thy thought so in the letter. I am thine—
But . . . *so* much to thee? Can I pour thy wine
While my hands tremble? Then my soul, instead
Of dreams of death, resumes life's lower range.
Then, love me, Love! Look on me—breathe on me!
As brighter ladies do not count it strange,
For love, to give up acres and degree,
I yield the grave for thy sake, and exchange
My near sweet view of Heaven, for earth with thee!

XXIV

LET the world's sharpness, like a clasping knife,
Shut in upon itself and do no harm
In this close hand of Love, now soft and warm,
And let us hear no sound of human strife
After the click of the shutting. Life to life—
I lean upon thee, Dear, without alarm,
And feel as safe as guarded by a charm
Against the stab of worldlings, who if rife
Are weak to injure. Very whitely still
The lilies of our lives may reassure
Their blossoms from their roots, accessible
Alone to heavenly dews that drop not fewer;
Growing straight, out of man's reach, on the hill.
God only, who made us rich, can make us poor.

XXV

A HEAVY heart, Belovëd, have I borne
From year to year until I saw thy face,
And sorrow after sorrow took the place
Of all those natural joys as lightly worn
As the stringed pearls, each lifted in its turn
By a beating heart at dance-time. Hopes apace
Were changed to long despairs, till God's own grace
Could scarcely lift above the world forlorn
My heavy heart. Then *thou* didst bid me bring
And let it drop adown thy calmly great
Deep being! Fast it sinketh, as a thing
Which its own nature doth precipitate,
While thine doth close above it, mediating
Betwixt the stars and the unaccomplished fate.

XXVI

I LIVED with visions for my company
Instead of men and women, years ago,
And found them gentle mates, nor thought to know
A sweeter music than they played to me.
But soon their trailing purple was not free
Of this world's dust, their lutes did silent grow,
And I myself grew faint and blind below
Their vanishing eyes. Then THOU didst come—to be,
Belovëd, what they seemed. Their shining fronts,
Their songs, their splendours (better, yet the same,
As river-water hallowed into fonts),
Met in thee, and from out thee overcame
My soul with satisfaction of all wants:
Because God's gifts put man's best dreams to shame.

XXVII

My own Belovëd, who hast lifted me
From this drear flat of earth where I was thrown,
And, in betwixt the languid ringlets, blown
A life-breath, till the forehead hopefully
Shines out again, as all the angels see,

Before thy saving kiss! My own, my own,
Who camest to me when the world was gone,
And I who looked for only God, found *thee!*
I find thee; I am safe, and strong, and glad.
As one who stands in dewless asphodel
Looks backward on the tedious time he had
In the upper life,—so I, with bosom-swell,
Make witness, here, between the good and bad,
That Love, as strong as Death, retrieves as well.

XXVIII

My letters! all dead paper, mute and white!
And yet they seem alive and quivering
Against my tremulous hands which loose the string
And let them drop down on my knee to-night,
This said,—he wished to have me in his sight
Once, as a friend: this fixed a day in spring
To come and touch my hand . . . a simple thing,
Yet I wept for it!—this, . . . the paper's light . . .
Said, *Dear, I love thee;* and I sank and quailed
As if God's future thundered on my past.
This said, *I am thine*—and so its ink has paled
With lying at my heart that beat too fast.
And this . . . O Love, thy words have ill availed
If, what this said, I dared repeat at last!

XXIX

I THINK of thee!—my thoughts do twine and bud
About thee, as wild vines, about a tree,
Put out broad leaves, and soon there's nought to see
Except the straggling green which hides the wood.
Yet, O my palm-tree, be it understood
I will not have my thoughts instead of thee
Who art dearer, better! Rather, instantly
Renew thy presence; as a strong tree should,
Rustle thy boughs and set thy trunk all bare,
And let these bands of greenery which insphere thee
Drop heavily down,—burst, shattered, everywhere!

Because, in this deep joy to see and hear thee
And breathe within thy shadow a new air,
I do not think of thee—I am too near thee.

XXX

I SEE thine image through my tears to-night,
And yet to-day I saw thee smiling. How
Refer the cause?—Belovëd, is it thou
Or I, who makes me sad? The acolyte
Amid the chanted joy and thankful rite
May so fall flat, with pale insensate brow
On the altar-stair. I hear thy voice and vow,
Perplexed, uncertain, since thou art out of sight,
As he, in his swooning ears, the choir's amen.
Belovëd, dost thou love? or did I see all
The glory as I dreamed, and fainted when
Too vehement light dilated my ideal,
For my soul's eyes? Will that light come again,
As now these tears come—falling hot and real?

XXXI

THOU comest! all is said without a word.
I sit beneath thy looks, as children do
In the noon-sun, with souls that tremble through
Their happy eyelids from an unaverred
Yet prodigal inward joy. Behold, I erred
In that last doubt! and yet I cannot rue
The sin most, but the occasion—that we two
Should for a moment stand unministered
By a mutual presence. Ah, keep near and close,
Thou dovelike help! and, when my fears would rise,
With thy broad heart serenely interpose:
Brood down with thy divine sufficiencies
These thoughts which tremble when bereft of those,
Like callow birds left desert to the skies.

XXXII

THE first time that the sun rose on thine oath
To love me, I looked forward to the moon

To slacken all those bonds which seemed too soon
And quickly tied to make a lasting troth.
Quick-loving hearts, I thought, may quickly loathe;
And, looking on myself, I seemed not one
For such man's love!—more like an out-of-tune
Worn viol, a good singer would be wroth
To spoil his song with, and which, snatched in haste,
Is laid down at the first ill-sounding note.
I did not wrong myself so, but I placed
A wrong on *thee*. For perfect strains may float
'Neath master-hands, from instruments defaced,—
And great souls, at one stroke, may do and doat.

XXXIII

Yes, call me by my pet-name! let me hear
The name I used to run at, when a child,
From innocent play, and leave the cowslips piled,
To glance up in some face that proved me dear
With the look of its eyes. I miss the clear
Fond voices which, being drawn and reconciled
Into the music of Heaven's undefiled,
Call me no longer. Silence on the bier,
While I call God—call God!—So let thy mouth
Be heir to those who are now exanimate.
Gather the north flowers to complete the south,
And catch the early love up in the late.
Yes, call me by that name,—and I, in truth,
With the same heart, will answer and not wait.

XXXIV

With the same heart, I said, I'll answer thee
As those, when thou shalt call me by my name—
Lo, the vain promise! is the same, the same,
Perplexed and ruffled by life's strategy?
When called before, I told how hastily
I dropped my flowers or brake off from a game,
To run and answer with the smile that came
At play last moment, and went on with me
Through my obedience. When I answer now,

I drop a grave thought, break from solitude;
Yet still my heart goes to thee—ponder how—
Not as to a single good, but all my good!
Lay thy hand on it, best one, and allow
That no child's foot could run fast as this blood.

XXXV

IF I leave all for thee, wilt thou exchange
And be all to me? Shall I never miss
Home-talk and blessing and the common kiss
That comes to each in turn, nor count it strange,
When I look up, to drop on a new range
Of walls and floors, another home than this?
Nay, wilt thou fill that place by me which is
Filled by dead eyes too tender to know change?
That's hardest. If to conquer love, has tried,
To conquer grief, tries more, as all things prove;
For grief indeed is love and grief beside.
Alas, I have grieved so I am hard to love.
Yet love me—wilt thou? Open thine heart wide,
And fold within the wet wings of thy dove.

XXXVI

WHEN we met first and loved, I did not build
Upon the event with marble. Could it mean
To last, a love set pendulous between
Sorrow and sorrow? Nay, I rather thrilled,
Distrusting every light that seemed to gild
The onward path, and feared to over-lean
A finger even. And, though I have grown serene
And strong since then, I think that God has willed
A still renewable fear ... O love, O troth ...
Lest these en-laspëd hands should never hold,
This mutual kiss drop down between us both
As an unowned thing, once the lips being cold.
And Love, be false! if he, to keep one oath,
Must lose one joy, by his life's star foretold.

XXXVII

Pardon, oh, pardon, that my soul should make,
Of all that strong divineness which I know
For thine and thee, an image only so
Formed of the sand, and fit to shift and break.
It is that distant years which did not take
Thy sovranty, recoiling with a blow,
Have forced my swimming brain to undergo
Their doubt and dread, and blindly to forsake
Thy purity of likeness and distort
Thy worthiest love to a worthless counterfeit:
As if a shipwrecked Pagan, safe in port,
His guardian sea-god to commemorate,
Should set a sculptured porpoise, gills a-snort
And vibrant tail, within the temple-gate.

XXXVIII

First time he kissed me, he but only kissed
The fingers of this hand wherewith I write;
And ever since, it grew more clean and white,
Slow to world-greetings, quick with its "Oh, list,"
When the angels speak. A ring of amethyst
I could not wear here, plainer to my sight,
Than that first kiss. The second passed in height
The first, and sought the forehead, and half missed,
Half falling on the hair. O beyond meed!
That was the chrism of love, which love's own crown,
With sanctifying sweetness, did precede.
The third upon my lips was folded down
In perfect, purple state; since when, indeed,
I have been proud and said, "My love, my own."

XXXIX

Because thou hast the power and own'st the grace
To look through and behind this mask of me
(Against which years have beat thus blanchingly
With their rains), and behold my soul's true face,
The dim and weary witness of life's race,

Because thou hast the faith and love to see,
Through that same soul's distracting lethargy,
The patient angel waiting for a place
In the new Heavens,—because nor sin nor woe,
Nor God's infliction, nor death's neighbourhood,
Nor all which others viewing, turn to go,
Nor all of which makes me tired of all, self-viewed,—
Nothing repels thee, . . . Dearest, teach me so
To pour out gratitude, as thou dost, good!

XL

OH, yes! they love through all this world of ours!
I will not gainsay love, called love forsooth.
I have heard love talked in my early youth,
And since, not so long back but that the flowers
Then gathered, smell still. Mussulmans and Giaours,
Throw kerchiefs at a smile, and have no ruth
For any weeping. Polypheme's white tooth
Slips on the nut if, after frequent showers,
The shell is over-smooth,—and not so much
Will turn the thing called love, aside to hate
Or else to oblivion. But thou art not such
A lover, my Belovëd! thou canst wait
Through sorrow and sickness, to bring souls to touch,
And think it soon when others cry "Too late."

XLI

I THANK all who have loved me in their hearts,
With thanks and love from mine. Deep thanks to all
Who paused a little near the prison-wall
To hear my music in its louder parts
Ere they went onward, each one to the mart's
Or temple's occupation, beyond call.
But thou, who, in my voice's sink and fall
When the sob took it, thy divinest Art's
Own instrument didst drop down at thy foot
To hearken what I said between my tears, . . .
Instruct me how to thank thee! Oh, to shoot

My soul's full meaning into future years,
That *they* should lend it utterance, and salute
Love that endures, from Life that disappears!

XLII

"*My future will not copy fair my past*"—
I wrote that once; and thinking at my side
My ministering life-angel justified
The word by his appealing look upcast
To the white throne of God, I turned at last,
And there, instead, saw thee, not unallied
To angels in thy soul! Then I, long tried
By natural ills, received the comfort fast,
While budding, at thy sight, my pilgrim's staff
Gave out green leaves with morning dews impearled.
I seek no copy now of life's first half:
Leave here the pages with long musing curled,
And write me new my future's epigraph,
New angel mine, unhoped for in the world!

XLIII

How do I love thee? Let me count the ways.
I love thee to the depth and breadth and height
My soul can reach, when feeling out of sight
For the ends of Being and ideal Grace.
I love thee to the level of everyday's
Most quiet need, by sun and candle-light.
I love thee freely, as men strive for Right;
I love thee purely, as they turn from Praise.
I love thee with the passion put to use
In my old griefs, and with my childhood's faith.
I love thee with a love I seemed to lose
With my lost saints,—I love thee with the breath,
Smiles, tears, of all my life!—and, if God choose,
I shall but love thee better after death.

XLIV

Belovèd, thou hast brought me many flowers
Plucked in the garden, all the summer through

And winter, and it seemed as if they grew
In this close room, nor missed the sun and showers.
So, in the like name of that love of ours,
Take back these thoughts which here unfolded too,
And which on warm and cold days I withdrew
From my heart's ground. Indeed, those beds and bowers
Be overgrown with bitter weeds and rue,
And wait thy weeding; yet here's eglantine,
Here's ivy!—take them, as I used to do
Thy flowers, and keep them where they shall not pine.
Instruct thine eyes to keep their colours true,
And tell thy soul, their roots are left in mine.

ROBERT BROWNING

YOU'LL LOVE ME YET

You'll love me yet!—and I can tarry
    Your love's protracted growing:
June rear'd that bunch of flowers you carry,
    From seeds of April's sowing.

I plant a heartful now: some seed
    At least is sure to strike,
And yield—what you'll not pluck indeed,
    Not love, but, may be, like.

You'll look at least on love's remains,
    A grave's one violet:
Your look?—that pays a thousand pains.
    What's death? You'll love me yet!

THE PIED PIPER OF HAMELIN

Hamelin Town's in Brunswick,
    By famous Hanover city;
The river Weser, deep and wide,
Washes its wall on the southern side;

A pleasanter spot you never spied;
But when begins my ditty,
   Almost five hundred years ago,
   To see the townsfolk suffer so
From vermin, was a pity.

   Rats!
They fought the dogs, and killed the cats,
   And bit the babies in the cradles,
And ate the cheeses out of the vats,
   And licked the soup from the cook's own ladles,
Split open the kegs of salted sprats,
Made nests inside men's Sunday hats,
And even spoiled the women's chats,
    By drowning their speaking
    With shrieking and squeaking
In fifty different sharps and flats.

At last the people in a body
   To the Town Hall came flocking:
" 'Tis clear," cried they, "our Mayor's a noddy;
   And as for our Corporation—shocking
To think we buy gowns lined with ermine
For dolts that can't or won't determine
What's best to rid us of our vermin!
You hope, because you're old and obese,
To find in the furry civic robe ease?
Rouse up, Sirs! Give your brains a racking
To find the remedy we're lacking,
Or, sure as fate, we'll send you packing!"
At this the Mayor and Corporation
Quaked with a mighty consternation.

An hour they sate in counsel—
   At length the Mayor broke silence:
"For a guilder I'd my ermine gown sell;
   I wish I were a mile hence!
It's easy to bid one rack one's brain—
I'm sure my poor head aches again,
I've scratched it so, and all in vain.

Oh for a trap, a trap, a trap!"
Just as he said this, what should hap
At the chamber door but a gentle tap?
"Bless us," cried the Mayor, "what's that?"
(With the Corporation as he sat,
Looking little, though wondrous fat;
Nor brighter was his eye, nor moister
Than a too-long-opened oyster,
Save when at noon his paunch grew mutinous
For a plate of turtle, green and glutinous,)
"Only a scraping of shoes on the mat?
Anything like the sound of a rat
Makes my heart go pit-a-pat!"

"Come in!"—the Mayor cried, looking bigger:
And in did come the strangest figure!
His queer long coat from heel to head
Was half of yellow and half of red;
And he himself was tall and thin;
With sharp blue eyes, each like a pin;
And light loose hair, yet swarthy skin;
No tuft on cheek nor beard on chin,
But lips where smiles went out and in—
There was no guessing his kith or kin!
And nobody could enough admire
The tall man and his quaint attire.
Quoth one: "It's as my great-grandsire,
Starting up at the Trump of Doom's tone,
Had walked this way from his painted tombstone!"

He advanced to the council-table:
And, "Please your honours," said he, "I'm able,
By means of a secret charm, to draw
All creatures living beneath the sun,
That creep, or swim, or fly, or run,
After me so as you never saw!
And I chiefly use my charm
On creatures that do people harm—
The mole, and toad, and newt, and viper—
And people call me the Pied Piper."

(And here they noticed round his neck
A scarf of red and yellow stripe,
To match with his coat of the self-same check;
And at the scarf's end hung a pipe;
And his fingers, they noticed, were ever straying
As if impatient to be playing
Upon this pipe, as low it dangled
Over his vesture so old-fangled.)
"Yet," said he, "poor piper as I am,
In Tartary I freed the Cham,
Last June, from his huge swarm of gnats;
I eased in Asia the Nizam
Of a monstrous brood of vampire-bats;
And, as for what your brain bewilders—
If I can rid your town of rats,
Will you give me a thousand guilders?"
"One? fifty thousand!"—was the exclamation
Of the astonished Mayor and Corporation.

Into the street the Piper stept,
    Smiling first a little smile,
As if he knew what magic slept
    In his quiet pipe the while;
Then, like a musical adept,
To blow the pipe his lips he wrinkled,
And green and blue his sharp eyes twinkled,
Like a candle flame where salt is sprinkled;
And ere three shrill notes the pipe uttered,
You heard as if an army muttered;
And the muttering grew to a grumbling;
And the grumbling grew to a mighty rumbling;
And out of the houses the rats came tumbling.
Great rats, small rats, lean rats, brawny rats,
Brown rats, black rats, grey rats, tawny rats,
Grave old plodders, gay young friskers,
    Fathers, mothers, uncles, cousins,
Cocking tails and pricking whiskers;
    Families by tens and dozens,
Brothers, sisters, husbands, wives—
Followed the Piper for their lives.

From street to street he piped advancing,
And step for step they followed dancing,
Until they came to the river Weser,
Wherein all plunged and perished
—Save one who, stout as Julius Cæsar,
Swam across and lived to carry
(As he the manuscript he cherished)
To Rat-land home his commentary,
Which was: "At the first shrill notes of the pipe,
I heard a sound as of scraping tripe,
And putting apples, wondrous ripe,
Into a cider-press's gripe—
And a moving away of pickle-tub-boards,
And a leaving ajar of conserve-cupboards,
And a drawing the corks of train-oil-flasks,
And a breaking the hoops of butter-casks;
And it seemed as if a voice
(Sweeter far than by harp or by psaltery
Is breathed) called out, O rats, rejoice!
The world is grown to one vast drysaltery!
So munch on, crunch on, take your nuncheon,
Breakfast, supper, dinner, luncheon!
And just as a bulky sugar-puncheon,
All ready staved, like a great sun shone
Glorious, scarce an inch before me,
Just as methought it said, Come, bore me!
—I found the Weser rolling o'er me."

You should have heard the Hamelin people
Ringing the bells till they rocked the steeple;
"Go," cried the Mayor, "and get long poles!
Poke out the nests and block up the holes!
Consult with carpenters and builders,
And leave in our town not even a trace
Of the rats!"—when suddenly up the face
Of the Piper perked in the market-place,
With a "First, if you please, my thousand guilders!"

A thousand guilders! The Mayor looked blue;
So did the Corporation too.

For council dinners made rare havock
With Claret, Moselle, Vin-de-Grave, Hock;
And half the money would replenish
Their cellar's biggest butt with Rhenish.
To pay this sum to a wandering fellow
With a gipsy coat of red and yellow!
"Beside," quoth the Mayor, with a knowing wink,
"Our business was done at the river's brink;
We saw with our eyes the vermin sink,
And what's dead can't come to life, I think.
So, friend, we're not the folks to shrink
From the duty of giving you something for drink,
And a matter of money to put in your poke;
But, as for the guilders, what we spoke
Of them, as you very well know, was in joke.
Beside, our losses have made us thrifty;
A thousand guilders! Come, take fifty!"

The piper's face fell, and he cried,
"No trifling! I can't wait! Beside,
I've promised to visit by dinner time
Bagdad, and accept the prime
Of the Head Cook's pottage, all he's rich in,
For having left, in the Caliph's kitchen,
Of a nest of scorpions no survivor—
With him I proved no bargain-driver;
With you, don't think I'll bate a stiver!
And folks who put me in a passion
May find me pipe to another fashion."

"How?" cried the Mayor, "d'ye think I'll brook
Being worse treated than a cook?
Insulted by a lazy ribald
With idle pipe and vesture piebald?
You threaten us, fellow? Do your worst,
Blow your pipe there till you burst!"

Once more he stept into the street;
And to his lips again
Laid his long pipe of smooth straight cane;

And ere he blew three notes (such sweet
Soft notes as yet musician's cunning
  Never gave the enraptured air)
There was a rustling that seemed like a bustling
Of merry crowds justling at pitching and hustling;
Small feet were pattering, wooden shoes clattering,
Little hands clapping, and little tongues chattering;
And, like fowls in a farm-yard when barley is scattering,
Out came the children running.
All the little boys and girls,
With rosy cheeks and flaxen curls,
And sparkling eyes and teeth like pearls,
Tripping and skipping, ran merrily after
The wonderful music with shouting and laughter.

The Mayor was dumb, and the Council stood
As if they were changed into blocks of wood,
Unable to move a step, or cry
To the children merrily skipping by—
And could only follow with the eye
That joyous crowd at the Piper's back.
But how the Mayor was on the rack,
And the wretched Council's bosoms beat,
As the Piper turned from the High Street
To where the Weser rolled its waters
Right in the way of their sons and daughters!
However, he turned from South to West,
And to Koppelberg Hill his steps addressed,
And after him the children pressed;
Great was the joy in every breast.
"He never can cross that mighty top!
He's forced to let the piping drop,
And we shall see our children stop!"
When, lo, as they reached the mountain's side,
A wondrous portal opened wide,
As if a cavern was suddenly hollowed;
And the Piper advanced and the children followed;
And when all were in, to the very last,
The door in the mountain side shut fast.
Did I say all? No! One was lame,
And could not dance the whole of the way!

And in after years, if you would blame
His sadness, he was used to say,—
"It's dull in our town since my playmates left!
I can't forget that I'm bereft
Of all the pleasant sights they see,
Which the Piper also promised me;
For he led us, he said, to a joyous land,
Joining the town and just at hand,
Where waters gushed and fruit-trees grew,
And flowers put forth a fairer hue,
And everything was strange and new;
The sparrows were brighter than peacocks here,
And their dogs outran our fallow deer,
And honey-bees had lost their stings,
And horses were born with eagles' wings;
And just as I became assured
My lame foot would be speedily cured,
The music stopped and I stood still,
And found myself outside the Hill,
Left alone against my will,
To go now limping as before,
And never hear of that country more!"

Alas, alas for Hamelin!
    There came into many a burgher's pate
    A text which says, that Heaven's gate
    Opes to the rich at as easy a rate
As the needle's eye takes a camel in!
The Mayor sent East, West, North, and South,
To offer the piper by word of mouth,
    Wherever it was men's lot to find him,
Silver and gold to his heart's content,
If he'd only return the way he went,
    And bring the children behind him.
But when they saw 'twas a lost endeavor,
And Piper and dancers were gone forever,
They made a decree that lawyers never
    Should think their records dated duly
If, after the day of the month and year,
These words did not as well appear,
"And so long after what happened here

On the Twenty-second of July,
Thirteen Hundred and Seventy-six:"
And the better in memory to fix
The place of the children's last retreat
They called it the Pied Piper's Street—
Where any one playing on pipe or tabor
Was sure for the future to lose his labor.
Nor suffered they hostelry or tavern
    To shock with mirth a street so solemn;
But opposite the place of the cavern
    They wrote the story on a column,
And on the Great Church window painted
The same, to make the world acquainted
How their children were stolen away;
And there it stands to this very day.
And I must not omit to say
That in Transylvania there's a tribe
Of alien people, that ascribe
The outlandish ways and dress
On which their neighbors lay such stress
To their fathers and mothers having risen
Out of some subterranean prison,
Into which they were trepanned
Long time ago, in a mighty band,
Out of Hamelin Town in Brunswick Land,
But how or why, they don't understand.

So, Willy, let you and me be wipers
Of scores out with all men—especially pipers:
And, whether they pipe us free from rats or from mice,
If we promised them aught, let us keep our promise.

HOW THEY BROUGHT THE GOOD NEWS
FROM GHENT TO AIX

I SPRANG to the stirrup, and Joris, and he:
I galloped, Dirck galloped, we galloped all three;
"Good speed!" cried the watch as the gate-bolts undrew;
"Speed!" echoed the wall to us galloping through.
Behind shut the postern, the lights sank to rest,
And into the midnight we galloped abreast.

Not a word to each other: we kept the great pace—
Neck by neck, stride by stride, never changing our place;
I turned in my saddle and made its girths tight,
Then shortened each stirrup and set the pique right,
Rebuckled the check-strap, chained slacker the bit,
Nor galloped less steadily Roland a whit.

'Twas moonset at starting; but while we drew near
Lokeren, the cocks crew and twilight dawned clear;
At Boom a great yellow star came out to see;
At Düffeld 'twas morning as plain as could be;
And from Mecheln church-steeple we heard the half-chime—
So Joris broke silence with "Yet there is time!"

At Aerschot up leaped of a sudden the sun,
And against him the cattle stood black every one,
To stare through the mist at us galloping past;
And I saw my stout galloper Roland at last,
With resolute shoulders, each butting away
The haze, as some bluff river headland its spray;

And his low head and crest, just one sharp ear bent back
For my voice, and the other pricked out on his track;
And one eye's black intelligence,—ever that glance
O'er its white edge at me, its own master, askance;
And the thick heavy spume-flakes, which aye and anon
His fierce lips shook upward in galloping on.

By Hasselt Dirck groaned; and cried Joris, "Stay spur!
Your Roos galloped bravely, the fault's not in her;
We'll remember at Aix"—for one heard the quick wheeze
Of her chest, saw the stretched neck, and staggering knees
And sunk tail, and horrible heave of the flank,
As down on her haunches she shuddered and sank.

So we were left galloping, Joris and I,
Past Looz and past Tongres, no cloud in the sky;
The broad sun above laughed a pitiless laugh;
'Neath our feet broke the brittle, bright stubble like chaff;
Till over by Dalhem a dome-spire sprang white,
And "Gallop" gasped Joris, "for Aix is in sight!"

"How they'll greet us!"—and all in a moment his roan
Rolled neck and croup over, lay dead as a stone;
And there was my Roland to bear the whole weight
Of the news which alone could save Aix from her fate,
With his nostrils like pits full of blood to the brim,
And with circles of red for his eye-sockets' rim.

Then I cast loose my buff-coat, each holster let fall,
Shook off both my jack-boots, let go belt and all,
Stood up in the stirrup, leaned, patted his ear,
Called my Roland his pet-name, my horse without peer—
Clapped my hands, laughed and sung, any noise, bad or good,
Till at length into Aix Roland galloped and stood.

And all I remember is friends flocking round,
As I sate with his head 'twixt my knees on the ground;
And no voice but was praising this Roland of mine,
As I poured down his throat our last measure of wine,
Which (the burgesses voted by common consent)
Was no more than his due who brought good news from Ghent.

WILLIAM CULLEN BRYANT

THANATOPSIS

To him who in the love of Nature holds
Communion with her visible forms, she speaks
A various language: for his gayer hours
She has a voice of gladness, and a smile
And eloquence of beauty; and she glides
Into his darker musings with a mild
And healing sympathy, that steals away
Their sharpness ere he is aware. When thoughts
Of the last bitter hour come like a blight
Over thy spirit, and sad images
Of the stern agony, and shroud, and pall,
And breathless darkness, and the narrow house,
Make thee to shudder, and grow sick at heart—
Go forth under the open sky, and list

ROBERT BROWNING

WILLIAM CULLEN BRYANT

To Nature's teachings, while from all around—
Earth and her waters, and the depths of air—
Comes a still voice: Yet a few days, and thee
The all-beholding sun shall see no more
In all his course; nor yet in the cold ground,
Where thy pale form was laid, with many tears,
Nor in the embrace of ocean, shall exist
Thy image. Earth, that nourished thee, shall claim
Thy growth, to be resolved to earth again;
And, lost each human trace, surrendering up
Thine individual being, shalt thou go
To mix forever with the elements—
To be a brother to the insensible rock,
And to the sluggish clod, which the rude swain
Turns with his share, and treads upon. The oak
Shall send his roots abroad; and pierce thy mould.
  Yet not to thine eternal resting-place
Shalt thou retire alone; nor couldst thou wish
Couch more magnificent. Thou shalt lie down
With patriarchs of the infant world,—with kings,
The powerful of the earth, the wise, the good,
Fair forms, and hoary seers of ages past,
All in one mighty sepulchre. The hills,
Rock-ribbed, and ancient as the sun; the vales
Stretching in pensive quietness between;
The venerable woods; rivers that move
In majesty, and the complaining brooks,
That make the meadows green; and, poured round all,
Old ocean's gray and melancholy waste,—
Are but the solemn decorations all
Of the great tomb of man. The golden sun,
The planets, all the infinite host of heaven,
Are shining on the sad abodes of death,
Through the still lapse of ages. All that tread
The globe are but a handful to the tribes
That slumber in its bosom. Take the wings
Of morning, traverse Barca's desert sands,
Or lose thyself in the continuous woods
Where rolls the Oregon, and hears no sound
Save his own dashings—yet the dead are there;

And millions in those solitudes, since first
The flight of years began, have laid them down
In their last sleep—the dead reign there alone.
So shalt thou rest; and what if thou withdraw
In silence from the living, and no friend
Take note of thy departure? All that breathe
Will share thy destiny. The gay will laugh
When thou art gone, the solemn brood of care
Plod on, and each one as before will chase
His favorite phantom; yet all these shall leave
Their mirth and their employments, and shall come
And make their bed with thee. As the long train
Of ages glide away, the sons of men—
The youth in life's green spring, and he who goes
In the full strength of years, matron and maid,
And the sweet babe, and the gray-headed man—
Shall one by one be gathered to thy side
By those who in their turn shall follow them.

    So live, that when thy summons comes to join
The innumerable caravan that moves
To that mysterious realm where each shall take
His chamber in the silent halls of death,
Thou go not like the quarry-slave at night,
Scourged to his dungeon; but, sustained and soothed
By an unfaltering trust, approach thy grave
Like one who wraps the drapery of his couch
About him, and lies down to pleasant dreams.

TO A WATERFOWL

WHITHER, 'midst falling dew,
While glow the heavens with the lasts steps of day,
Far, through their rosy depths, dost thou pursue
    Thy solitary way?

    Vainly the fowler's eye
Might mark thy distant flight to do thee wrong,
As, darkly seen against the crimson sky,
    Thy figure floats along.

Seek'st thou the plashy brink
Of weedy lake, or marge of river wide,
Or where the rocking billows rise and sink
    On the chafed ocean side?

There is a Power whose care
Teaches thy way along that pathless coast,
The desert and illimitable air,
    Lone wandering, but not lost.

All day thy wings have fann'd,
At that far height, the cold, thin atmosphere,
Yet stoop not, weary, to the welcome land,
    Though the dark night is near.

And soon that toil shall end;
Soon shalt thou find a summer home and rest,
And scream among thy fellows; reeds shall bend
    Soon o'er thy shelter'd nest.

Thou'rt gone, the abyss of heaven
Hath swallow'd up thy form; yet, on my heart,
Deeply hath sunk the lesson thou hast given,
    And shall not soon depart.

He who, from zone to zone,
Guides through the boundless sky thy certain flight,
In the long way that I must tread alone,
    Will lead my steps aright.

THE DEATH OF THE FLOWERS

The melancholy days are come, the saddest of the year,
Of wailing winds, and naked woods, and meadows brown and sere.
Heaped in the hollows of the grove, the autumn leaves lie dead;
They rustle to the eddying gust, and to the rabbit's tread.
The robin and the wren are flown, and from the shrubs the jay,
And from the wood-top calls the crow through all the gloomy day.

Where are the flowers, the fair young flowers, that lately sprang and
    stood
In brighter light, and softer airs, a beauteous sisterhood?
Alas! they all are in their graves; the gentle race of flowers
Are lying in their lowly beds, with the fair and good of ours.
The rain is falling where they lie; but the cold November rain
Calls not from out the gloomy earth the lovely ones again.

The wind-flower and the violet, they perished long ago,
And the brier-rose and the orchis died amid the summer glow;
But on the hill the golden-rod, and the aster in the wood,
And the yellow sun-flower by the brook in autumn beauty stood,
Till fell the frost from the clear cold heaven, as falls the plague on
    men,
And the brightness of their smile was gone, from upland, glade, and
    glen.

And now, when comes the calm mild day, as still such days will come,
To call the squirrel and the bee from out their winter home;
When the sound of dropping nuts is heard, though all the trees are
    still,
And twinkle in the smoky light the waters of the rill,
The south wind searches for the flowers whose fragrance late he bore,
And sighs to find them in the wood and by the stream no more.

And then I think of one who in her youthful beauty died,
The fair meek blossom that grew up and faded by my side.
In the cold moist earth we laid her, when the forests cast the leaf,
And we wept that one so lovely should have a life so brief;
Yet not unmeet it was that one like that young friend of ours,
So gentle and so beautiful, should perish with the flowers.

ROBERT BURNS

BONNIE DOON

Ye banks and braes o' bonnie Doon
How can ye blume sae fair!
How can ye chant, ye little birds,
And I sae fu' o' care!

Thou'll break my heart, thou bonnie bird
   That sings upon the bough;
Thou minds me o' the happy days
   When my fause Luve was true.

Thou'll break my heart, thou bonnie bird
   That sings beside thy mate;
For sae I sat, and sae I sang,
   And wist na o' my fate.

Aft hae I roved by bonnie Doon
   To see the woodbine twine,
And ilka bird sang o' its love;
   And sae did I o' mine.

Wi' lightsome heart I pu'd a rose,
   Frae aff its thorny tree;
And my fause luver staw the rose,
   But left the thorn wi' me.

TO A MOUSE

On turning her up in her nest, with the plough,
November, 1785

Wee, sleekit, cow'rin', tim'rous beastie,
O what a panic's in thy breastie!
Thou need na start awa sae hasty,
   Wi' bickering brattle!
I wad be laith to rin an' chase thee
   Wi' murd'ring pattle!

I'm truly sorry man's dominion
Has broken Nature's social union,
An' justifies that ill opinion
   Which makes thee startle
At me, thy poor earth-born companion,
   An' fellow-mortal!

I doubt na, whiles, but thou may thieve;
What then? poor beastie, thou maun live!
A daimen-icker in a thrave
'S a sma' request:
I'll get a blessin' wi' the lave,
And never miss't!

Thy wee bit housie, too, in ruin!
Its silly wa's the win's are strewin:
And naething, now, to big a new ane,
O' foggage green!
An' bleak December's winds ensuin'
Baith snell an' keen!

Thou saw the fields laid bare an' waste
An' weary winter comin' fast,
An' cozie here, beneath the blast,
Thou thought to dwell
Till, crash! the cruel coulter past
Out thro' thy cell.

That wee bit heap o' leaves an' stibble
Has cost thee mony a weary nibble!
Now thou's turn'd out, for a' thy trouble,
But house or hald,
To thole the winter's sleety dribble
An' cranreuch cauld!

But, Mousie, thou art no thy lane
In proving foresight may be vain:
The best laid schemes o' mice an' men
Gang aft a-gley,
An' lea'e us nought but grief an' pain,
For promised joy.

Still thou art blest, compared wi' me!
The present only toucheth thee:
But, Och! I backward cast my e'e
On prospects drear!
An' forward, tho' I canna see,
I guess an' fear!

THE COTTER'S SATURDAY NIGHT

> Let not ambition mock their useful toil,
> Their homely joys and destiny obscure;
> Nor grandeur hear, with a disdainful smile,
> The short and simple annals of the poor.
>   GRAY.

My loved, my honored, much-respected friend!
  No mercenary bard his homage pays;
With honest pride I scorn each selfish end,
  My dearest meed a friend's esteem and praise.
To you I sing, in simple Scottish lays,
  The lowly train in life's sequestered scene;
The native feelings strong, the guileless ways—
  What Aiken in a cottage would have been;
Ah! tho' his worth unknown, far happier there, I ween!

November chill blaws loud wi' angry sugh;
  The shortening winter day is near a close;
The miry beasts retreating frae the pleugh,
  The blackening trains o' craws to their repose.
The toil-worn cotter frae his labor goes—
  This night his weekly moil is at an end—
Collect his spades, his mattocks, and his hoes,
  Hoping the morn in ease and rest to spend;
  And weary, o'er the moor, his course does hameward
    bend.

At length his lonely cot appears in view,
  Beneath the shelter of an aged tree;
The expectant wee things, todlin, stacher thro'
  To meet their dad wi' flichterin noise and glee.
His wee bit ingle blinkin' bonnilie,
  His clean hearth-stane, his thriftie wifie's smile,
The lisping infant prattling on his knee,
  Does a' his weary, carking cares beguile,
  An' makes him quite forget his labor and his toil.

Belyve the elder bairns come drappin' in—
  At service out, amang the farmers roun;
Some ca' the pleugh, some herd, some tentie rin
  A cannie errand to a neebor town.

Their eldest hope, their Jenny, woman grown,
  In youthfu' bloom, love sparkling in her e'e,
Comes hame, perhaps, to shew a braw new gown,
  Or deposite her sair-won penny fee,
  To help her parents dear, if they in hardship be.

Wi' joy unfeigned, brothers and sisters meet,
  An' each for other's weelfare kindly spiers;
The social hours, swift-winged, unnoticed fleet;
  Each tells the uncos that he sees or hears;
The parents, partial, eye their hopeful years—
  Anticipation forward points the view.
The mother, wi' her needle an' her shears,
  Gars auld claes look amaist as weel's the new;
  The father mixes a' wi' admonition due.

Their masters' and their mistresses' command
  The younkers a' are warned to obey,
An' mind their labors wi' an eydent hand,
  An' ne'er, tho' out o' sight, to jauk or play;
An' O! be sure to fear the Lord alway!
  An' mind your duty, duly, morn an' night!
Lest in temptation's path ye gang astray,
  Implore His counsel and assisting might:
  They never sought in vain that sought the Lord aright!

But hark! a rap comes gently to the door;
  Jenny, wha kens the meaning o' the same,
Tells how a neebor lad cam o'er the moor
  To do some errands, and convoy her hame.
The wily mother sees the conscious flame
  Sparkle in Jenny's e'e, and flush her cheek:
Wi' heart-struck, anxious care, inquires his name,
  While Jenny hafflins is afraid to speak;
  Weel pleased the mother hears its nae wild, worthless
    rake.

Wi' kindly welcome, Jenny brings him ben—
  A strappan youth, he takes the mother's eye;
Blythe Jenny sees the visit 's no ill ta'en;
  The father cracks of horses, pleughs, and kye;

By Oppression's woes and pains!
By your sons in servile chains!
We will drain our dearest veins,
   But they shall be free!

Lay the proud usurpers low!
Tyrants fall in every foe!
Liberty's in every blow!
   Let us do, or die!

HIGHLAND MARY

Ye banks, and braes, and streams around
   The castle o' Montgomery,
Green be your woods, and fair your flowers,
   Your waters never drumlie!
There simmer first unfauld her robes,
   And there the langest tarry!
For there I took the last fareweel
   O' my sweet Highland Mary.

How sweetly bloomed the gay green birk!
   How rich the hawthorn blossom!
As, underneath their fragrant shade,
   I clasped her to my bosom!
The golden hours, on angel wings,
   Flew o'er me and my dearie;
For dear to me as light and life
   Was my sweet Highland Mary.

Wi' monie a vow and locked embrace
   Our parting was fu' tender;
And pledging aft to meet again,
   We tore ourselves asunder;
But oh! fell death's untimely frost,
   That nipt my flower sae early!
Now green's the sod, and cauld's the clay,
   That wraps my Highland Mary!

O pale, pale now, those rosy lips
   I aft hae kissed sae fondly!
And closed for aye the sparkling glance
   That dwelt on me sae kindly!
And mouldering now in silent dust
   That heart that lo'ed me dearly!
But still within my bosom's core
   Shall live my Highland Mary.

TAM O'SHANTER

A TALE

Of brownyis and of bogilis full is this buke.
                      GAWIN DOUGLAS.

WHEN chapman billies leave the street,
And drouthy neebors neebors meet,
As market-days are wearing late,
An' folk begin to tak the gate;
While we sit bousing at the nappy,
An' getting fou and unco happy,
We think na on the lang Scots miles,
The mosses, waters, slaps, and stiles,
That lie between us and our hame,
Whare sits our sulky, sullen dame,
Gathering her brows like gathering storm,
Nursing her wrath to keep it warm.

   This truth fand honest Tam O'Shanter,
As he frae Ayr ae night did canter,
(Auld Ayr, whom ne'er a town surpasses,
For honest men and bonny lasses.)

   O Tam! hadst thou but been sae wise,
As ta'en thy ain wife Kate's advice!
She tauld thee weel thou was a skellum,
A blethering, blustering, drunken blellum;
That frae November till October,
Ae market-day thou was nae sober;
That ilka melder, wi' the miller,
Thou sat as lang as thou had siller;
That every naig was ca'd a shoe on,

The smith and thee gat roaring fou on;
That at the L—d's house, e'en on Sunday,
Thou drank wi' Kirton Jean till Monday.
She prophesied, that late or soon,
Thou would be found deep drowned in **Doon**;
Or catch'd wi' warlocks in the mirk,
By Alloway's auld haunted kirk.

Ah, gentle dames! it gars me greet,
To think how mony counsels sweet,
How mony lengthened, sage advices,
The husband frae the wife despises!

But to our tale: Ae market night,
Tam had got planted unco right;
Fast by an ingle, bleezing finely,
Wi' reaming swats, that drank divinely;
And at his elbow souter Johnny,
His ancient, trusty, drouthy crony;
Tam lo'ed him like a vera brither;
They had been fou for weeks thegither.
The night drave on wi' sangs an' clatter;
And aye the ale was growing better;
The landlady and Tam grew gracious,
Wi' favors secret, sweet, and precious;
The souter tauld his queerest stories;
The landlord's laugh was ready chorus:
The storm without might rair and rustle,
Tam did na mind the storm a whistle.

Care, mad to see a man sae happy,
E'en drowned himself amang the nappy;
As bees flee hame wi' lades o' treasure,
The minutes winged their way wi' pleasure;
Kings may be blest, but Tam was glorious,
O'er a' the ills o' life victorious.

But pleasures are like poppies spread,
You seize the flower, its bloom is shed;
Or like the snow-falls in the river,
A moment white—then melts forever;

Or like the Borealis race,
That flit ere you can point their place;
Or like the rainbow's lovely form,
Evanishing amid the storm.—
Nae man can tether time or tide;
The hour approaches Tam maun ride;
That hour, o' night's black arch the key-stane,
That dreary hour he mounts his beast in;
And sic a night he taks the road in,
As ne'er poor sinner was abroad in.

   The wind blew as 'twad blawn its last;
The rattling showers rose on the blast;
The speedy gleams the darkness swallowed;
Loud, deep, and lang the thunder bellowed:
That night, a child might understand,
The deil had business on his hand.

   Weel mounted on his gray mare Meg—
A better never lifted leg—
Tam skelpit on through dub and mire,
Despising wind, and rain, and fire;
Whiles holding fast his guid blue bonnet:
Whiles crooning o'er some auld Scots sonnet;
Whiles glowering round wi' prudent cares,
Lest bogles catch him unawares;
Kirk-Alloway was drawing nigh,
Whare ghaists and howlets nightly cry.

   By this time he was cross the ford,
Whare in the snaw the chapman smoored;
And past the birks an' meikle stane,
Whare drunken Charlie brak's neck-bane;
And through the whins, and by the cairn,
Whare hunters fand the murdered bairn;
And near the thorn, aboon the well,
Whare Mungo's mither hanged hersel.—
Before him Doon pours all his floods;
The doubling storm roars through the woods:
The lightnings flash from pole to pole;

Near and more near the thunders roll;
When, glimmering through the groaning trees,
Kirk-Alloway seemed in a bleeze;
Through ilka bore the beams were glancing;
And loud resounded mirth and dancing.—

Inspiring bold John Barleycorn!
What dangers thou canst make us scorn!
Wi' tippenny we fear nae evil;
Wi' usquabae we'll face the devil!—
The swats sae ream'd in Tammie's noddle,
Fair play,—he cared na deils a boddle.
But Maggie stood right sair astonished,
Till by the heel and hand admonished,
She ventured forward on the light;
And, vow! Tam saw an unco sight!
Warlocks and witches in a dance;
Nae cotillon brent new frae France,
But hornpipes, jigs, strathspeys, and reels,
Put life and mettle in their heels.
A winnock-bunker in the east,
There sat auld Nick, in shape o' beast;
A towzie tyke, black, grim, and large,
To gie them music was his charge;
He screwed the pipes, and gart them skirl,
Till roof and rafters a' did dirl.—
Coffins stood round like open presses,
That shawed the dead in their last dresses;
And by some devilish cantraip slight,
Each in its cauld hand held a light,—
By which heroic Tam was able
To note upon the haly table,
A murderer's banes in gibbet airns;
Twa span-lang, wee, unchristened bairns;
A thief new cutted frae a rape,
Wi' his last gasp his gab did gape;
Five tomahawks, wi' bluid red rusted;
Five cimiters, wi' murder crusted;
A garter, which a babe had strangled;
A knife, a father's throat had mangled,

Whom his ain son o' life bereft,
The gray hairs yet stack to the heft;
Wi' mair o' horrible and awfu',
Which e'en to name wad be unlawfu'.

As Tammie glowred, amazed and curious,
The mirth and fun grew fast and furious:
The piper loud and louder blew;
The dancers quick and quicker flew;
They reeled, they set, they crossed, they cleekit,
Till ilka carlin swat and reekit,
And coost her duddies to the wark,
And linket at it in her sark!

Now Tam, O Tam! had they been queans,
A' plump and strapping, in their teens;
Their sarks, instead o' creeshie flannen,
Been snaw-white seventeen hunder linen!
Thir breeks o' mine, my only pair,
That ance were plush, o' guid blue hair,
I wad hae gien them aff my hurdies
For ae blink o' the bonnie burdies!
But withered beldams, auld and droll,
Rigwoodie hags wad spean a foal,
Lowping an' flinging on a crummock,
I wonder didna turn thy stomach!

But Tam kenned what was what fu' brawlie,
There was ae winsome wench and walie,
That night enlisted in the core,
(Lang after kenned on Carrick shore!
For mony a beast to dead she shot,
And perished mony a bonnie boat,
And shook baith meikle corn and bear,
And kept the county side in fear.)
Her cuttie sark, o' Paisley harn,
That while a lassie she had worn,
In longitude though sorely scanty,
It was her best and she was vauntie.—

Ah! little kenned thy reverend grannie,
That sark she coft for her wee Nannie,
Wi' twa pund Scots, ('twas a' her riches,)
Wad ever graced a dance of witches!

But here my muse her wing maun cour;
Sic flights are far beyond her power;
To sing how Nannie lap and flang,
(A souple jade she was and strang,)
And how Tam stood like ane bewitched,
And thought his very een enriched;
E'en Satan glowred, and fidged fu' fain,
And hotched and blew wi' might and main:
Till first ae caper, syne anither,
Tam tint his reason a' thegither,
And roars out, "Weel done, Cutty-sark!"—
And in an instant all was dark:
And scarcely had he Maggie rallied,
When out the hellish legion sallied.

As bees bizz out wi' angry fyke,
When plundering herds assail their byke;
As open pussie's mortal foes,
When, pop! she starts before their nose;
As eager runs the market-crowd,
When "Catch the thief!" resounds aloud;
So Maggie runs, the witches follow,
Wi' mony an eldritch skreech and hollow.

Ah, Tam! ah, Tam! thou'll get thy fairin!
In hell they'll roast thee like a herrin!
In vain thy Kate awaits thy comin!
Kate soon will be a wofu' woman!
Now do thy speedy utmost, Meg,
And win the key-stane of the brig;
There at them thou thy tail may toss,
A running stream they dare na cross.
But ere the key-stane she could make,
The fient a tail she had to shake!

For Nannie, far before the rest,
Hard upon noble Maggie pressed,
And flew at Tam wi' furious ettle;
But little wist she Maggie's mettle—
Ae spring brought off her master hale
But left behind her ain gray tail:
The carlin caught her by the rump,
And left poor Maggie scarce a stump.

Now, wha this tale o' truth shall read,
Ilk man and mother's son, take heed:
Whene'er to drink you are inclined,
Or cutty-sarks run in your mind,
Think, ye may buy the joys o'er dear,—
Remember Tam O'Shanter's mare.

LORD BYRON

THE ISLES OF GREECE

The isles of Greece, the isles of Greece!
  Where burning Sappho loved and sung,
Where grew the arts of war and peace—
  Where Delos rose, and Phœbus sprung!
Eternal summer gilds them yet;
But all, except their sun, is set.

The Scian and the Teian muse,
  The hero's harp, the lover's lute,
Have found the fame your shores refuse;
  Their place of birth alone is mute
To sounds which echo farther west
Than your sires' "Islands of the Blest."

The mountains look on Marathon,
  And Marathon looks on the sea;
And musing there an hour alone,
  I dreamed that Greece might still be free;
For standing on the Persian's grave,
I could not deem myself a slave.

ROBERT BURNS

LORD BYRON

A king sat on the rocky brow
  Which looks o'er sea-born Salamis;
And ships, by thousands, lay below,
  And men in nations—all were his!
He counted them at break of day—
And when the sun set, where were they?

And where are they? and where art thou,
  My country? On thy voiceless shore
The heroic lay is tuneless now—
  The heroic bosom beats no more!
And must thy lyre, so long divine,
Degenerate into hands like mine?

'Tis something, in the dearth of fame,
  Though linked among a fettered race,
To feel at least a patriot's shame,
  Ev'n as I sing, suffuse my face;
For what is left the poet here?
For Greeks a blush—for Greece a tear.

Must we but weep o'er days more blest?
  Must we but blush?—Our fathers bled.
Earth! render back from out thy breast
  A remnant of our Spartan dead!
Of the three hundred grant but three,
To make a new Thermopylæ!

What! silent still? and silent all?
  Ah no!—the voices of the dead
Sound like a distant torrent's fall,
  And answer, "Let one living head,
But one, arise—we come, we come!"
'Tis but the living who are dumb.

In vain! in vain! strike other chords;
  Fill high the cup with Samian wine!
Leave battles to the Turkish hordes,
And shed the blood of Scio's vine!
Hark! rising to the ignoble call,
How answers each bold Bacchanal!

You have the Pyrrhic dance as yet,—
  Where is the Pyrrhic phalanx gone?
Of two such lessons, why forget
  The nobler and the manlier one?
You have the letters Cadmus gave—
Think ye he meant them for a slave?

Fill high the bowl with Samian wine!
  We will not think of themes like these!
It made Anacreon's song divine;
  He served—but several Polycrates—
A tyrant; but our masters then
Were still at least our countrymen.

The tyrant of the Chersonese
  Was freedom's best and bravest friend;
That tyrant was Miltiades!
  Of that the present hour would lend
Another despot of the kind!
Such chains as his were sure to bind.

Fill high the bowl with Samian wine!
  On Suli's rock, and Parga's shore,
Exists the remnant of a line
  Such as the Doric mothers bore;
And there perhaps some seed is sown
The Heracleidan blood might own.

Trust not for freedom to the Franks—
  They have a king who buys and sells;
In native swords, and native ranks,
  The only hope of courage dwells;
But Turkish force, and Latin fraud,
Would break your shield, however broad.

Fill high the bowl with Samian wine!
  Our virgins dance beneath the shade—
I see their glorious black eyes shine;
  But gazing on each glowing maid,
My own the burning tear-drop laves,
To think such breasts must suckle slaves.

Place me on Sunium's marbled steep,
  Where nothing, save the waves and I,
May hear our mutual murmurs sweep;
  There, swan-like, let me sing and die.
A land of slaves shall ne'er be mine—
Dash down yon cup of Samian wine!

THE DESTRUCTION OF SENNACHERIB

The Assyrian came down like the wolf on the fold,
And his cohorts were gleaming in purple and gold;
And the sheen of their spears was like stars on the sea,
When the blue wave rolls nightly, on deep Galilee.

Like the leaves of the forest when summer is green,
That host with their banners at sunset were seen;
Like the leaves of the forest when autumn hath blown,
That host on the morrow lay withered and strewn.

For the Angel of death spread his wings on the blast,
And breathed in the face of the foe as he passed;
And the eyes of the sleepers waxed deadly and chill,
And their hearts but once heaved—and forever grew still.

And there lay the steed with his nostril all wide,
But through it there rolled not the breath of his pride;
And the foam of his gasping lay white on the turf,
And cold as the spray of the rock-beating surf.

And there lay the rider distorted and pale,
With the dew on his brow, and the rust on his mail;
And the tents were all silent, the banners alone,
The lances unlifted, the trumpet unblown.

And the widows of Ashur are loud in their wail,
And the idols are broke in the temple of Baal;
And the might of the Gentile, unsmote by the sword,
Hath melted like snow in the glance of the Lord!

CHILLON

ETERNAL Spirit of the chainless mind!
Brightest in dungeons, Liberty, thou art;
For there thy habitation is the heart,
The heart which love of thee alone can bind;
And when thy sons to fetters are consigned,
To fetters, and the damp vault's dayless gloom,
Their country conquers with their martyrdom,
And Freedom's fame finds wings on every wind.
Chillon! thy prison is a holy place,
And thy sad floor an altar, for 'twas trod,
Until his very steps have left a trace
Worn as if thy cold pavement were a sod,
By Bonnivard! May none those marks efface!
For they appeal from tyranny to God.

THE GLADIATOR

I SEE before me the gladiator lie:
He leans upon his hand;—his manly brow
Consents to death, but conquers agony,
And his drooped head sinks gradually low—
And through his side the last drops, ebbing slow
From the red gash, fall heavy, one by one,
Like the first of a thunder-shower; and now
The arena swims around him—he is gone,
Ere ceased the inhuman shout which hailed the wretch
    who won.

He heard it, but he heeded not,—his eyes
Were with his heart, and that was far away;
He recked not of the life he lost, nor prize,
But where his rude hut by the Danube lay,
There were his young barbarians all at play,
There was their Dacian mother,—he, their sire,
Butchered to make a Roman holiday;—
All this rushed with his blood;—Shall he expire,
And unavenged?—Arise! ye Goths, and glut your ire!

MY NATIVE LAND, GOOD NIGHT

ADIEU, adieu! my native shore
 Fades o'er the waters blue;
The night-winds sigh, the breakers roar,
 And shrieks the wild sea-mew.
Yon sun that sets upon the sea
 We follow in his flight:
Farewell awhile to him and thee,
 My native Land—Good Night!

A few short hours, and he will rise
 To give the morrow birth;
And I shall hail the main and skies,
 But not my mother earth.
Deserted is my own good hall,
 Its hearth is desolate:
Wild weeds are gathering on the wall;
 My dog howls at the gate.

Come hither, hither, my little page,
 Why dost thou weep and wail?
Or dost thou dread the billow's rage,
 Or tremble at the gale?
But dash the tear-drop from thine eye;
 Our ship is swift and strong:
Our fleetest falcon scarce can fly
 More merrily along.

"Let winds be shrill, let waves roll high,
 I fear not wave nor wind:
Yet marvel not, Sir Childe, that I
 Am sorrowful in mind;
For I have from my father gone,
 A mother whom I love,
And have no friend, save these alone,
 But thee—and One above.

"My father blessed me fervently,
 Yet did not much complain;
But sorely will my mother sigh
 Till I come back again."

Enough, enough, my little lad!
  Such tears become thine eye;
If I thy guileless bosom had,
  My own would not be dry.

Come hither, hither, my stanch yeoman,
  Why dost thou look so pale?
Or dost thou dread a French foeman?
  Or shiver at the gale?—
"Deem'st thou I tremble for my life?
  Sir Childe, I'm not so weak;
But thinking on an absent wife
  Will blanch a faithful cheek.

"My spouse and boys dwell near thy hall,
  Along the bordering lake,
And when they on their father call,
  What answer shall she make?"
Enough, enough, my yeoman good,
  Thy grief let none gainsay:
But I, who am of lighter mood,
  Will laugh to flee away.

For who would trust the seeming sighs
  Of wife or paramour?
Fresh feres will dry the bright blue eyes
  We late saw streaming o'er.
For pleasures past I do not grieve,
  Nor perils gathering near;
My greatest grief is that I leave
  No thing that claims a tear.

And now I'm in the world alone,
  Upon the wide, wide sea;
But why should I for others groan,
  When none will sigh for me?
Perchance my dog will whine in vain,
  Till fed by stranger hands;
But long ere I come back again
  He'd tear me where he stands.

With thee, my bark, I'll swiftly go
  Athwart the foaming brine;
Nor care what land thou bear'st me to,
  So not again to mine.
Welcome, welcome, ye dark-blue waves!
  And when you fail my sight,
Welcome, ye deserts, and ye caves!
  My native Land—Good Night!

SHE WALKS IN BEAUTY

She walks in beauty like the night
  Of cloudless climes and starry skies;
And all that's best of dark and bright
  Meets in her aspect and her eyes;
Thus mellowed to that tender light
  Which heaven to gaudy day denies.

One shade the more, one ray the less,
  Had half impaired the nameless grace
Which waves in every raven tress,
  Or softly lightens o'er her face;
Where thoughts serenely sweet express
  How pure, how dear their dwelling-place.

And on that cheek, and o'er that brow,
  So soft, so calm, yet eloquent,
The smiles that win, the tints that glow,
  But tell of days in goodness spent,
A mind at peace with all below,
  A heart whose love is innocent.

TO THOMAS MOORE

My boat is on the shore,
  And my bark is on the sea;
But, before I go, Tom Moore,
  Here's a double health to thee!

Here's a sigh for those that love me,
　　And a smile for those who hate;
And, whatever sky's above me,
　　Here's a heart for every fate.

Though the ocean roar around me,
　　Yet it still shall bear me on;
Though a desert should surround me,
　　It hath springs that may be won.

Were 't the last drop in the well,
　　As I gasped upon the brink,
Ere my fainting spirit fell
　　'T is to thee that I would drink.

With that water, as this wine,
　　The libation I would pour
Should be,—Peace with thine and mine,
　　And a health to thee, Tom Moore!

WATERLOO

(FROM CHILDE HAROLD)

STOP!—for thy tread is on an Empire's dust!
An Earthquake's spoil is sepulchred below!
Is the spot marked with no colossal bust?
Nor column trophied for triumphal show?
None: but the moral's truth tells simpler so.
As the ground was before, thus let it be;—
How that red rain hath made the harvest grow!
And is this all the world has gained by thee,
Thou first and last of fields! king-making Victory?

And Harold stands upon this place of skulls,
The grave of France, the deadly Waterloo!
How in an hour the power which gave annuls
Its gifts, transferring fame as fleeting too!

In "pride of place" here last the eagle flew,
Then tore with bloody talon the rent plain,
Pierced by the shaft of banded nations through;
Ambition's life and labors all were vain;
He wears the shattered links of the world's broken chain.

There was a sound of revelry by night,
And Belgium's capital had gathered then
Her Beauty and her Chivalry, and bright
The lamps shone o'er fair women and brave men;
A thousand hearts beat happily; and when
Music arose with its voluptuous swell,
Soft eyes looked love to eyes which spake again,
And all went merry as a marriage-bell;
But hush! hark! a deep sound strikes like a rising knell!

Did ye not hear it?—No; 'twas but the wind,
Or the car rattling o'er the stony street;
On with the dance! let joy be unconfined,
No sleep till morn, when Youth and Pleasure meet,
To chase the glowing Hours with flying feet—
But, hark!—that heavy sound breaks in once more,
As if the clouds its echo would repeat;
And nearer, clearer, deadlier than before!
Arm! arm! it is—it is—the cannon's opening roar!

Within a windowed niche of that high hall,
Sat Brunswick's fated chieftain; he did hear
That sound the first amid the festival,
And caught its tone with death's prophetic ear;
And when they smiled because he deemed it near,
His heart more truly knew that peal too well
Which stretched his father on a bloody bier,
And roused the vengeance blood alone could quell:
He rushed into the field, and, foremost fighting, fell.

Ah! then and there was hurrying to and fro,
And gathering tears, and tremblings of distress,
And cheeks all pale, which but an hour ago
Blushed at the praise of their own loveliness!

And there were sudden partings, such as press
The life from out young hearts, and choking sighs
Which ne'er might be repeated: who could guess
If ever more should meet those mutual eyes,
Since upon night so sweet such awful morn could rise!

And there was mounting in hot haste: the steed,
The mustering squadron, and the clattering car,
Went pouring forward with impetuous speed,
And swiftly forming in the ranks of war;
And the deep thunder peal on peal afar,
And near, the beat of the alarming drum,
Roused up the soldier ere the morning star;
While thronged the citizens with terror dumb,
Or whispering with white lips—"The foe! They come!
        they come!"

And wild and high the "Cameron's gathering" rose,
The war-note of Lochiel, which Albyn's hills
Have heard, and heard, too, have her Saxon foes:
How in the noon of night that pibroch thrills
Savage and shrill! But with the breath which fills
Their mountain-pipe, so fill the mountaineers
With the fierce native daring which instils
The stirring memory of a thousand years,
And Evan's, Donald's fame rings in each clansman's ear!

And Ardennes waves above them her green leaves,
Dewy with nature's tear-drops, as they pass,
Grieving, if aught inanimate e'er grieves,
Over the unreturning brave,—alas!
Ere evening to be trodden like the grass
Which, now beneath them, but above shall grow
In its next verdure, when this fiery mass
Of living valor, rolling on the foe,
And burning with high hope, shall moulder cold and low!

Last noon beheld them full of lusty life,
Last eve in Beauty's circle proudly gay;
The midnight brought the signal sound of strife,

The morn the marshalling in arms,—the day
Battle's magnificently-stern array!
The thunder-clouds close o'er it, which when rent,
The earth is covered thick with other clay,
Which her own clay shall cover, heaped and pent,
Rider and horse,—friend, foe,—in one red burial blent!

Their praise is hymned by loftier harps than mine;
Yet one I would select from that proud throng,
Partly because they blend me with his line,
And partly that I did his sire some wrong,
And partly that bright names will hallow song!
And his was of the bravest, and when showered
The death-bolts deadliest the thinned files along,
Even where the thickest of war's tempest lowered,
They reached no nobler breast than thine, young, gallant
      Howard!

There have been tears and breaking hearts for thee,
And mine were nothing, had I such to give;
But when I stood beneath the fresh green tree,
Which, living, waves where thou didst cease to live,
And saw around me the wide field revive
With fruits and fertile promise, and the Spring
Come forth her work of gladness to contrive,
With all her reckless birds upon the wing,
I turned from all she brought to those she could not bring!

THOMAS CAMPBELL

YE MARINERS OF ENGLAND

I.

YE Mariners of England!
That guard our native seas;
Whose flag has braved, a thousand years,
The battle and the breeze!

Your glorious standard launch again,
To match another foe!
And sweep through the deep
While the stormy winds do blow—
While the battle rages loud and long,
And the stormy winds do blow.

II.

The spirits of your fathers
Shall start from every wave!—
For the deck it was their field of fame,
And Ocean was their grave.
Where Blake and mighty Nelson fell
Your manly hearts shall glow,
As ye sweep through the deep,
While the stormy winds do blow—
While the battle rages loud and long,
And the stormy winds do blow.

III.

Britannia needs no bulwarks,
No towers along the steep;
Her march is o'er the mountain-wave,
Her home is on the deep.
With thunders from her native oak
She quells the floods below,
As they roar on the shore,
When the stormy winds do blow—
When the battle rages loud and long,
And the stormy winds do blow.

IV.

The meteor flag of England
Shall yet terrific burn,
Till danger's troubled night depart,
And the star of peace return.
Then, then, ye ocean-warriors!

Our song and feast shall flow
  To the fame of your name,
When the storm has ceased to blow—
When the fiery fight is heard no more,
  And the storm has ceased to blow.

LORD ULLIN'S DAUGHTER

A CHIEFTAIN, to the Highlands bound,
  Cries, "Boatman, do not tarry!
And I'll give thee a silver pound
  To row us o'er the ferry."

"Now who be ye, would cross Lochgyle,
  This dark and stormy water?"
"O, I'm the chief of Ulva's isle,
  And this Lord Ullin's daughter.

"And fast before her father's men
  Three days we've fled together;
For should he find us in the glen,
  My blood would stain the heather.

"His horsemen hard behind us ride;
  Should they our steps discover,
Then who will cheer my bonny bride
  When they have slain her lover?"—

Out spoke the hardy Highland wight,
  "I'll go, my chief—I'm ready.
It is not for your silver bright,
  But for your winsome lady.

"And by my word! the bonny bird
  In danger shall not tarry;
So though the waves are raging white,
  I'll row you o'er the ferry."

By this the storm grew loud apace;
  The water-wraith was shrieking;
And in the scowl of heaven each face
  Grew dark as they were speaking.

But still as wilder blew the wind,
  And as the night grew drearer,
Adown the glen rode armèd men—
  Their trampling sounded nearer.

"O haste thee, haste!" the lady cries;
  "Though tempests round us gather;
I'll meet the raging of the skies,
  But not an angry father."

The boat has left a stormy land,
  A stormy sea before her—
When, oh! too strong for human hand,
  The tempest gathered o'er her.

And still they rowed amidst the roar
  Of waters fast prevailing;—
Lord Ullin reached that fatal shore;
  His wrath was changed to wailing.

For sore dismayed, through storm and shade
  His child he did discover;
One lovely hand she stretched for aid,
  And one was round her lover.

"Come back! come back!" he cried in grief,
  "Across this stormy water;
And I'll forgive your Highland chief,
  My daughter!—Oh, my daughter!"

'Twas vain:—the loud waves lashed the shore,
  Return or aid preventing:
The waters wild went o'er his child,
  And he was left lamenting.

HENRY CAREY

SALLY IN OUR ALLEY

Of all the girls that are so smart
  There's none like pretty Sally;
She is the darling of my heart,
  And she lives in our alley.

There is no lady in the land
  Is half so sweet as Sally;
She is the darling of my heart,
  And she lives in our alley.

Her father he makes cabbage-nets
  And through the streets does cry 'em;
Her mother she sells laces long
  To such as please to buy 'em:
But sure such folks could ne'er beget
  So sweet a girl as Sally!
She is the darling of my heart,
  And she lives in our alley.

When she is by, I leave my work,
  I love her so sincerely;
My master comes like any Turk,
  And bangs me most severely—
But let him bang his bellyful,
  I'll bear it all for Sally;
She is the darling of my heart,
  And she lives in our alley.

Of all the days that's in the week
  I dearly love but one day—
And that's the day that comes betwixt
  A Saturday and Monday;
For then I'm drest all in my best
  To walk abroad with Sally;
She is the darling of my heart,
  And she lives in our alley.

My master carries me to church,
  And often am I blamed
Because I leave him in the lurch
  As soon as text is named;
I leave the church in sermon-time
  And slink away to Sally;
She is the darling of my heart,
  And she lives in our alley.

When Christmas comes about again
  O then I shall have money;
I'll hoard it up, and box it all,
  I'll give it to my honey:
I would it were ten thousand pound,
  I'd give it all to Sally;
She is the darling of my heart,
  And she lives in our alley.

My master and the neighbours all
  Make game of me and Sally,
And, but for her, I'd better be
  A slave and row a galley;
But when my seven long years are out
  O then I'll marry Sally,—
O then we'll wed, and then we'll bed . . .
  But not in our alley!

GEOFFREY CHAUCER

THE COMPLAINT TO HIS EMPTY PURSE

To you, my purse, and to none other wight
Complain I, for ye be my lady dear!
I am so sorrow, now that ye be light;
For certes, but ye make me heavy cheer,
Me were as leif be laid upon my bier;
For which unto your mercy thus I cry:
Be heavy again, or elles might I die!

Now voucheth safe this day, or it be night,
That I of you the blissful sound may hear,
Or see your colour like the sun bright
That of yellowness had never a peer.
Ye be my life, ye be my hertes stere,
Queen of comfort and of good company:
Be heavy again, or elles might I die!

SAMUEL TAYLOR COLERIDGE

Samuel Taylor Coleridge

Now purse, that be to me my life's light,
And saviour, as down in this world here,
Out of this toune help me through your might,
Since that ye wole not be my treasurer;
For I am shaved as nigh as any frere.
But yet I pray unto your courtesy
Be heavy again, or elles might I die!

O Conqueror of Brute's Albion
Which that by line and free election
Be very king, this song to you I send;
And ye, that mighten all our harm amend,
Have mind upon my supplication!

SAMUEL TAYLOR COLERIDGE

KUBLA KHAN

IN Xanadu did Kubla Khan
A stately pleasure-dome decree:
Where Alph, the sacred river, ran,
Through caverns measureless to man,
Down to a sunless sea.
So twice five miles of fertile ground
With walls and towers were girdled round:
And here were gardens bright with sinuous rills,
Where blossomed many an incense-bearing tree;
And here were forests ancient as the hills,
Infolding sunny spots of greenery.

But oh! that deep romantic chasm which slanted
Down the green hill athwart a cedarn cover!
A savage place! as holy and enchanted
As e'er beneath a waning moon was haunted
By woman wailing for her demon-lover!
And from this chasm, with ceaseless turmoil seething,

As if this earth in fast thick pants were breathing,
A mighty fountain momently was forced:
Amid whose swift half-intermitted burst
Huge fragments vaulted like rebounding hail,
Or chaffy grain beneath the thresher's flail:

And 'mid these dancing rocks at once and ever
It flung up momently the sacred river.
Five miles meandering with a mazy motion
Through wood and dale the sacred river ran,
Then reached the caverns measureless to man,
And sank in tumult to a lifeless ocean:
And 'mid this tumult Kubla heard from far
Ancestral voices prophesying war!

The shadow of the dome of pleasure
Floated midway on the waves;
Where was heard the mingled measure
From the fountain and the caves.
It was a miracle of rare device,
A sunny pleasure-dome with caves of ice!

A damsel with a dulcimer
In a vision once I saw:
It was an Abyssinian maid,
And on her dulcimer she played,
Singing of Mount Abora.
Could I revive within me
Her symphony and song,
To such a deep delight 't would win me,
That with music loud and long,
I would build that dome in air,
That sunny dome! those caves of ice!
And all who heard should see them there,
And all should cry, Beware! Beware!
His flashing eyes, his floating hair.
Weave a circle round him thrice,
And close your eyes with holy dread,
For he on honey-dew hath fed,
And drunk the milk of Paradise.

THE RIME OF
THE ANCIENT MARINER

PART I

An ancient Mariner meeteth three gallants bidden to a wedding feast, and detaineth one.

IT is an ancient Mariner,
  And he stoppeth one of three.
"By thy long grey beard and glittering eye,
  Now wherefore stopp'st thou me?

The Bridegroom's doors are opened wide,
  And I am next of kin;
The guests are met, the feast is set:
  May'st hear the merry din."

He holds him with his skinny hand,
  "There was a ship," quoth he.
"Hold off! unhand me, grey beard loon!"
  Eftsoons his hand dropt he.

The wedding-guest is spell-bound by the eye of the old sea-faring man, and constrained to hear his tale.

He holds him with his glittering eye—
  The Wedding-Guest stood still,
And listens like a three years' child:
  The Mariner hath his will.

The Wedding-Guest sat on a stone:
  He cannot choose but hear;
And thus spake on that ancient man,
  The bright-eyed Mariner.

"The ship was cheered, the harbor cleared,
  Merrily did we drop
Below the kirk, below the hill,
  Below the light-house top.

The Mariner tells how the ship sailed southward with a good wind and fair weather, till it reached the Line.

The Sun came up upon the left,
  Out of the sea came he!
And he shone bright, and on the right
  Went down into the sea.

Higher and higher every day,
   Till over the mast at noon"—
The Wedding-Guest here beat his breast,
   For he heard the loud bassoon.

The wedding-guest
heareth the bridal
music, but the
Mariner continu-
eth his tale.

The bride hath paced into the hall,
   Red as a rose is she;
Nodding their heads before her goes
   The merry minstrelsy.

The Wedding-Guest he beat his breast,
   Yet he cannot choose but hear;
And thus spake on that ancient man,
   The bright-eyed Mariner.

The ship drawn
[driven] by a
storm toward the
south pole.

"And now the storm-blast came, and he
   Was tyrannous and strong:
He struck with his o'ertaking wings,
   And chased us south along.

With sloping masts and dipping prow,
As who pursued with yell and blow
Still treads the shadow of his foe,
   And forward bends his head,
The ship drove fast, loud roared the blast,
   And southward aye we fled.

And now there came both mist and snow,
   And it grew wondrous cold:
And ice, mast-high, came floating by,
   As green as emerald.

The land of ice
and of fearful
sounds, where no
living thing was
to be seen.

And through the drifts the snowy clifts
   Did send a dismal sheen:
Nor shapes of men nor beasts we ken—
   The ice was all between.

The ice was here, the ice was there,
   The ice was all around:
It cracked and growled, and roared and howled,
   Like noises in a swound!

Till a great sea-bird called the Albatross came through the snow-fog, and was received with great joy and hospitality.

At length did cross an Albatross:
　Thorough the fog it came;
As if it had been a Christian soul,
　We hailed it in God's name.

It ate the food it ne'er had eat,
　And round and round it flew.
The ice did split with a thunder-fit;
　The helmsman steered us through!

And lo! the Albatross proveth a bird of good omen, and followeth the ship, as it returned northward through fog and floating ice.

And a good south wind sprung up behind;
　The Albatross did follow,
And every day, for food or play,
　Came to the mariner's hollo!

In mist or cloud, on mast or shroud,
　It perched for vespers nine;
Whiles all the night, through fog-smoke white,
　Glimmered the white moon-shine."

The ancient Mariner inhospitably killeth the pious bird of good omen.

"God save thee, ancient Mariner!
　From the fiends, that plague thee thus!—
Why look'st thou so?"—"With my cross-bow
　I shot the Albatross.

PART II

The Sun now rose upon the right:
　Out of the sea came he,
Still hid in mist, and on the left
　Went down into the sea.

And the good south wind still blew behind,
　But no sweet bird did follow,
Nor any day for food or play
　Came to the Mariner's hollo!

His shipmates cry out against the ancient Mariner for killing the bird of good luck.

And I had done a hellish thing,
　And it would work 'em woe:
For all averred, I had killed the bird
　That made the breeze to blow.

'Ah, wretch!' said they, 'the bird to slay,
That made the breeze to blow!'

But when the fog cleared off, they justify the same, and thus make themselves accomplices in the crime.

Nor dim nor red, like God's own head,
The glorious Sun uprist:
Then all averred, I had killed the bird
That brought the fog and mist.
' 'T was right,' said they, 'such birds to slay,
That bring the fog and mist.'

The fair breeze continues; the ship enters the Pacific Ocean, and sails northward, even until it reaches the Line.

The fair breeze blew, the white foam flew,
The furrow followed free;
We were the first that ever burst
Into that silent sea.

The ship hath been suddenly becalmed.

Down dropt the breeze, the sails dropt down,
'T was sad as sad could be;
And we did speak only to break
The silence of the sea!

All in a hot and copper sky,
The bloody Sun, at noon,
Right up above the mast did stand,
No bigger than the Moon.

Day after day, day after day,
We stuck, nor breath nor motion;
As idle as a painted ship
Upon a painted ocean.

And the Albatross begins to be avenged.

Water, water, everywhere,
And all the boards did shrink;
Water, water, everywhere,
Nor any drop to drink.

The very deep did rot: O Christ!
That ever this should be!
Yea, slimy things did crawl with legs
Upon the slimy sea.

About, about, in reel and rout
The death-fires danced at night;
The water, like a witch's oils,
Burnt green, and blue, and white.

A spirit had fol-
lowed them ; one
of the invisible in-
habitants of this
planet, neither de-
parted souls nor
angels; concerning
whom the learned
Jew, Josephus, and
the Platonic Constantinopolitan, Michael Psellus, may be consulted. They are very numerous,
and there is no climate or element without one or more.

And some in dreams assurèd were
Of the spirit that plagued us so;
Nine fathom deep he had followed us
From the land of mist and snow.

And every tongue, through utter drought,
Was withered at the root;
We could not speak, no more than if
We had been choked with soot.

The shipmates in
their sore distress
would fain throw
the whole guilt on
the ancient Mari-
ner; in sign
whereof they hang
the dead sea-bird
round his neck.

Ah! well-a-day! what evil looks
Had I from old and young!
Instead of the cross, the Albatross
About my neck was hung.

PART III

The ancient Mari-
ner beholdeth a
sign in the element
afar off.

There passed a weary time. Each throat
Was parched, and glazed each eye.
A weary time! a weary time!
How glazed each weary eye,
When looking westward, I beheld
A something in the sky.

At first it seemed a little speck,
And then it seemed a mist;
It moved and moved, and took at last
A certain shape, I wist.

A speck, a mist, a shape, I wist!
And still it neared and neared:
As if it dodged a water-sprite,
It plunged and tacked and veered.

At its nearer approach, it seemeth him to be a ship; and at a dear ransom he freeth his speech from the bonds of thirst.

With throats unslaked, with black lips baked,
　We could not laugh nor wail;
Through utter drought all dumb we stood!
I bit my arm, I sucked the blood,
　And cried, 'A sail! a sail!'

With throats unslaked, with black lips baked,
　Agape they heard me call:

A flash of joy.

Gramercy! they for joy did grin,
And all at once their breath drew in,
　As they were drinking all.

And horror follows. For can it be a ship that comes onward without wind or tide?

'See! see! (I cried) she tacks no more!
　Hither to work us weal;
Without a breeze, without a tide,
　She steadies with upright keel!'

The western wave was all a-flame.
　The day was well-nigh done!
Almost upon the western wave
　Rested the broad bright Sun;
When that strange shape drove suddenly
　Betwixt us and the Sun.

It seemeth him but the skeleton of a ship.

And straight the Sun was flecked with bars,
　(Heaven's Mother send us grace!)
As if through a dungeon-grate he peered
　With broad and burning face.

Alas! (thought I, and my heart beat loud)
　How fast she nears and nears!
Are those her sails that glance in the Sun,
　Like restless gossameres?

And its ribs are seen as bars on the face of the setting Sun. The spectre-woman and her death-mate, and no other on board the skeleton-ship.

Are those her ribs through which the Sun
　Did peer, as through a grate?
And is that Woman all her crew?
Is that a Death? and are there two?
　Is Death that woman's mate?

Like vessel, like crew!

Her lips were red, her looks were free,
Her locks were yellow as gold:
Her skin was as white as leprosy,
The Night-mare Life-in-Death was she,
Who thicks man's blood with cold.

Death and Life-in-Death have diced for the ship's crew, and she (the latter) winneth the ancient Mariner.

The naked hulk alongside came,
And the twain were casting dice;
'The game is done! I've won, I've won!'
Quoth she, and whistles thrice.

No twilight within the courts of the Sun.

The Sun's rim dips; the stars rush out:
At one stride comes the dark;
With far-heard whisper, o'er the sea,
Off shot the spectre-bark.

At the rising of the Moon.

We listened and looked sideways up!
Fear at my heart, as at a cup,
My life-blood seemed to sip!
The stars were dim, and thick the night,
The steerman's face by his lamp gleamed white;
From the sails the dew did drip—
Till clomb above the eastern bar
The hornëd Moon, with one bright star
Within the nether tip.

One after another.

One after one, by the star-dogged Moon,
Too quick for groan or sigh,
Each turned his face with a ghastly pang,
And cursed me with his eye.

His shipmates drop down dead;

Four times fifty living men,
(And I heard nor sigh nor groan)
With heavy thump, a lifeless lump,
They dropped down one by one.

But Life-in-Death begins her work on the ancient Mariner.

The souls did from the bodies fly—
They fled to bliss or woe!
And every soul, it passed me by,
Like the whizz of my cross-bow!"

PART IV

"I fear thee, ancient Mariner!
    I fear thy skinny hand!
And thou art long, and lank, and brown,
    As is the ribbed sea-sand.

I fear thee and thy glittering eye,
    And thy skinny hand, so brown."—
"Fear not, fear not, thou Wedding-Guest!
    This body dropt not down.

Alone, alone; all, all alone,
    Alone on a wide wide sea!
And never a saint took pity on
    My soul in agony.

The many men, so beautiful!
    And they all dead did lie;
And a thousand thousand slimy things
    Lived on; and so did I.

I looked upon the rotting sea,
    And drew my eyes away;
I looked upon the rotting deck,
    And there the dead men lay.

I looked to Heaven, and tried to pray;
    But or ever a prayer had gusht,
A wicked whisper came and made
    My heart as dry as dust.

I closed my lids, and kept them close,
    And the balls like pulses beat;
For the sky and the sea, and the sea and the sky
Lay like a load on my weary eye,
    And the dead were at my feet.

The cold sweat melted from their limbs,
    Nor rot nor reek did they:
The look with which they looked on me
    Had never passed away.

An orphan's curse would drag to Hell
  A spirit from on high;
But oh! more horrible than that
  Is a curse in a dead man's eye!
Seven days, seven nights, I saw that curse,
  And yet I could not die.

In his loneliness and fixedness he yearneth towards the journeying Moon, and the stars that still sojourn, yet still move onward; and everywhere the

The moving Moon went up the sky,
  And no where did abide:
Softly she was going up,
  And a star or two beside—

blue sky belongs to them, and is their appointed rest, and their native country and their own natural homes, which they enter unannounced, as lords that are certainly expected, and yet there is a silent joy at their arrival.

Her beams bemocked the sultry main,
  Like April hoar-frost spread;
But where the ship's huge shadow lay,
The charmèd water burnt alway
  A still and awful red.

By the light of the Moon, he beholdeth God's creatures of the great calm.

Beyond the shadow of the ship,
  I watched the water-snakes:
They moved in tracks of shining white,
And when they reared, the elfish light
  Fell off in hoary flakes.

Within the shadow of the ship,
  I watched their rich attire:
Blue, glossy green, and velvet black,
They coiled and swam; and every track
  Was a flash of golden fire.

Their beauty and their happiness.

O happy living things! no tongue
  Their beauty might declare:
A spring of love gushed from my heart,

He blesseth them in his heart.

  And I blessed them unaware:
Sure my kind saint took pity on me,
  And I blessed them unaware.

The selfsame moment I could pray;
   And from my neck so free
The Albatross fell off and sank
   Like lead into the sea.

PART V

Oh sleep! it is a gentle thing,
   Beloved from pole to pole!
To Mary Queen the praise be given!
She sent the gentle sleep from Heaven,
   That slid into my soul.

By grace of the
holy Mother, the
ancient Mariner
is refreshed with
rain.
The silly buckets on the deck,
   That had so long remained,
I dreamt that they were filled with dew;
   And when I awoke, it rained.

My lips were wet, my throat was cold
   My garments all were dank;
Sure I had drunken in my dreams,
   And still my body drank.

I moved, and could not feel my limbs:
   I was so light—almost
I thought that I had died in sleep,
   And was a blessèd ghost.

He heareth sounds
and seeth strange
sights and commo-
tions in the sky
and the element.
And soon I heard a roaring wind:
   It did not come anear;
But with its sound it shook the sails,
   That were so thin and sere.

The upper air burst into life!
   And a hundred fire-flags sheen,
To and fro they were hurried about!
And to and fro, and in and out,
   The wan stars danced between.

And the coming wind did roar more loud,
   And the sails did sigh like sedge;

And the rain poured down from one black cloud;
The Moon was at its edge.

The thick black cloud was cleft, and still
   The Moon was at its side:
Like waters shot from some high crag,
The lightning fell with never a jag,
   A river steep and wide.

The loud wind never reached the ship,
   Yet now the ship moved on!
Beneath the lightning and the Moon
   The dead men gave a groan.

They groaned, they stirred, they all uprose,
   Nor spoke, nor moved their eyes;
It had been strange, even in a dream,
   To have seen those dead men rise.

The helmsman steered, the ship moved on;
   Yet never a breeze up blew;
The mariners all 'gan work the ropes,
   Where they were wont to do;
They raised their limbs like lifeless tools—
   We were a ghastly crew.

The body of my brother's son
   Stood by me, knee to knee:
The body and I pulled at one rope,
   But he said nought to me."

"I fear thee, ancient Mariner!"
"Be calm, thou Wedding-Guest!
'T was not those souls that fled in pain,
Which to their corses came again,
   But a troop of spirits blest:

For when it dawned—they dropped their arms,
   And clustered round the mast;
Sweet sounds rose slowly through their mouths,
   And from their bodies passed.

The bodies of the ship's crew are inspired, and the ship moves on;

But not by the souls of the men, nor by dæmons of earth or middle air, but by a blessed troop of angelic spirits, sent down by the invocation of the guardian saint.

If he may know which way to go;
  For she guides him smooth or grim.
See brother, see! how graciously
  She looketh down on him.'

First Voice

The Mariner hath
been cast into a
trance; for the an-
gelic power caus-
eth the vessel to
drive northward
faster than human
life could endure.

'But why drives on that ship so fast,
  Without or wave or wind?'

Second Voice

'The air is cut away before,
  And closes from behind.

Fly, brother, fly! more high, more high!
  Or we shall be belated:
For slow and slow that ship will go,
  When the Mariner's trance is abated.'

The supernatural
motion is retarded;
the ancient Mari-
ner awakes and his
penance begins
anew.

I woke, and we were sailing on
  As in a gentle weather:
'T was night, calm night, the Moon was high;
  The dead men stood together.

All stood together on the deck,
  For a charnel-dungeon fitter:
All fixed on me their stony eyes,
  That in the Moon did glitter.

The pang, the curse, with which they died,
  Had never passed away:
I could not draw my eyes from theirs,
  Nor turn them up to pray.

The curse is finally
expiated.

And now this spell was snapt: once more
  I viewed the ocean green,
And looked far forth, yet little saw
  Of what had else been seen—

Like one, that on a lonesome road
 Doth walk in fear and dread,
And having once turned round walks on,
 And turns no more his head;
Because he knows a frightful fiend
 Doth close behind him tread.

But soon there breathed a wind on me,
 Nor sound nor motion made:
Its path was not upon the sea,
 In ripple or in shade.

It raised my hair, it fanned my cheek
 Like a meadow-gale of spring—
It mingled strangely with my fears,
 Yet it felt like a welcoming.

Swiftly, swiftly flew the ship,
 Yet she sailed softly too:
Sweetly, sweetly blew the breeze—
 On me alone it blew.

And the ancient Mariner beholdeth his native country. Oh! dream of joy! is this indeed
 The light-house top I see?
Is this the hill? is this the kirk?
 Is this mine own countree?

We drifted o'er the harbour-bar,
 And I with sobs did pray—
'O let me be awake, my God!
 Or let me sleep alway.'

The harbour-bay was clear as glass,
 So smoothly it was strewn!
And on the bay the moonlight lay,
 And the shadow of the Moon.

The rock shone bright, the kirk no less,
 That stands above the rock:
The moonlight steeped in silentness
 The steady weathercock.

The angelic spirits
leave the dead
bodies.
And the bay was white with silent light,
    Till rising from the same,
Full many shapes, that shadows were,
    In crimson colors came.

And appear in
their own forms
of light.
A little distance from the prow
    Those crimson shadows were:
I turned my eyes upon the deck—
    Oh, Christ! what saw I there!

Each corse lay flat, lifeless and flat,
    And by the holy rood!
A man all light, a seraph-man,
    On every corse there stood.

This seraph-band, each waved his hand:
    It was a heavenly sight!
They stood as signals to the land,
    Each one a lovely light;

This seraph-band, each waved his hand:
    No voice did they impart—
No voice; but oh! the silence sank
    Like music on my heart.

But soon I heard the dash of oars,
    I heard the Pilot's cheer;
My head was turned perforce away,
    And I saw a boat appear.

The Pilot and the Pilot's boy,
    I heard them coming fast:
Dear Lord in Heaven! it was a joy
    The dead men could not blast.

I saw a third—I heard his voice:
    It is the Hermit good!
He singeth loud his godly hymns
That he makes in the wood.
He'll shrieve my soul, he'll wash away
    The Albatross's blood.

PART VII

The Hermit of
the Wood.

This Hermit good lives in that wood
  Which slopes down to the sea.
How loudly his sweet voice he rears!
He loves to talk with marineres
  That come from a far countree.

He kneels at morn, at noon and eve—
  He hath a cushion plump:
It is the moss that wholly hides
  The rotted old oak stump.

The skiff-boat neared: I heard them talk,
  'Why, this is strange, I trow!
Where are those lights so many and fair,
  That signal made but now?'

Approacheth the
ship with wonder.

'Strange, by my faith!' the Hermit said—
  'And they answered not our cheer!
The planks look warped! and see those sails,
  How thin they are and sere!
I never saw aught like to them,
  Unless perchance it were

Brown skeletons of leaves that lag
  My forest-brook along;
When the ivy-tod is heavy with snow,
And the owlet whoops to the wolf below,
  That eats the she-wolf's young.'

'Dear Lord! it hath a fiendish look—
  (The Pilot made reply)
I am a-feared'—'Push on, push on!'
  Said the Hermit cheerily.

The boat came closer to the ship,
  But I nor spake nor stirred;
The boat came close beneath the ship,
  And straight a sound was heard.

The ship suddenly
sinketh.

Under the water it rumbled on,
  Still louder and more dread:
It reached the ship; it split the bay;
  The ship went down like lead.

The ancient Mari-
ner is saved in the
Pilot's boat.

Stunned by that loud and dreadful sound,
  Which sky and ocean smote,
Like one that hath been seven days drowned
  My body lay afloat;
But swift as dreams, myself I found
  Within the Pilot's boat.

Upon the whirl, where sank the ship,
  The boat spun round and round;
And all was still, save that the hill
  Was telling of the sound.

I moved my lips—the Pilot shrieked
  And fell down in a fit;
The holy Hermit raised his eyes,
  And prayed where he did sit.

I took the oars: the Pilot's boy,
  Who now doth crazy go,
Laughed loud and long, and all the while
  His eyes went to and fro.
'Ha! ha!' quoth he, 'full plain I see,
  The Devil knows how to row.'

And now, all in my own countree,
  I stood on the firm land!
The Hermit stepped forth from the boat,
  And scarcely he could stand.

The ancient Mari-
ner earnestly en-
treateth the Her-
mit to shrieve him;
and the penance
of life falls on
him.

'O shrieve me, shrieve me, holy man!'
  The Hermit crossed his brow.
'Say quick,' quoth he, 'I bid thee say—
  What manner of man art thou?'

Forthwith this frame of mine was wrenched
  With a woeful agony,

Which forced me to begin my tale;
  And then it left me free.

And ever and anon throughout his future life an agony constraineth him to travel from land to land. Since then, at an uncertain hour,
  That agony returns:
And till my ghastly tale is told,
  This heart within me burns.

I pass, like night, from land to land;
  I have strange power of speech;
That moment that his face I see,
I know the man that must hear me:
  To him my tale I teach.

What loud uproar bursts from that door!
  The wedding-guests are there:
But in the garden-bower the bride
  And bride-maids singing are:
And hark the little vesper-bell,
  Which biddeth me to prayer!

Oh Wedding-Guest! this soul hath been
  Alone on a wide wide sea:
So lonely 'twas, that God himself
  Scarce seemèd there to be.

Oh sweeter than the marriage feast,
  'Tis sweeter far to me,
To walk together to the kirk
  With goodly company!—

To walk together to the kirk,
  And all together pray,
While each to his great Father bends,
Old men, and babes, and loving friends,
  And youths and maidens gay!

And to teach, by his own example, love and reverence to all things that God made and loveth. Farewell, farewell! but this I tell
  To thee, thou Wedding-Guest!
He prayeth well, who loveth well
  Both man and bird and beast.

He prayeth best, who loveth best
  All things both great and small;
For the dear God who loveth us,
  He made and loveth all."

The Mariner, whose eye is bright,
  Whose beard with age is hoar,
Is gone: and now the Wedding-Guest
Turned from the bridegroom's door.

He went like one that hath been stunned,
  And is of sense forlorn;
A sadder and a wiser man,
  He rose the morrow morn.

WILLIAM CONGREVE

FROM "THE MOURNING BRIDE"

Music hath charms to sooth a savage beast,
To soften rocks, or bend a knotted oak.
I've read that things inanimate have moved,
And, as with living souls, have been informed,
By magic numbers and persuasive sound.

JAMES FENIMORE COOPER

MY BRIGANTINE

My brigantine!
Just in thy mould and beauteous in thy form,
Gentle in roll and buoyant on the surge,
Light as the sea-fowl rocking in the storm,
In breeze and gale thy onward course we urge,
  My water-queen!

Lady of mine!
More light and swift than thou none thread the sea,
With surer keel or steadier on its path;
We brave each waste of ocean-mystery
And laugh to hear the howling tempest's wrath,
    For we are thine!

    My brigantine!
Trust to the mystic power that points thy way,
Trust to the eye that pierces from afar,
Trust to the red meteors that around thee play,
And, fearless, trust the Sea-Green Lady's Star,
    Thou bark divine!

WILLIAM COWPER

TO MARY UNWIN

Mary! I want a lyre with other strings,
Such aid from Heaven as some have feign'd they drew,
An eloquence scarce given to mortals, new
And undebased by praise of meaner things,

That ere through age or woe I shed my wings
I may record thy worth with honour due,
In verse as musical as thou art true,
And that immortalizes whom it sings:—

But thou hast little need. There is a Book
By seraphs writ with beams of heavenly light,
On which the eyes of God not rarely look,

A chronicle of actions just and bright—
There all thy deeds, my faithful Mary, shine;
And since thou own'st that praise, I spare thee mine.

VERSES

I AM monarch of all I survey,
  My right there is none to dispute;
From the centre all round to the sea,
  I am lord of the fowl and the brute.
O Solitude! where are the charms
  That sages have seen in thy face?
Better dwell in the midst of alarms,
  Than reign in this horrible place.

I am out of humanity's reach,
  I must finish my journey alone,
Never hear the sweet music of speech,
  I start at the sound of my own.
The beasts, that roam over the plain,
  My form with indifference see;
They are so unacquainted with man,
  Their tameness is shocking to me.

Society, friendship, and love,
  Divinely bestowed upon man,
Oh, had I the wings of a dove,
  How soon would I taste you again!
My sorrows I then might assuage
  In the ways of religion and truth,
Might learn from the wisdom of age,
  And be cheered by the sallies of youth.

Religion! what treasure untold
  Resides in that heavenly word!
More precious than silver and gold,
  Or all that this earth can afford.
But the sound of the church-going bell
  These valleys and rocks never heard,
Never sighed at the sound of a knell,
  Or smiled when a sabbath appeared.

Ye winds, that have made me your sport,
  Convey to this desolate shore
Some cordial endearing report
  Of a land I shall visit no more.
My friends, do they now and then send
  A wish or a thought after me?
Oh, tell me I yet have a friend,
  Though a friend I am never to see.

How fleet is a glance of the mind!
  Compared with the speed of its flight
The tempest itself lags behind,
  And the swift-wingèd arrows of light.
When I think of my own native land,
  In a moment I seem to be there;
But alas! recollection at hand
  Soon hurries me back to despair.

But the sea-fowl is gone to her nest,
  The beast is laid down in his lair;
Even here is a season of rest,
  And I to my cabin repair.
There's mercy in every place,
  And mercy, encouraging thought!
Gives even affliction a grace,
  And reconciles man to his lot.

LOSS OF THE ROYAL GEORGE

TOLL for the Brave!
The brave that are no more!
All sunk beneath the wave
Fast by their native shore!

Eight hundred of the brave
Whose courage well was tried,
Had made the vessel heel
And laid her on her side.

A land-breeze shook the shrouds
And she was overset;
Down went the Royal George,
With all her crew complete.

Toll for the brave!
Brave Kempenfelt is gone;
His last sea-fight is fought,
His work of glory done.

It was not in the battle;
No tempest gave the shock;
She sprang no fatal leak,
She ran upon no rock.

His sword was in the sheath,
His fingers held the pen,
When Kempenfelt went down
With twice four hundred men.

—Weigh the vessel up
Once dreaded by our foes!
And mingle with our cup
The tears that England owes.

Her timbers yet are sound,
And she may float again
Full charged with England's thunder,
And plough the distant main:

But Kempenfelt is gone,
His victories are o'er;
And he and his eight hundred
Must plough the wave no more.

JOHN DRYDEN

ALEXANDER'S FEAST;

OR, THE POWER OF MUSIC.—AN ODE IN HONOR OF ST. CECILIA'S DAY

'T was at the royal feast for Persia won
  By Philip's warlike son:
  Aloft, in awful state,
  The godlike hero sate
    On his imperial throne;
His valiant peers were placed around,
Their brows with roses and with myrtles bound;
(So should desert in arms be crowned);
  The lovely Thais by his side
  Sate, like a blooming eastern bride,
  In flower of youth and beauty's pride.
    Happy, happy, happy pair!
      None but the brave,
      None but the brave,
  None but the brave deserves the fair.

CHORUS

Happy, happy, happy pair!
  None but the brave,
  None but the brave,
None but the brave deserves the fair.

Timotheus, placed on high
  Amid the tuneful quire,
  With flying fingers touched the lyre;
The trembling notes ascend the sky,
  And heavenly joys inspire.
The song began from Jove,
Who left his blissful seats above,
(Such is the power of mighty Love).
A dragon's fiery form belied the god;
Sublime on radiant spires he rode,
  When he to fair Olympia pressed,
  And while he sought her snowy breast;

Then, round her slender waist he curled,
And stamped an image of himself, a sovereign of the world.
The listening crowd admire the lofty sound—
A present deity! they shout around;
A present deity! the vaulted roofs rebound.
      With ravished ears
      The monarch hears,
        Assumes the god,
        Affects to nod,
      And seems to shake the spheres.

CHORUS

With ravished ears
The monarch hears,
  Assumes the god,
  Affects to nod,
And seems to shake the spheres.

The praise of Bacchus, then, the sweet musician sung—
  Of Bacchus ever fair and ever young;
    The jolly god in triumph comes:
    Sound the trumpets! beat the drums!
      Flushed with a purple grace,
      He shows his honest face;
Now give the hautboys breath—he comes, he comes!
Bacchus, ever fair and young,
  Drinking joys did first ordain;
Bacchus' blessings are a treasure;
Drinking is the soldier's pleasure:
    Rich the treasure,
    Sweet the pleasure;
Sweet is pleasure after pain.

CHORUS

Bacchus' blessings are a treasure;
Drinking is the soldier's pleasure:
  Rich the treasure,
  Sweet the pleasure;
Sweet is pleasure after pain.

Soothed with the sound, the king grew vain;
Fought all his battles o'er again;
And thrice he routed all his foes, and thrice he slew the slain.
The master saw the madness rise—
His glowing cheeks, his ardent eyes;
And while he Heaven and Earth defied,
Changed his hand, and checked his pride.
    He chose a mournful Muse,
      Soft pity to infuse;
He sung Darius great and good,
    By too severe a fate
Fallen, fallen, fallen, fallen—
Fallen from his high estate,
    And weltering in his blood;
Deserted, at his utmost need,
By those his former bounty fed;
On the bare earth exposed he lies,
With not a friend to close his eyes.
With downcast looks the joyless victor sate
    Revolving in his altered soul
      The various turns of chance below;
    And, now and then, a sigh he stole;
    And tears began to flow.

CHORUS

*   Revolving in his altered soul*
*   The various turns of chance below;*
*   And, now and then, a sigh he stole;*
*   And tears began to flow.*

The mighty master smiled, to see
That Love was in the next degree;
'Twas but a kindred sound to move,
For pity melts the mind to love.
    Softly sweet, in Lydian measures,
    Soon he soothed his soul to pleasures.
War, he sung, is toil and trouble;
Honor but an empty bubble—
    Never ending, still beginning—
Fighting still, and still destroying;

If the world be worth thy winning,
Think, O think it worth enjoying!
Lovely Thais sits beside thee—
Take the goods the gods provide thee.
The many rend the sky with loud applause;
So Love was crowned, but Music won the cause.
The prince, unable to conceal his pain,
    Gazed on the fair
    Who caused his care,
And sighed and looked, sighed and looked
Sighed and looked, and sighed again.
At length, with love and wine at once oppressed,
The vanquished victor sunk upon her breast.

CHORUS

The prince, unable to conceal his pain,
    Gazed on the fair
    Who caused his care,
And sighed and looked, sighed and looked,
Sighed and looked, and sighed again.
At length, with love and wine at once oppressed,
The vanquished victor sunk upon her breast.

Now strike the golden lyre again!
A louder yet, and yet a louder strain,
Break his bands of sleep asunder,
And rouse him, like a rattling peal of thunder.
    Hark, hark! the horrid sound
    Has raised up his head!
    As awaked from the dead,
    And amazed, he stares around.
Revenge! revenge! Timotheus cries;
    See the Furies arise!
    See the snakes that they rear,
    How they hiss in their hair,
And the sparkles that flash from their eyes!
    Behold a ghastly band,
    Each a torch in his hand!

These are Grecian ghosts, that in battle were slain,
        And unburied remain,
        Inglorious, on the plain!
        Give the vengeance due
        To the valiant crew.
Behold how they toss their torches on high,
    How they point to the Persian abodes,
And glittering temples of their hostile gods!
The princes applaud with a furious joy,
And the king seized a flambeau with zeal to destroy;
        Thais led the way
        To light him to his prey,
And, like another Helen, fired another Troy.

CHORUS

And the king seized a flambeau with zeal to destroy;
        Thais led the way
        To light him to his prey,
And, like another Helen, fired another Troy.

        Thus, long ago—
    Ere heaving bellows learned to blow,
        While organs yet were mute—
    Timotheus, to his breathing flute,
        And sounding lyre,
Could swell the soul to rage, or kindle soft desire.
    At last divine Cecilia came,
    Inventress of the vocal frame;
The sweet enthusiast, from her sacred store,
    Enlarged the former narrow bounds,
    And added length to solemn sounds,
With nature's mother-wit, and arts unknown before.
    Let old Timotheus yield the prize,
        Or both divide the crown;
    He raised a mortal to the skies,
        She drew an angel down.

GRAND CHORUS

At last divine Cecilia came,
Inventress of the vocal frame;
The sweet enthusiast, from her sacred store,
Enlarged the former narrow bounds,
And added length to solemn sounds,
With nature's mother-wit and arts unknown before.
Let old Timotheus yield the prize,
Or both divide the crown;
He raised a mortal to the skies,
She drew an angel down.

UNDER THE PORTRAIT OF MILTON

THREE Poets, in three distant ages born,
Greece, Italy, and England did adorn.
The first in loftiness of thought surpassed;
The next in majesty; in both the last.
The force of Nature could no further go:
To make a third she joined the former two.

RALPH WALDO EMERSON

EACH AND ALL

LITTLE thinks, in the field, yon red-cloaked clown
Of thee from the hill-top looking down;
The heifer that lows in the upland farm,
Far-heard, lows not thine ear to charm;
The sexton, tolling his bell at noon,
Deems not that great Napoleon
Stops his horse, and lists with delight,
Whilst his files sweep round yon Alpine height.
Nor knowest thou what argument
Thy life to thy neighbor's creed has lent.
All are needed by each one—
Nothing is fair or good alone.

RALPH WALDO EMERSON

I thought the sparrow's note from heaven,
Singing at dawn on the alder bough;
I brought him home, in his nest, at even;
He sings the song, but it pleases not now;
For I did not bring home the river and sky;
He sang to my ear—they sang to my eye.

The delicate shells lay on the shore;
The bubbles of the latest wave
Fresh pearls to their enamel gave,
And the bellowing of the savage sea
Greeted their safe escape to me.
I wiped away the weeds and foam—
I fetched my sea-born treasures home;
But the poor, unsightly, noisome things
Had left their beauty on the shore,
With the sun, and the sand, and the wild uproar.

The lover watched his graceful maid,
As 'mid the virgin train she strayed;
Nor knew her beauty's best attire
Was woven still by the snow-white choir.
At last she came to his hermitage,
Like the bird from the woodlands to the cage;
The gay enchantment was undone—
A gentle wife, but fairy none.

Then I said, "I covet truth;
Beauty is unripe childhood's cheat;
I leave it behind with the games of youth."—
As I spoke, beneath my feet
The ground-pine curled its pretty wreath,
Running over the club-moss burrs;
I inhaled the violet's breath;
Around me stood the oaks and firs;
Pine-cones and acorns lay on the ground;
Over me soared the eternal sky,
Full of light and of deity;

Again I saw, again I heard,
The rolling river, the morning bird;
Beauty through my senses stole—
I yielded myself to the perfect whole.

THE DAY'S RATION

WHEN I was born,
From all the seas of strength Fate filled a chalice,
Saying, "This be thy portion, child; this chalice.
Less than a lily's, thou shalt daily draw
From my great arteries—nor less nor more."
All substances the cunning chemist Time
Melts down into that liquor of my life—
Friends, foes, joys, fortunes, beauty, and disgust;
And whether I am angry or content,
Indebted or insulted, loved or hurt,
All he distills into sidereal wine,
And brims my little cup; heedless, alas!
Of all he sheds, how little it will hold,
How much rains over on the desert sands.
If a new Muse draw me with splendid ray,
And I uplift myself into its heaven,
The needs of the first sight absorb my blood,
And all the following hours of the day
Drag a ridiculous age.
To-day, when friends approach, and every hour
Brings book, or star-bright scroll of genius,
The little cup will hold not a bead more,
And all the costly liquor runs to waste;
Nor gives the jealous lord one diamond-drop,
So to be husbanded for future days.
Why need I volumes, if one word suffice?
Why need I galleries, when a pupil's draught,
After the master's sketch, fills and o'erfills
My apprehension? Why seek Italy,
Who cannot circumnavigate the sea
Of thoughts and things at home, but still adjourn
The nearest matters for a thousand days?

EDWARD FITZGERALD

THE RUBÁIYÁT OF
OMAR KHÁYYÁM

I

WAKE! For the Sun who scatter'd into flight
The Stars before him from the Field of Night,
   Drives Night along with them from Heav'n, and strikes
The Sultán's Turret with a Shaft of Light.

II

Before the phantom of False morning died,
Methought a Voice within the Tavern cried,
   "When all the Temple is prepared within,
Why nods the drowsy Worshipper outside?"

III

And, as the Cock crew, those who stood before
The Tavern shouted—"Open then the door!
   You know how little while we have to stay,
And, once departed, may return no more."

IV

Now the New Year reviving old Desires,
The thoughtful Soul to Solitude retires,
   Where the WHITE HAND OF MOSES on the Bough
Puts out, and Jesus from the Ground suspires.

V

Iram indeed is gone with all his Rose,
And Jamshyd's Sev'n-ring'd Cup where no one knows;
   But still a Ruby gushes from the Vine,
And many a Garden by the Water blows.

VI

And David's lips are lockt; but in divine
High-piping Péhlevi, with "Wine! Wine! Wine!
    Red Wine!"—the Nightingale cries to the Rose
That sallow cheek of hers to incarnadine.

VII

Come, fill the Cup, and in the fire of Spring
Your Winter-garment of Repentance fling:
    The Bird of Time has but a little way
To flutter—and the Bird is on the Wing.

VIII

Whether at Naishápúr or Babylon,
Whether the Cup with sweet or bitter run,
    The Wine of Life keeps oozing drop by drop,
The Leaves of Life keep falling one by one.

IX

Each Morn a thousand Roses brings, you say;
Yes, but where leaves the Rose of Yesterday?
    And this first Summer month that brings the Rose
Shall take Jamshyd and Kaikobád away.

X

Well, let it take them! What have we to do
With Kaikobád the Great, or Kaikhosrú?
    Let Zál and Rustum thunder as they will,
Or Hátim call to Supper—heed not you.

XI

With me along the strip of Herbage strown
That just divides the desert from the sown,
    Where name of Slave and Sultán is forgot—
And Peace to Máhmúd on his golden Throne!

XII

A Book of Verses underneath the Bough,
A Jug of Wine, a Loaf of Bread—and Thou
   Beside me singing in the Wilderness—
Oh, Wilderness were Paradise enow!

XIII

Some for the Glories of This World; and some
Sigh for the Prophet's Paradise to come;
   Ah, take the Cash, and let the Credit go,
Nor heed the rumble of a distant Drum!

XIV

Look to the blowing Rose about us—"Lo,
Laughing," she says, "into the world I blow,
   At once the silken tassel of my Purse
Tear, and its Treasure on the Garden throw."

XV

And those who husbanded the Golden grain,
And those who flung it to the winds like Rain,
   Alike to no such aureate Earth are turn'd
As, buried once, Men want dug up again.

XVI

The Worldly Hope men set their Hearts upon
Turns Ashes—or it prospers; and anon,
   Like Snow upon the Desert's dusty Face,
Lighting a little hour or two—was gone.

XVII

Think, in this batter'd Caravanserai
Whose Portals are alternate Night and Day,
   How Sultán after Sultán with his Pomp
Abode his destin'd Hour, and went his way.

XVIII

They say the Lion and the Lizard keep
The Courts where Jamshyd gloried and drank deep:
And Bahrám, that great Hunter—the Wild Ass
Stamps o'er his Head, but cannot break his Sleep.

XIX

I sometimes think that never blows so red
The Rose as where some buried Cæsar bled;
That every Hyacinth the Garden wears
Dropt in her Lap from some once lovely Head.

XX

And this reviving Herb whose tender Green
Fledges the River-Lip on which we lean—
Ah, lean upon it lightly! for who knows
From what once lovely Lip it springs unseen!

XXI

Ah, my Belovéd, fill the cup that clears
To-DAY of past Regret and future Fears:
To-morrow!—Why, To-morrow I may be
Myself with Yesterday's Sev'n thousand Years.

XXII

For some we loved, the loveliest and the best
That from his Vintage rolling Time has prest,
Have drunk their Cup a Round or two before,
And one by one crept silently to rest.

XXIII

And we, that now make merry in the Room
They left, and Summer dresses in new bloom,
Ourselves must we beneath the Couch of Earth
Descend—ourselves to make a Couch—for whom?

XXIV

Ah, make the most of what we yet may spend,
Before we too into the Dust descend;
     Dust into Dust, and under Dust, to lie,
Sans Wine, sans Song, sans Singer, and—sans End!

XXV

Alike for those who for To-DAY prepare,
And those that after some To-MORROW stare,
     A Muezzín from the Tower of Darkness cries,
"Fools, your Reward is neither Here nor There."

XXVI

Why, all the Saints and Sages who discuss'd
Of the Two Worlds so learnedly are thrust
     Like foolish Prophets forth; their Words to Scorn
Are scatter'd, and their Mouths are stopt with Dust.

XXVII

Myself when young did eagerly frequent
Doctor and Saint, and heard great argument
     About it and about: but evermore
Came out by the same door where in I went.

XXVIII

With them the seed of Wisdom did I sow,
And with my own hand wrought to make it grow;
     And this was all the Harvest that I reap'd—
"I came like Water, and like Wind I go."

XXIX

Into this Universe, and *Why* not knowing,
Nor *Whence*, like Water willy-nilly flowing;
     And out of it, as Wind along the Waste,
I know not *Whither*, willy-nilly blowing.

XXX

What, without asking, hither hurried *Whence?*
And, without asking, *Whither* hurried hence!
  Oh, many a Cup of this forbidden Wine
Must drown the memory of that insolence!

XXXI

Up from Earth's Centre through the Seventh Gate
I rose, and on the Throne of Saturn sate,
  And many a Knot unravell'd by the Road;
But not the Master-knot of Human Fate.

XXXII

There was the Door to which I found no Key;
There was the Veil through which I could not see:
  Some little talk awhile of ME and THEE
There was—and then no more of THEE and ME.

XXXIII

Earth could not answer; nor the Seas that mourn
In flowing Purple, of their Lord forlorn;
  Nor rolling Heaven, with all his Signs reveal'd
And hidden by the sleeve of Night and Morn.

XXXIV

Then of the THEE IN ME who works behind
The Veil, I lifted up my hands to find
  A Lamp amid the Darkness; and I heard,
As from Without—"THE ME WITHIN THEE BLIND!"

XXXV

Then to the Lip of this poor earthen Urn
I lean'd, the Secret of my Life to learn:
  And Lip to Lip it murmur'd—"While you live,
Drink!—for, once dead, you never shall return."

XXXVI

I think the Vessel, that with fugitive
Articulation answer'd, once did live,
   And drink; and Ah! the passive Lip I kiss'd,
How many Kisses might it take—and give!

XXXVII

For I remember stopping by the way
To watch a Potter thumping his wet Clay:
   And with its all-obliterated Tongue
It murmur'd—"Gently, Brother, gently, pray!"

XXXVIII

"And has not such a Story from of Old
Down Man's successive generations rolled
   Of such a clod of saturated Earth
Cast by the Maker into Human mould?"

XXXIX

And not a drop that from our Cups we throw
For Earth to drink of, but may steal below
   To quench the fire of Anguish in some Eye
There hidden—far beneath, and long ago.

XL

As then the Tulip for her morning sup
Of Heav'nly Vintage from the soil looks up,
   Do you devoutly do the like, till Heav'n
To Earth invert you like an empty Cup.

XLI

Perplext no more with Human or Divine,
To-morrow's tangle to the winds resign,
   And lose your fingers in the tresses of
The Cypress-slender Minister of Wine.

XLII

And if the Wine you drink, the Lip you press,
End in what All begins and ends in—Yes;
   Think then you are TO-DAY what YESTERDAY
You were—TO-MORROW you shall not be less.

XLIII

So when the Angel of the darker Drink
At last shall find you by the river-brink,
   And, offering his Cup, invite your Soul
Forth to your Lips to quaff—you shall not shrink.

XLIV

Why, if the Soul can fling the Dust aside,
And naked on the Air of Heaven ride,
   Wer't not a Shame—wer't not a Shame for him
In this clay carcase crippled to abide?

XLV

'T is but a Tent where takes his one-day's rest
A Sultan to the realm of Death addrest;
   The Sultán rises, and the dark Ferrásh
Strikes, and prepares it for another Guest.

XLVI

And fear not lest Existence closing your
Account, and mine, should know the like no more;
   The Eternal Sáki from that Bowl has pour'd
Millions of Bubbles like us, and will pour.

XLVII

When You and I behind the Veil are past,
Oh but the long long while the World shall last,
   Which of our Coming and Departure heeds
As the SEV'N SEAS should heed a pebble cast.

XLVIII

A Moment's Halt—a momentary taste
Of Being from the Well amid the Waste—
    And Lo!—the phantom Caravan has reach'd
The Nothing it set out from—Oh, make haste!

XLIX

Would you that spangle of Existence spend
About the secret—quick about it, Friend!
    A Hair perhaps divides the False and True—
And upon what, prithee, does Life depend?

L

A Hair perhaps divides the False and True;
Yes; and a single Alif were the clue—
    Could you but find it—to the Treasure-house,
And peradventure to The Master too;

LI

Whose secret Presence, through Creation's veins
Running Quicksilver-like eludes your pains;
    Taking all shapes from Máh and Máhi; and
They change and perish all—but He remains;

LII

A moment guess'd—then back behind the Fold
Immerst of Darkness round the Drama roll'd
    Which, for the Pastime of Eternity,
He does Himself contrive, enact, behold.

LIII

But if in vain, down on the stubborn floor
Of Earth, and up to Heav'n's unopening Door,
    You gaze To-day, while You are You—how then
To-morrow, when You shall be You no more?

LIV

Waste not your Hour, nor in the vain pursuit
Of This and That endeavour and dispute;
  Better be jocund with the fruitful Grape
Than sadden after none, or bitter, Fruit.

LV

You know, my Friends, with what a brave Carouse
I made a Second Marriage in my house;
  Divorced old barren Reason from my Bed,
And took the Daughter of the Vine to Spouse.

LVI

For "Is" and "Is-NOT" though with Rule and Line,
And "UP-AND-DOWN" by Logic I define,
  Of all that one should care to fathom, I
Was never deep in anything but—Wine.

LVII

Ah, but my Computations, People say,
Reduced the Year to better reckoning?—Nay,
  'T was only striking from the Calendar
Unborn To-morrow, and dead Yesterday.

LVIII

And lately, by the Tavern Door agape,
Came shining through the Dusk an Angel Shape
  Bearing a Vessel on his Shoulder; and
He bid me taste of it; and 't was—the Grape!

LIX

The Grape that can with Logic absolute
The Two-and-Seventy jarring Sects confute:
  The sovereign Alchemist that in a trice
Life's leaden metal into Gold transmute:

LX

The mighty Máhmúd, Allah-breathing Lord,
That all the misbelieving and black Horde
  Of Fears and Sorrows that infest the Soul
Scatters before him with his whirlwind Sword.

LXI

Why, be this Juice the growth of God, who dare
Blaspheme the twisted tendril as a Snare!
  A Blessing, we should use it, should we not?
And if a Curse—why, then, Who set it there?

LXII

I must abjure the Balm of Life, I must,
Scared by some After-reckoning ta'en on trust,
  Or lured with Hope of some Diviner Drink,
To fill the Cup—when crumbled into Dust!

LXIII

O threats of Hell and hopes of Paradise!
One thing at least is certain,—*This* Life flies;
  One thing is certain and the rest is Lies;
The Flower that once has blown forever dies.

LXIV

Strange, is it not? that of the myriads who
Before us pass'd the door of Darkness through
  Not one returns to tell us of the Road,
Which to discover we must travel too.

LXV

The Revelations of Devout and Learn'd
Who rose before us, and as Prophets burn'd,
  Are all but Stories, which, awoke from Sleep
They told their fellows, and to Sleep return'd.

LXVI

I sent my Soul through the Invisible,
Some letter of that After-life to spell:
   And by and by my Soul return'd to me,
And answer'd "I myself am Heav'n and Hell."

LXVII

Heav'n but the Vision of fulfill'd Desire,
And Hell the Shadow of a Soul on fire,
   Cast on the Darkness into which Ourselves,
So late emerg'd from, shall so soon expire.

LXVIII

We are no other than a moving row
Of Magic Shadow-shapes that come and go
   Round with this Sun-illumin'd Lantern held
In Midnight by the Master of the Show;

LXIX

Impotent Pieces of the Game He plays
Upon this Checker-board of Nights and Days;
   Hither and thither moves, and checks, and slays,
And one by one back in the Closet lays.

LXX

The Ball no question makes of Ayes and Noes
But Right or Left as strikes the Player goes;
   And He that toss'd you down into the Field,
He knows about it all—HE knows—HE knows!

LXXI

The Moving Finger writes; and, having writ,
Moves on: nor all your Piety nor Wit
   Shall lure it back to cancel half a Line,
Nor all your Tears wash out a Word of it.

LXXII

And that inverted Bowl they call the Sky,
Whereunder crawling coop'd we live and die,
   Lift not your hands to *It* for help—for It
As impotently rolls as you or I.

LXXIII

With Earth's first Clay They did the Last Man knead,
And there of the Last Harvest sow'd the Seed:
   And the first Morning of Creation wrote
What the Last Dawn of Reckoning shall read.

LXXIV

YESTERDAY *This* Day's Madness did prepare;
To-MORROW's Silence, Triumph, or Despair:
   Drink! for you know not whence you came, nor why:
Drink! for you know not why you go, nor where.

LXXV

I tell you this—When, started from the Goal,
Over the flaming shoulders of the Foal
   Of Heav'n Parwín and Mushtari they flung,
In my predestin'd Plot of Dust and Soul

LXXVI

The Vine had struck a fibre: which about
If clings my Being—let the Dervish flout;
   Of my Base metal may be filed a Key,
That shall unlock the Door he howls without.

LXXVII

And this I know: whether the one True Light
Kindle to Love, or Wrath-consume me quite,
   One Flash of It within the Tavern caught
Better than in the Temple lost outright.

LXXVIII

What! out of senseless Nothing to provoke
A conscious Something to resent the yoke
   Of unpermitted Pleasure, under pain
Of Everlasting Penalties, if broke!

LXXIX

What, from his helpless Creature be repaid
Pure Gold for what he lent us dross-allay'd—
   Sue for a Debt we never did contract,
And cannot answer—Oh the sorry trade!

LXXX

Oh Thou, who didst with pitfall and with gin
Beset the Road I was to wander in,
   Thou wilt not with Predestin'd Evil round
Enmesh, and then impute my Fall to Sin!

LXXXI

Oh, Thou, who Man of baser Earth didst make
And ev'n with Paradise devise the Snake:
   For all the Sin wherewith the Face of Man
Is blacken'd—Man's Forgiveness give—and take!

      *   *   *   *

LXXXII

As under cover of departing Day
Slunk hunger-stricken Ramazán away,
   Once more within the Potter's house alone
I stood, surrounded by the Shapes of Clay.

LXXXIII

Shapes of all Sorts and Sizes, great and small,
That stood along the floor and by the wall;
   And some loquacious Vessels were; and some
Listen'd perhaps, but never talk'd at all.

LXXXIV

Said one among them—"Surely not in vain
My substance of the common Earth was ta'en
    And to this Figure moulded, to be broke,
Or trampled back to shapeless Earth again."

LXXXV

Then said a Second—"Ne'er a peevish Boy
Would break the Bowl from which he drank in joy:
    And He that with his hand the Vessel made
Will surely not in after Wrath destroy."

LXXXVI

After a momentary silence spake
Some Vessel of a more ungainly Make,
    "They sneer at me for leaning all awry:
What! did the Hand then of the Potter shake?"

LXXXVII

Whereat some of the loquacious Lot—
I think a Súfi pipkin—waxing hot—
    "All this of Pot and Potter—Tell me then,
Who is the Potter, pray, and who the Pot?"

LXXXVIII

"Why," said another, "Some there are who tell
Of one who threatens he will toss to Hell
    The luckless Pots he marr'd in making—Pish!
He's a Good Fellow, and 't will all be well."

LXXXIX

"Well," murmur'd one, "Let whoso make or buy,
My Clay with long Oblivion is gone dry:
    But fill me with the old familiar Juice,
Methinks I might recover by and by."

XC

So while the Vessels one by one were speaking,
The little Moon look'd in that all were seeking:
　　And then they jogg'd each other, "Brother! Brother!
Now for the Porter's shoulder-knot a-creaking!"

*　　*　　*　　*

XCI

Ah, with the Grape my fading Life provide,
And wash the Body whence the Life has died,
　　And lay me, shrouded in the living Leaf,
By some not unfrequented Garden-side.

XCII

That ev'n my buried Ashes such a snare
Of Vintage shall fling up into the Air
　　As not a True-believer passing by
But shall be overtaken unaware.

XCIII

Indeed the idols I have loved so long
Have done my credit in this world much **wrong:**
　　Have drown'd my Glory in a shallow Cup,
And sold my Reputation for a Song.

XCIV

Indeed, indeed, Repentance oft before
I swore—but was I sober when I swore?
　　And then and then came Spring, and Rose-in-**hand**
My threadbare Penitence apieces tore.

XCV

And much as Wine has play'd the Infidel,
And robb'd me of my Robe of Honour—Well,
　　I wonder often what the Vintners buy
One-half so precious as the stuff they sell.

XCVI

Yet Ah, that Spring should vanish with the Rose!
That Youth's sweet-scented manuscript should close!
  The Nightingale that in the branches sang,
Ah whence, and whither flown again, who knows!

XCVII

Would but the Desert of the Fountain yield
One glimpse—if dimly, yet indeed, reveal'd,
  To which the fainting Traveller might spring,
As springs the trampled herbage of the field!

XCVIII

Would but some wingéd Angel ere too late
Arrest the yet unfolded Roll of Fate,
  And make the stern Recorder otherwise
Enregister, or quite obliterate!

XCIX

Ah Love! could you and I with Him conspire
To grasp this sorry Scheme of Things entire,
  Would not we shatter it to bits—and then
Re-mould it nearer to the Heart's Desire!

*   *   *   *

C

Yon rising Moon that looks for us again—
How oft hereafter will she wax and wane;
  How oft hereafter rising look for us
Through this same Garden—and for *one* in vain!

CI

And when like her, oh Sáki, you shall pass
Among the Guests Star-scatter'd on the Grass,
  And in your blissful errand reach the spot
Where I made One—turn down an empty Glass!

STEPHEN COLLINS FOSTER

MY OLD KENTUCKY HOME, GOOD-NIGHT

The sun shines bright in the old Kentucky home;
  'Tis summer, the darkeys are gay;
The corn top's ripe, and the meadow's in the bloom,
  While the birds make music all the day.
The young folks roll on the little cabin floor,
  All merry, all happy and bright;
By-'n'-by hard times comes a-knocking at the door:—
  Then my old Kentucky home, good-night!

        Weep no more my lady,
        O, weep no more to-day!
      We will sing one song for the old Kentucky home,
      For the old Kentucky home, far away.

They hunt no more for the possum and the coon,
  On the meadow, the hill, and the shore;
They sing no more by the glimmer of the moon,
  On the bench by the old cabin door.
The day goes by like a shadow o'er the heart,
  With sorrow, where all was delight;
The time has come when the darkeys have to part:—
  Then my old Kentucky home, good-night!

The head must bow, and the back will have to bend,
  Wherever the darkey may go;
A few more days, and the trouble all will end,
  In the field where the sugar-canes grow.

A few more days for to tote the weary load,—
No matter, 'twill never be light;
A few more days till we totter on the road:—
Then my old Kentucky home, good-night!

Weep no more my lady,
O, weep no more to-day!
We will sing one song for the old Kentucky home,
For the old Kentucky home, far away.

MASSA'S IN DE COLD GROUND

Round de meadows am a-ringing
    De darkeys' mournful song,
While de mocking-bird am singing,
    Happy as de day am long.
Where de ivy am a-creeping,
    O'er de grassy mound,
Dere old massa am a-sleeping,
    Sleeping in de cold, cold ground.

Down in de corn-field
    Hear dat mournful sound:
All de darkeys am a-weeping,—
    Massa's in de cold, cold ground.

When de autumn leaves were falling,
    When de days were cold,
'Twas hard to hear old massa calling,
    Cayse he was so weak and old.
Now de orange tree am blooming
    On de sandy shore,
Now de summer days am coming,—
    Massa nebber calls no more.

Massa make de darkeys love him,
    Cayse he was so kind;
Now dey sadly weep above him,
    Mourning cayse he leave dem behind.

I cannot work before tomorrow,
    Cayse de tear-drop flow;
I try to drive away my sorrow,
    Pickin on de old banjo.

Down in de corn-field
    Hear dat mournful sound:
All de darkeys am a-weeping,—
    Massa's in de cold, cold ground.

OLD FOLKS AT HOME

Way down upon de Swanee Ribber,
    Far, far away,
Dere's wha my heart is turning ebber,
    Dere's wha de old folks stay.
All up and down de whole creation
    Sadly I roam,
Still longing for de old plantation,
    And for de old folks at home.

All de world am sad and dreary,
    Eberywhere I rome;
O darkeys, how my heart grows weary,
    Far from de old folks at home!

All round de little farm I wandered
    When I was young,
Den many happy days I squandered,
    Many de songs I sung.
When I was playing wid my brudder,
    Happy was I;
Oh, take me to my kind old mudder!
    Dere let me live and die.

One little hut among de bushes,
  One dat I love,
Still sadly to my memory rushes,
  No matter where I rove.
When will I see de bees a-humming
  All round de comb?
When will I hear de banjo tumming,
  Down in my good old home?

All de world am sad and dreary,
  Eberywhere I rome;
O darkeys, how my heart grows weary,
  Far from de old folks at home!

SIR WILLIAM S. GILBERT

THE YARN OF THE "NANCY BELL"

'Twas on the shores that round our coast
  From Deal to Ramsgate span,
That I found alone on a piece of stone
  An elderly naval man.

His hair was weedy, his beard was long,
  And weedy and long was he,
And I heard this wight, on the shore recite,
  In a singular minor key:

"Oh, I am a cook and a captain bold,
  And the mate of the *Nancy* brig,
And a bo'sun tight, and a midshipmite,
  And the crew of the captain's gig."

And he shook his fists and he tore his hair,
  Till I really felt afraid,
For I couldn't help thinking the man had been drinking,
  And so I simply said:

"Oh, elderly man, it's little I know
　　Of the duties of men of the sea,
And I'll eat my hand if I understand
　　However you can be

"At once a cook, and a captain bold,
　　And the mate of the *Nancy* brig,
And a bo'sun tight, and a midshipmite,
　　And the crew of the captain's gig."

Then he gave a hitch to his trousers, which
　　Is a trick all seamen larn,
And having got rid of a thumping quid,
　　He spun this painful yarn:

" 'Twas in the good ship *Nancy Bell*
　　That we sailed to the Indian Sea,
And there on a reef we come to grief,
　　Which has often occurred to me.

"And pretty nigh all the crew was drowned
　　(There was seventy-seven o' soul),
And only ten of the *Nancy's* men
　　Said 'Here!' to the muster-roll.

"There was me and the cook and the captain bold,
　　And the mate of the *Nancy* brig,
And the bo'sun tight, and a midshipmite,
　　And the crew of the captain's gig.

"For a month we'd neither wittles nor drink,
　　Till a-hungry we did feel,
So we drawed a lot, and, accordin' shot
　　The captain for our meal.

"The next lot fell to the *Nancy's* mate,
　　And a delicate dish he made;
And then our appetite with the midshipmite
　　We seven survivors stayed.

"And then we murdered the bo'sun tight,
   And he much resembled pig;
Then we wittled free, did the cook and me,
   On the crew of the captain's gig.

"Then only the cook and me was left,
   And the delicate question, 'Which
Of us two goes to the kettle?' arose
   And we argued it out as sich.

"For I loved that cook as a brother, I did,
   And the cook he worshipped me;
But we'd both be blowed if we'd either be stowed
   In the other chap's hold, you see.

" 'I'll be eat if you dines off me,' says Tom,
   'Yes, that,' says I, 'you'll be,'—
'I'm boiled if I die, my friend,' quoth I,
   And 'Exactly so,' quoth he.

"Says he, 'Dear James, to murder me
   Were a foolish thing to do,
For don't you see that you can't cook *me,*
   While I can—and will—cook *you!*'

"So he boils the water, and takes the salt
   And the pepper in portions true
(Which he never forgot), and some chopped shalot,
   And some sage and parsley too.

" 'Come here,' says he, with a proper pride,
   Which his smiling features tell,
' 'Twill soothing be if I let you see
   How extremely nice you'll smell.'

"And he stirred it round and round and round,
   And he sniffed at the foaming froth;
When I ups with his heels, and smothers his squeals
   In the scum of the boiling broth.

"And I eat that cook in a week or less,
   And—as I eating be
The last of his chops, why, I almost drops,
   For a wessel in sight I see!

*   *   *   *   *

"And I never larf, and I never smile,
   And I never lark nor play,
But sit and croak, and a single joke
   I have—which is to say:

" 'Oh, I am a cook and a captain bold,
   And the mate of the *Nancy* brig,
And a bo'sun tight, and a midshipmite,
   And the crew of the captain's gig!' "

GENTLE ALICE BROWN

IT was a robber's daughter, and her name was ALICE BROWN,
Her father was the terror of a small Italian town;
Her mother was a foolish, weak, but amiable old thing;
But it isn't of her parents that I'm going for to sing.

As ALICE was a-sitting at her window-sill one day,
A beautiful young gentleman he chanced to pass that way;
She cast her eyes upon him, and he looked so good and true,
That she thought, "I could be happy with a gentleman like you!"

And every morning passed her house that cream of gentlemen,
She knew she might expect him at a quarter unto ten,
A sorter in the Custom-house, it was his daily road
(The Custom-house was fifteen minutes' walk from her abode).

But ALICE was a pious girl, who knew it wasn't wise
To look at strange young sorters with expressive purple eyes;
So she sought the village priest to whom her family confessed—
The priest by whom their little sins were carefully assessed.

"Oh, holy father," Alice said, " 'twould grieve you, would it not?
To discover that I was a most disreputable lot!
Of all unhappy sinners I'm the most unhappy one!"
The padre said, "Whatever have you been and gone and done?"

"I have helped mamma to steal a little kiddy from its dad
I've assisted dear papa in cutting up a little lad.
I've planned a little burglary and forged a little cheque,
And slain a little baby for the coral on its neck!"

The worthy pastor heaved a sigh, and dropped a silent tear—
And said, "You mustn't judge yourself too heavily, my dear—
It's wrong to murder babies, little corals for to fleece;
But sins like these one expiates at half-a-crown apiece.

"Girls will be girls—you're very young, and flighty in your mind;
Old heads upon young shoulders we must not expect to find:
We mustn't be too hard upon these little girlish tricks—
Let's see—five crimes at half-a-crown—exactly twelve-and-six."

"Oh, father," little Alice cried, "your kindness makes me weep,
You do these little things for me so singularly cheap—
Your thoughtful liberality I never can forget;
But oh, there is another crime I haven't mentioned yet!

"A pleasant-looking gentleman, with pretty purple eyes,
I've noticed at my window, as I've sat a-catching flies;
He passes by it every day as certain as can be—
I blush to say I've winked at him, and he has winked at me!"

"For shame!" said Father Paul, "my erring daughter! On my word
This is the most distressing news that I have ever heard.
Why, naughty girl, your excellent papa has pledged your hand
To a promising young robber, the lieutenant of his band!

"This dreadful piece of news will pain your worthy parents so!
They are the most remunerative customers I know;
For many many years they've kept starvation from my doors:
I never knew so criminal a family as yours!

"The common country folk in this insipid neighbourhood
Have nothing to confess, they're so ridiculously good;
And if you marry any one respectable at all,
Why, you'll reform, and what will then become of FATHER PAUL?"

The worthy priest, he up and drew his cowl upon his crown,
And started off in haste to tell the news to ROBBER BROWN;
To tell him how his daughter, who was now for marriage fit,
Had winked upon a sorter, who reciprocated it.

Good ROBBER BROWN he muffled up his anger pretty well,
He said, "I have a notion, and that notion I will tell;
I will nab this gay young sorter, terrify him into fits,
And get my gentle wife to chop him into little bits.

"I've studied human nature, and I know a thing or two;
Though a girl may fondly love a living gent, as many do,
A feeling of disgust upon her senses there will fall
When she looks upon his body chopped particularly small."

He traced that gallant sorter to a still suburban square;
He watched his opportunity and seized him unaware;
He took a life-preserver and he hit him on the head,
And MRS. BROWN dissected him before she went to bed.

And pretty little ALICE grew more settled in her mind,
She never more was guilty of a weakness of the kind,
Until at length good ROBBER BROWN bestowed her pretty hand
On the promising young robber, the lieutenant of his band.

SIR GUY THE CRUSADER

SIR GUY was a doughty crusader,
    A muscular knight,
    Ever ready to fight,
A very determined invader,
    And DICKEY DE LION's delight.

Lenore was a Saracen maiden,
    Brunette, statuesque,
      The reverse of grotesque,
Her pa was a bagman from Aden,
    Her mother she played in burlesque.

A *coryphée*, pretty and loyal,
    In amber and red
      The ballet she led;
Her mother performed at the Royal,
    Lenore at the Saracen's Head.

Of face and of figure majestic,
    She dazzled the cits—
      Ecstaticised pits;—
Her troubles were only domestic,
    But drove her half out of her wits.

Her father incessantly lashed her,
    On water and bread
      She was grudgingly fed;
Whenever her father he thrashed her
    Her mother sat down on her head.

Guy saw her, and loved her, with reason,
    For beauty so bright
      Sent him mad with delight;
He purchased a stall for the season,
    And sat in it every night.

His views were exceedingly proper,
    He wanted to wed,
      So he called at her shed
And saw her progenitor whop her—
    Her mother sit down on her head.

"So pretty," said he, "and so trusting!
    You brute of a dad,
      You unprincipled cad,
Your conduct is really disgusting,
    Come, come, now admit it's too bad!

"You're a turbaned old Turk, and malignant—
    Your daughter LENORE
      I intensely adore,
And I cannot help feeling indignant,
    A fact that I hinted before;

"To see a fond father employing
    A deuce of a knout
      For to bang her about,
To a sensitive lover's annoying."
    Said the bagman, "Crusader, get out."

Says GUY, "Shall a warrior laden
    With a big spiky knob,
      Sit in peace on his cob
While a beautiful Saracen maiden
    Is whipped by a Saracen snob?

"To London I'll go from my charmer."
    Which he did, with his loot
      (Seven hats and a flute)
And was nabbed for his Sydenham armour
    At MR. BEN-SAMUEL's suit.

SIR GUY he was lodged in the Compter,
    Her pa, in a rage,
      Died (don't know his age),
His daughter, she married the prompter,
    Grew bulky and quitted the stage.

OLIVER GOLDSMITH

THE DESERTED VILLAGE

SWEET Auburn! loveliest village of the plain,
Where health and plenty cheered the laboring swain,
Where smiling Spring its earliest visit paid,
And parting Summer's lingering blooms delayed!

Dear lovely bowers of innocence and ease—
Seats of my youth, when every sport could please!
How often have I loitered o'er thy green,
Where humble happiness endeared each scene!
How often have I paused on every charm—
The sheltered cot, the cultivated farm,
The never-failing brook, the busy mill,
The decent church that topt the neighboring hill,
The hawthorn bush, with seats beneath the shade—
For talking age and whispering lovers made!
How often have I blest the coming day,
When toil, remitting, lent its turn to play,
And all the village train, from labor free,
Led up their sports beneath the spreading tree;
While many a pastime circled in the shade,
The young contending as the old surveyed;
And many a gambol frolicked o'er the ground,
And sleights of art and feats of strength went round;
And still, as each repeated pleasure tired,
Succeeding sports the mirthful band inspired;
The dancing pair, that simply sought renown
By holding out, to tire each other down;
The swain, mistrustless of his smutted face,
While secret laughter tittered round the place;
The bashful virgin's sidelong looks of love,
The matron's glance that would those looks reprove:
These were thy charms, sweet village! sports like these,
With sweet succession, taught e'en toil to please;
These round thy bowers their cheerful influence shed;
These were thy charms—but all these charms are fled.

Sweet-smiling village, loveliest of the lawn!
Thy sports are fled, and all thy charms withdrawn;
Amidst thy bowers the tyrant's hand is seen,
And desolation saddens all thy green;
One only master grasps the whole domain,
And half a tillage stints thy smiling plain.
No more thy glassy brook reflects the day,
But, choked with sedges, works its weedy way;
Along thy glades, a solitary guest,
The hollow-sounding bittern guards its nest;

Amidst thy desert walks the lapwing flies,
And tires their echoes with unvaried cries;
Sunk are thy bowers in shapeless ruin all,
And the long grass o'ertops the mouldering wall;
And, trembling, shrinking from the spoiler's hand,
Far, far away thy children leave the land.

Ill fares the land, to hastening ills a prey,
Where wealth accumulates, and men decay;
Princes and lords may flourish, or may fade—
A breath can make them, as a breath has made;
But a bold peasantry, their country's pride,
When once destroyed, can never be supplied.

A time there was, ere England's griefs began,
When every rood of ground maintained its man:
For him light labor spread her wholesome store—
Just gave what life required, but gave no more;
His best companions, innocence and health;
And his best riches, ignorance of wealth.

But times are altered: trade's unfeeling train
Usurp the land, and dispossess the swain;
Along the lawn, where scattered hamlets rose,
Unwieldy wealth and cumbrous pomp repose;
And every want to luxury allied,
And every pang that folly pays to pride.
Those gentle hours that plenty bade to bloom,
Those calm desires that asked but little room,
Those healthful sports that graced the peaceful scene,
Lived in each look, and brightened all the green—
These, far departing, seek a kinder shore,
And rural mirth and manners are no more.

Sweet Auburn! parent of the blissful hour,
Thy glades forlorn confess the tyrant's power.
Here, as I take my solitary rounds
Amidst thy tangling walks and ruined grounds,
And, many a year elapsed, return to view
Where once the cottage stood, the hawthorn grew,
Remembrance wakes with all her busy train,
Swells at my breast, and turns the past to pain.

In all my wanderings round this world of care,
In all my griefs—and God has given my share—
I still had hopes my latest hours to crown,
Amidst these humble bowers to lay me down;
To husband out life's taper at the close,
And keep the flame from wasting by repose.
I still had hopes—for pride attends us still—
Amidst the swains to show my book-learned skill,
Around my fire an evening group to draw,
And tell of all I felt, and all I saw;
And, as a hare, whom hounds and horns pursue,
Pants to the place from whence at first she flew,
I still had hopes, my long vexations past,
Here to return—and die at home at last.

O blest retirement! friend to life's decline!
Retreats from care, that never must be mine!
How blest is he who crowns, in shades like these,
A youth of labor with an age of ease;
Who quits a world where strong temptations try,
And, since 't is hard to combat, learns to fly!
For him no wretches, born to work and weep,
Explore the mine, or tempt the dangerous deep;
No surly porter stands in guilty state,
To spurn imploring famine from the gate;
But on he moves to meet his latter end,
Angels around befriending virtue's friend;
Sinks to the grave with unperceived decay,
While resignation gently slopes the way;
And, all his prospects brightening to the last,
His heaven commences ere the world be past.

Sweet was the sound, when oft at evening's close
Up yonder hill the village murmur rose;
There, as I passed with careless steps and slow,
The mingling notes came softened from below:
The swain responsive as the milkmaid sung,
The sober herd that lowed to meet their young,
The noisy geese that gabbled o'er the pool,
The playful children just let loose from school,

The watch-dog's voice that bayed the whispering wind,
And the loud laugh that spoke the vacant mind.
These all in sweet confusion sought the shade,
And filled each pause the nightingale had made.
But now the sounds of population fail;
No cheerful murmurs fluctuate in the gale;
No busy steps the grass-grown footway tread—
But all the bloomy blush of life is fled.
All but one widowed, solitary thing,
That feebly bends beside the plashy spring;
She, wretched matron, forced in age, for bread,
To strip the brook with mantling cresses spread,
To pick her wintry fagot from the thorn,
To seek her nightly shed, and weep till morn—
She only left of all the harmless train,
The sad historian of the pensive plain.

Near yonder copse, where once the garden smiled,
And still where many a garden-flower grows wild,
There, where a few torn shrubs the place disclose,
The village preacher's modest mansion rose.
A man he was to all the country dear,
And passing rich with forty pounds a year;
Remote from towns he ran his godly race,
Nor e'er had changed, nor wished to change, his place;
Unskilful he to fawn, or seek for power
By doctrines fashioned to the varying hour;
Far other aims his heart had learned to prize—
More bent to raise the wretched than to rise.
His house was known to all the vagrant train;
He chid their wanderings, but relieved their pain.
The long-remembered beggar was his guest,
Whose beard, descending, swept his aged breast;
The ruined spendthrift, now no longer proud,
Claimed kindred there, and had his claims allowed;
The broken soldier, kindly bade to stay,
Sate by his fire, and talked the night away—
Wept o'er his wounds, or, tales of sorrow done,
Shouldered his crutch, and showed how fields were won.

Pleased with his guests, the good man learned to glow,
And quite forgot their vices in their woe;
Careless their merits or their faults to scan,
His pity gave ere charity began.

Thus to relieve the wretched was his pride,
And even his failings leaned to virtue's side;
But in his duty prompt at every call,
He watched and wept, he prayed and felt for all;
And, as a bird each fond endearment tries
To tempt its new-fledged offspring to the skies,
He tried each art, reproved each dull delay,
Allured to brighter worlds, and led the way.

Beside the bed where parting life was laid,
And sorrow, guilt, and pain by turns dismayed,
The reverend champion stood. At his control
Despair and anguish fled the struggling soul;
Comfort came down the trembling wretch to raise,
And his last faltering accents whispered praise.

At church, with meek and unaffected grace,
His looks adorned the venerable place;
Truth from his lips prevailed with double sway,
And fools, who came to scoff, remained to pray.
The service past, around the pious man,
With ready zeal, each honest rustic ran;
Even children followed, with endearing wile,
And plucked his gown, to share the good man's smile.
His ready smile a parent's warmth expressed;
Their welfare pleased him, and their cares distressed;
To them his heart, his love, his griefs, were given—
But all his serious thoughts had rest in heaven.
As some tall cliff that lifts its awful form,
Swells from the vale, and midway leaves the storm,
Though round its breast the rolling clouds are spread,
Eternal sunshine settles on its head.

Beside yon straggling fence that skirts the way,
With blossomed furze unprofitably gay,

There, in his noisy mansion, skilled to rule,
The village master taught his little school.
A man severe he was, and stern to view—
I knew him well, and every truant knew;
Well had the boding tremblers learned to trace
The day's disasters in his morning face;
Full well they laughed with counterfeited glee,
At all his jokes, for many a joke had he;
Full well the busy whisper, circling round,
Conveyed the dismal tidings when he frowned;
Yet he was kind—or, if severe in aught,
The love he bore to learning was in fault.
The village all declared how much he knew;
'Twas certain he could write, and cipher too;
Lands he could measure, terms and tides presage,
And e'en the story ran that he could gauge.
In arguing too, the parson owned his skill,
For, even though vanquished, he could argue still;
While words of learned length and thundering sound
Amazed the gazing rustics ranged around;
And still they gazed, and still the wonder grew,
That one small head could carry all he knew.
But past is all his fame; the very spot
Where many a time he triumphed, is forgot.

Near yonder thorn, that lifts its head on high,
Where once the sign-post caught the passing eye,
Low lies that house where nut-brown draughts inspired,
Where gray-beard mirth and smiling toil retired,
Where village statesmen talked with looks profound,
And news much older than their ale went round.
Imagination fondly stoops to trace
The parlor splendors of that festive place:
The whitewashed wall, the nicely sanded floor,
The varnished clock that clicked behind the door,
The chest contrived a double debt to pay—
A bed by night, a chest of drawers by day,
The pictures placed for ornament and use,
The twelve good rules, the royal game of goose;
The hearth, except when winter chilled the day,
With aspen boughs and flowers and fennel gay;

While broken tea-cups, wisely kept for show,
Ranged o'er the chimney, glistened in a row.

Vain, transitory splendor! could not all
Reprieve the tottering mansion from its fall?
Obscure it sinks, nor shall it more impart
An hour's importance to the poor man's heart;
Thither no more the peasant shall repair
To sweet oblivion of his daily care;
No more the farmer's news, the barber's tale,
No more the woodman's ballad shall prevail;
No more the smith his dusky brow shall clear,
Relax his ponderous strength, and lean to hear;
The host himself no longer shall be found
Careful to see the mantling bliss go round;
Nor the coy maid, half willing to be pressed,
Shall kiss the cup to pass it to the rest.

Yes! let the rich deride, the proud disdain,
These simple blessings of the lowly train;
To me more dear, congenial to my heart,
One native charm than all the gloss of art:
Spontaneous joys, where nature has its play,
The soul adopts, and owns their first-born sway;
Lightly they frolic o'er the vacant mind,
Unenvied, unmolested, unconfined;
But the long pomp, the midnight masquerade,
With all the freaks of wanton wealth arrayed—
In these, ere triflers half their wish obtain,
The toiling pleasure sickens into pain;
And, even while fashion's brightest arts decoy,
The heart, distrusting, asks if this be joy.

Ye friends to truth, ye statesmen, who survey
The rich man's joys increase, the poor's decay!
'Tis yours to judge how wide the limits stand
Between a splendid and a happy land.
Proud swells the tide with loads of freighted ore,
And shouting Folly hails them from her shore;
Hoards, even beyond the miser's wish, abound,
And rich men flock from all the world around.

Yet count our gains: this wealth is but a name,
That leaves our useful products still the same.
Not so the loss: the man of wealth and pride
Takes up a space that many poor supplied—
Space for his lake, his park's extended bounds—
Space for his horses, equipage, and hounds;
The robe that wraps his limbs in silken sloth
Has robbed the neighboring fields of half their growth;
His seat, where solitary sports are seen,
Indignant spurns the cottage from the green;
Around the world each needful product flies,
For all the luxuries the world suppplies;
While thus the land, adorned for pleasure all,
In barren splendor, feebly waits the fall.

As some fair female, unadorned and plain,
Secure to please while youth confirms her reign,
Slights every borrowed charm that dress supplies,
Nor shares with art the triumph of her eyes;
But when those charms are past—for charms are frail—
When time advances, and when lovers fail,
She then shines forth, solicitous to bless,
In all the glaring impotence of dress:
Thus fares the land, by luxury betrayed,
In nature's simplest charms at first arrayed;
But, verging to decline, its splendors rise,
Its vistas strike, its palaces surprise;
While, scourged by famine, from the smiling land
The mournful peasant leads his humble band;
And while he sinks, without one arm to save,
The country blooms—a garden and a grave.

Where, then, ah! where, shall poverty reside,
To 'scape the pressure of contiguous pride?
If, to some common's fenceless limits strayed,
He drives his flock to pick the scanty blade,
Those fenceless fields the sons of wealth divide,
And even the bare-worn common is denied.
If to the city sped, what waits him there?
To see profusion that he must not share;

To see ten thousand baneful arts combined
To pamper luxury, and thin mankind;
To see each joy the sons of pleasure know
Extorted from his fellow-creatures' woe.
Here while the courtier glitters in brocade,
There the pale artist plies his sickly trade;
Here while the proud their long-drawn pomps display,
There the black gibbet glooms beside the way.
The dome where pleasure holds her midnight reign,
Here, richly decked, admits the gorgeous train:
Tumultuous grandeur crowds the blazing square—
The rattling chariots clash, the torches glare.
Sure, scenes like these no troubles e'er annoy!
Sure, these denote one universal joy!
Are these thy serious thoughts? Ah! turn thine eyes
Where the poor, houseless, shivering female lies:
She once, perhaps, in village plenty blessed,
Has wept at tales of innocence distressed;
Her modest looks the cottage might adorn,
Sweet as the primrose peeps beneath the thorn;
Now lost to all—her friends, her virtue fled—
Near her betrayer's door she lays her head;
And, pinched with cold, and shrinking from the shower,
With heavy heart deplores that luckless hour
When idly first, ambitious of the town,
She left her wheel, and robes of country brown.

Do thine, sweet Auburn—thine the loveliest train—
Do thy fair tribes participate her pain?
Even now, perhaps, by cold and hunger led,
At proud men's doors they ask a little bread.

Ah, no! To distant climes, a dreary scene,
Where half the convex world intrudes between,
Through torrid tracts with fainting steps they go,
Where wild Altama murmurs to their woe.
Far different there, from all that charmed before,
The various terrors of that horrid shore:
Those blazing suns that dart a downward ray,
And fiercely shed intolerable day;

Those matted woods where birds forget to sing,
But silent bats in drowsy clusters cling;
Those poisonous fields, with rank luxuriance crowned,
Where the dark scorpion gathers death around;
Where at each step the stranger fears to wake
The rattling terrors of the vengeful snake;
Where crouching tigers wait their hapless prey,
And savage men more murderous still than they;
While oft in whirls the mad tornado flies,
Mingling the ravaged landscape with the skies.
Far different these from every former scene—
The cooling brook, the grassy-vested green,
The breezy covert of the warbling grove,
That only sheltered thefts of harmless love.

Good Heaven! what sorrows gloomed that parting day
That called them from their native walks away;
When the poor exiles, every pleasure past,
Hung round the bowers, and fondly looked their last,
And took a long farewell, and wished in vain
For seats like these beyond the western main;
And, shuddering still to face the distant deep,
Returned and wept, and still returned to weep!
The good old sire the first prepared to go
To new-found worlds, and wept for others' woe;
But for himself, in conscious virtue brave,
He only wished for worlds beyond the grave.
His lovely daughter, lovelier in her tears,
The fond companion of his helpless years,
Silent went next, neglectful of her charms,
And left a lover's for her father's arms.
With louder plaints the mother spoke her woes,
And blessed the cot where every pleasure rose;
And kissed her thoughtless babes with many a tear,
And clasped them close, in sorrow doubly dear;
Whilst her fond husband strove to lend relief
In all the silent manliness of grief.

O luxury! thou cursed by Heaven's decree,
How ill exchanged are things like these for thee!

How do thy potions, with insidious joy,
Diffuse their pleasures only to destroy!
Kingdoms by thee, to sickly greatness grown,
Boast of a florid vigor not their own.
At every draught more large and large they grow,
A bloated mass of rank unwieldy woe;
Till sapped their strength, and every part unsound,
Down, down they sink, and spread a ruin round.

Even now the devastation is begun,
And half the business of destruction done;
Even now, methinks, as pondering here I stand,
I see the rural virtues leave the land.
Down where yon anchoring vessel spreads the sail
That, idly waiting, flaps with every gale—
Downward they move, a melancholy band,
Pass from the shore, and darken all the strand.
Contented toil, and hospitable care,
And kind connubial tenderness are there;
And piety with wishes placed above,
And steady loyalty, and faithful love.
And thou, sweet Poetry, thou loveliest maid,
Still first to fly where sensual joys invade—
Unfit, in these degenerate times of shame,
To catch the heart, or strike for honest fame!
Dear, charming nymph, neglected and decried,
My shame in crowds, my solitary pride!
Thou source of all my bliss and all my woe—
That found'st me poor at first, and keep'st me so!
Thou guide, by which the nobler arts excel!
Thou nurse of every virtue—fare thee well!
Farewell!—and O! where'er thy voice be tried,
On Torno's cliffs or Pambamarca's side—
Whether where equinoctial fervors glow,
Or winter wraps the polar world in snow—
Still let thy voice, prevailing over time,
Redress the rigors of the inclement clime;
Aid slighted truth with thy persuasive strain;
Teach erring man to spurn the rage of gain;
Teach him that states, of native strength possessed,
Though very poor, may still be very blest;

That trade's proud empire hastes to swift decay,
As ocean sweeps the labored mole away;
While self-dependent power can time defy,
As rocks resist the billows and the sky.

THE TRAVELLER,

OR, A PROSPECT OF SOCIETY

REMOTE, unfriended, melancholy, slow,
Or by the lazy Scheld, or wandering Po;
Or onward, where the rude Carinthian boor
Against the houseless stranger shuts the door;
Or where Campania's plain forsaken lies,
A weary waste expanding to the skies;
Where'er I roam, whatever realms to see,
My heart, untraveled, fondly turns to thee:
Still to my brother turns with ceaseless pain,
And drags at each remove a lengthening chain.

Eternal blessings crown my earliest friend,
And round his dwelling guardian saints attend.
Blest be that spot, where cheerful guests retire
To pause from toil, and trim their evening fire;
Blest that abode, where want and pain repair,
And every stranger finds a ready chair;
Blest be those feasts with simple plenty crowned,
Where all the ruddy family around
Laugh at the jests or pranks that never fail,
Or sigh with pity at some mournful tale;
Or press the bashful stranger to his food,
And learn the luxury of doing good.

But me, not destined such delights to share,
My prime of life in wandering spent and care;
Impelled with steps unceasing to pursue
Some fleeting good, that mocks me with the view;
That, like the circle bounding earth and skies,
Allures from far, yet, as I follow, flies;

My fortune leads to traverse realms alone,
And find no spot of all the world my own.

Even now, where Alpine solitudes ascend,
I sit me down a pensive hour to spend;
And, placed on high above the storm's career,
Look downward where an hundred realms appear;
Lakes, forests, cities, plains extending wide,
The pomp of kings, the shepherd's humbler pride.

When thus creation's charms around combine,
Amidst the store, should thankless pride repine?
Say, should the philosophic mind disdain
That good which makes each humbler bosom vain?
Let school-taught pride dissemble all it can,
These little things are great to little man;
And wiser he, whose sympathetic mind
Exults in all the good of all mankind.
Ye glittering towns, with wealth and splendor crowned,
Ye fields, where summer spreads profusion round,
Ye lakes, whose vessels catch the busy gale,
Ye bending swains, that dress the flowery vale,
For me your tributary stores combine;
Creation's heir, the world, the world is mine!

As some lone miser, visiting his store,
Bends at his treasure, counts, recounts it o'er;
Hoards after hoards his rising raptures fill,

Yet still he sighs, for hoards are wanting still;
Thus to my breast alternate passions rise,
Pleased with each good that Heaven to man supplies;
Yet oft a sigh prevails, and sorrows fall,
To see the hoard of human bliss so small;
And oft I wish, amidst the scene to find
Some spot to real happiness consigned,
Where my worn soul, each wandering hope at rest,
May gather bliss, to see my fellows blest.

But where to find that happiest spot below,
Who can direct, when all pretend to know?

The shuddering tenant of the frigid zone
Boldly proclaims that happiest spot his own;
Extols the treasures of his stormy seas,
And his long nights of revelry and ease:
The naked Negro, panting at the Line,
Boasts of his golden sands, and palmy wine,
Basks in the glare or stems the tepid wave,
And thanks his gods for all the good they gave.
Such is the patriot's boast, where'er we roam,
His first, best country ever is at home.
And yet, perhaps, if countries we compare,
And estimate the blessings which they share,
Though patriots flatter, still shall wisdom find
An equal portion dealt to all mankind:
As different good, by Art or Nature given
To different nations, makes their blessings even.

Nature, a mother kind alike to all,
Still grants her bliss at labor's earnest call;
With food as well the peasant is supplied
On Idra's cliff as Arno's shelvy side;
And though the rocky-crested summits frown,
These rocks, by custom, turn to beds of down.
From art more various are the blessings sent;
Wealth, commerce, honor, liberty, content:
Yet these each other's power so strong contest,
That either seems destructive of the rest.
Where wealth and freedom reign, contentment fails,
And honor sinks where commerce long prevails.
Hence every state, to one loved blessing prone,
Conforms and models life to that alone:
Each to the favorite happiness attends,
And spurns the plan that aims at other ends;
Till, carried to excess in each domain,
This favorite good begets peculiar pain.

But let us try these truths with closer eyes,
And trace them through the prospect as it lies:
Here for a while, my proper cares resigned,
Here let me sit in sorrow for mankind;

Like yon neglected shrub, at random cast,
That shades the steep, and sighs at every blast.

Far to the right, where Apennine ascends,
Bright as the summer, Italy extends:
Its uplands sloping deck the mountain's side,
Woods over woods in gay theatric pride;
While oft some temple's mouldering tops between
With memorable grandeur mark the scene.

Could Nature's bounty satisfy the breast,
The sons of Italy were surely blest.
Whatever fruits in different climes are found,
That proudly rise or humbly court the ground;
Whatever blooms in torrid tracts appear,
Whose bright succession decks the varied year;
Whatever sweets salute the northern sky
With vernal lives, that blossom but to die;
These here disporting own the kindred soil,
Nor ask luxuriance from the planter's toil;
While sea-born gales their gelid wings expand
To winnow fragrance round the smiling land.

But small the bliss that sense alone bestows,
And sensual bliss is all the nation knows.
In florid beauty groves and fields appear;
Man seems the only growth that dwindles here.
Contrasted faults through all his manners reign;
Though poor, luxurious; though submissive, vain;
Though grave, yet trifling; zealous, yet untrue;
And even in penance planning sins anew.
All evils here contaminate the mind,
That opulence departed leaves behind,
For wealth was theirs; not far removed the date,
When commerce proudly flourished through the state,
At her command the palace learnt to rise;
Again the long-fallen column sought the skies;
The canvas glowed, beyond e'en Nature warm;
The pregnant quarry teemed with human form;
Till, more unsteady than the southern gale,
Commerce on other shores displayed her sail;

While nought remained of all that riches gave,
But towns unmanned, and lords without a slave:
And late the nation found, with fruitless skill,
Its former strength was but plethoric ill.

  Yet still the loss of wealth is here supplied
By arts, the splendid wrecks of former pride;
From these the feeble heart and long-fallen mind
An easy compensation seem to find.
Here may be seen, in bloodless pomp arrayed,
The pasteboard triumph and the cavalcade:
Processions formed for piety and love,
A mistress or a saint in every grove.
By sports like these are all their cares beguiled,—
The sports of children satisfy the child:
Each nobler aim, represt by long control,
Now sinks at last, or feebly mans the soul;
While low delights, succeeding fast behind,
In happier meanness occupy the mind:
As in those domes, where Cæsars once bore sway,
Defaced by time, and tottering in decay,
There in the ruin, heedless of the dead,
The shelter-seeking peasant builds his shed;
And, wondering man could want the larger pile,
Exults and owns his cottage with a smile.

  My soul, turn from them, turn we to survey
Where rougher climes a nobler race display,
Where the bleak Swiss their stormy mansions tread,
And force a churlish soil for scanty bread:
No product here the barren hills afford,
But man and steel, the soldier and his sword:
No vernal blooms their torpid rocks array,
But winter lingering chills the lap of May:
No zephyr fondly sues the mountain's breast,
But meteors glare, and stormy glooms invest.

  Yet still, e'en here, content can spread a charm,
Redress the clime, and all its rage disarm.
Though poor the peasant's hut, his feasts tho' small,
He sees his little lot the lot of all;

Sees no contiguous palace rear its head,
To shame the meanness of his humble shed;
No costly lord the sumptuous banquet deal,
To make him loathe his vegetable meal;
But calm, and bred in ignorance and toil,
Each wish contracting, fits him to the soil.
Cheerful, at morn, he wakes from short repose,
Breathes the keen air, and carols as he goes;
With patient angle trolls the finny deep,
Or drives his venturous plowshare to the steep;
Or seeks the den where snow-tracks mark the way,
And drags the struggling savage into day.
At night returning, every labor sped,
He sits him down the monarch of a shed;
Smiles by his cheerful fire, and round surveys
His children's looks, that brighten at the blaze;
While his loved partner, boastful of her hoard,
Displays her cleanly platter on the board:
And haply too some pilgrim, thither led,
With many a tale repays the nightly bed.

  Thus every good his native wilds impart
Imprints the patriot passion on his heart;
And even those hills, that round his mansion rise,
Enhance the bliss his scanty fund supplies.
Dear is that shed to which his soul conforms,
And dear that hill which lifts him to the storms;
And as a child, when scaring sounds molest,
Clings close and closer to the mother's breast,
So the loud torrent, and the whirlwind's roar,
But bind him to his native mountains more.

  Such are the charms to barren states assigned;
Their wants but few, their wishes all confined.
Yet let them only share the praises due,
If few their wants their pleasures are but few;
For every want that stimulates the breast
Becomes a source of pleasure when redrest:
Whence from such lands each pleasing science flies
That first excites desire, and then supplies;

Unknown to them, when sensual pleasures cloy,
To fill the languid pause with finer joy;
Unknown those powers that raise the soul to flame,
Catch every nerve, and vibrate through the frame.
Their level life is but a mouldering fire,
Unquenched by want, unfanned by strong desire;
Unfit for raptures, or, if raptures cheer
On some high festival of once a year,
In wild excess the vulgar breast takes fire,
Till, buried in debauch, the bliss expire.

But not their joys alone thus coarsely flow;
Their morals, like their pleasures, are but low;
For, as refinement stops, from sire to son
Unaltered, unimproved, the manners run;
And love's and friendship's finely pointed dart
Falls blunted from each indurated heart.
Some sterner virtues o'er the mountain's breast
May sit, like falcons cowering on the nest:
But all the gentler morals, such as play
Thro' life's more cultured walks, and charm the way,
These, far dispersed, on timorous pinions fly,
To sport and flutter in a kinder sky.

To kinder skies, where gentler manners reign,
I turn; and France displays her bright domain:
Gay sprightly land of mirth and social ease,
Pleased with thyself, whom all the world can please!
How often have I led thy sportive choir,
With tuneless pipe, beside the murmuring Loire!
Where shading elms along the margin grew,
And freshened from the wave the zephyr flew:
And haply, though my harsh touch, faltering still,
But mocked all tune, and marred the dancers' skill,
Yet would the village praise my wondrous power,
And dance, forgetful of the noontide hour.
Alike all ages. Dames of ancient days
Have led their children through the mirthful maze;
And the gay grandsire, skilled in gestic lore,
Has frisked beneath the burthen of threescore.

So blest a life these thoughtless realms display,
Thus idly busy rolls their world away:
Theirs are those arts that mind to mind endear,
For honor forms the social temper here:
Honor, that praise which real merit gains,
Or even imaginary worth obtains,
Here passes current; paid from hand to hand,
It shifts, in splendid traffic, round the land:
From courts, to camps, to cottages it strays,
And all are taught an avarice of praise;
They please, are pleased, they give to get esteem,
Till, seeming blest, they grow to what they seem.

But while this softer art their bliss supplies,
It gives their follies also room to rise;
For praise too dearly loved, or warmly sought,
Enfeebles all internal strength of thought;
And the weak soul, within itself unblest,
Leans for all pleasure on another's breast.
Hence ostentation here, with tawdry art,
Pants for the vulgar praise which fools impart;
Here Vanity assumes her pert grimace,
And trims her robes of frieze with copper lace;
Here beggar pride defrauds her daily cheer,
To boast one splendid banquet once a year:
The mind still turns where shifting fashion draws,
Nor weighs the solid worth of self-applause.

To men of other minds my fancy flies,
Embosomed in the deep where Holland lies.
Methinks her patient sons before me stand,
Where the broad ocean leans against the land,
And, sedulous to stop the coming tide,
Lift the tall rampire's artificial pride.
Onward, methinks, and diligently slow,
The firm, connected bulwark seems to grow:
Spreads its long arms amidst the watery roar,
Scoops out an empire, and usurps the shore:
While the pent Ocean, rising o'er the pile,
Sees an amphibious world beneath him smile:

The slow canal, the yellow blossomed vale,
The willow-tufted bank, the gliding sail,
The crowded mart, the cultivated plain,
A new creation rescued from his reign.

Thus, while around the wave-subjected soil
Impels the native to repeated toil,
Industrious habits in each bosom reign,
And industry begets a love of gain.
Hence all the good from opulence that springs,
With all those ills superfluous treasure brings,
Are here displayed. Their much loved wealth imparts
Convenience, plenty, elegance, and arts!
But view them closer, craft and fraud appear,
Even liberty itself is bartered here.
At gold's superior charms all freedom flies,
The needy sell it, and the rich man buys;
A land of tyrants and a den of slaves,
Here wretches seek dishonorable graves,
And, calmly bent, to servitude conform,
Dull as their lakes that slumber in the storm.

Heavens! how unlike their Belgic sires of old!
Rough, poor, content, ungovernably bold;
War in each breast, and freedom on each brow;
How much unlike the sons of Britain now!

Fired at the sound, my genius spreads her wing,
And flies where Britain courts the western spring;
Where lawns extend that scorn Arcadian pride,
And brighter streams than famed Hydaspes glide;
There all around the gentlest breezes stray,
There gentle music melts on every spray;
Creation's mildest charms are there combined,
Extremes are only in the master's mind;
Stern o'er each bosom reason holds her state,
With daring aims irregularly great;
Pride in their port, defiance in their eye,
I see the lords of human-kind pass by;
Intent on high designs, a thoughtful band,
By forms unfashioned, fresh from nature's hand,

Fierce in their native hardiness of soul,
True to imagined right, above control;
While even the peasant boasts these rights to scan,
And learns to venerate himself as man.

   Thine, Freedom, thine the blessings pictured here,
Thine are those charms that dazzle and endear:
Too blest indeed were such without alloy;
But fostered even by freedom, ills annoy.
That independence Britons prize too high,
Keeps man from man, and breaks the social tie;
The self-dependent lordlings stand alone,
All claims that bind and sweeten life unknown.
Here, by the bonds of nature feebly held,
Minds combat minds, repelling and repelled;
Ferments arise, imprisoned factions roar,
Represt ambition struggles round her shore;
Till, over-wrought, the general system feels
Its motions stop, or frenzy fire the wheels.

   Nor this the worst. As nature's ties decay,
As duty, love, and honor, fail to sway,
Fictitious bonds, the bonds of wealth and law,
Still gather strength, and force unwilling awe.
Hence all obedience bows to these alone,
And talent sinks, and merit weeps unknown;
Till time may come, when, stript of all her charms,
The land of scholars, and the nurse of arms,
Where noble stems transmit the patriot flame,
Where kings have toiled, and poets wrote for fame,
One sink of level avarice shall lie,
And scholars, soldiers, kings, unhonored die.

   Yet think not, thus when freedom's ills I state,
I mean to flatter kings, or court the great:
Ye powers of truth, that bid my soul aspire,
Far from my bosom drive the low desire!
And thou, fair Freedom, taught alike to feel
The rabble's rage, the tyrant's angry steel;
Thou transitory flower, alike undone
By proud contempt, or favor's fostering sun;

Still may thy blooms the changeful clime endure!
I only would repress them to secure;
For just experience tells, in every soil,
That those who think must govern those that toil;
And all that freedom's highest aims can reach
Is but to lay proportioned loads on each.
Hence, should one order disproportioned grow,
Its double weight must ruin all below.

O then how blind to all that truth requires,
Who think it freedom when a part aspires!
Calm is my soul nor apt to rise in arms,
Except when fast approaching danger warns:
But when contending chiefs blockade the throne,
Contracting regal power to stretch their own;
When I behold a factious band agree
To call it freedom when themselves are free;
Each wanton judge new penal statutes draw,
Laws grind the poor, and rich men rule the law;
The wealth of climes, where savage nations roam,
Pillaged from slaves to purchase slaves at home;
Fear, pity, justice, indignation start,
Tear off reserve, and bare my swelling heart;
Till, half a patriot, half a coward grown,
I fly from petty tyrants to the throne.

Yes, brother, curse with me that baleful hour,
When first ambition struck at regal power;
And thus, polluting honor in its source,
Gave wealth to sway the mind with double force.
Have we not seen, round Britain's peopled shore,
Her useful sons exchanged for useless ore?
Seen all her triumphs but destruction haste,
Like flaring tapers brightening as they waste?
Seen Opulence, her grandeur to maintain,
Lead stern Depopulation in her train,
And over fields where scattered hamlets rose,
In barren solitary pomp repose?
Have we not seen, at pleasure's lordly call,
The smiling long-frequented village fall?

Beheld the duteous son, the sire decayed,
The modest matron, and the blushing maid,
Forced from their homes, a melancholy train,
To traverse climes beyond the western main,
Where wild Oswego spreads her swamps around,
And Niagara stuns with thundering sound?

Even now, perhaps, as there some pilgrim strays
Through tangled forests, and through dangerous ways;
While beasts with man divided empire claim,
And the brown Indian marks with murderous aim;
There, while above the giddy tempest flies,
And all around distressful yells arise,
The pensive exile, bending with his woe,
To stop too fearful, and too faint to go,
Casts a long look where England's glories shine,
And bids his bosom sympathize with mine.

Vain, very vain, my weary search to find
That bliss which only centres in the mind.
Why have I strayed from pleasure and repose,
To seek a good each government bestows?
In every government, though terrors reign,
Though tyrant kings or tyrant laws restrain,
How small, of all that human hearts endure,
That part which laws or kings can cause or cure!
Still to ourselves in every place consigned,
Our own felicity we make or find:
With secret course, which no loud storms annoy,
Glides the smooth current of domestic joy.
The lifted ax, the agonizing wheel,
Luke's iron crown, and Damien's bed of steel,
To men remote from power but rarely known,
Leave reason, faith, and conscience, all our own.

THOMAS GRAY

ELEGY WRITTEN IN A COUNTRY CHURCHYARD

THE curfew tolls the knell of parting day,
    The lowing herd winds slowly o'er the lea,
The plowman homeward plods his weary way,
    And leaves the world to darkness and to me.

Now fades the glimmering landscape on the sight,
    And all the air a solemn stillness holds,
Save where the beetle wheels his droning flight,
    And drowsy tinklings lull the distant folds;

Save that from yonder ivy-mantled tower
    The moping owl does to the moon complain
Of such as, wandering near her secret bower,
    Molest her ancient solitary reign.

Beneath those rugged elms, that yew-tree's shade,
    Where heaves the turf in many a mouldering heap,
Each in his narrow cell forever laid,
    The rude forefathers of the hamlet sleep.

The breezy call of incense-breathing morn,
    The swallow twittering from the straw-built shed,
The cock's shrill clarion, or the echoing horn,
    No more shall rouse them from their lowly bed.

For them no more the blazing hearth shall burn,
    Or busy housewife ply her evening care;
No children run to lisp their sire's return,
    Or climb his knees, the envied kiss to share.

Oft did the harvest to their sickle yield,
    Their furrow oft the stubborn glebe has broke:
How jocund did they drive their team afield!
    How bowed the woods beneath their sturdy stroke!

Let not Ambition mock their useful toil,
  Their homely joys, and destiny obscure;
Nor Grandeur hear with a disdainful smile
  The short and simple annals of the poor.

The boast of heraldry, the pomp of power,
  And all that beauty, all that wealth, e'er gave,
Await alike the inevitable hour:
  The paths of glory lead but to the grave.

Nor you, ye proud, impute to these the fault,
  If Memory o'er their tomb no trophies raise,
Where through the long-drawn aisle and fretted vault
  The pealing anthem swells the note of praise.

Can storied urn, or animated bust,
  Back to its mansion call the fleeting breath?
Can Honor's voice provoke the silent dust,
  Or Flattery soothe the dull, cold ear of death?

Perhaps in this neglected spot is laid
  Some heart once pregnant with celestial fire;
Hands that the rod of empire might have swayed,
  Or waked to ecstasy the living lyre.

But Knowledge to their eyes her ample page,
  Rich with the spoils of time, did ne'er unroll;
Chill Penury repressed their noble rage,
  And froze the genial current of the soul.

Full many a gem, of purest ray serene,
  The dark, unfathomed caves of ocean bear;
Full many a flower is born to blush unseen,
  And waste its sweetness on the desert air.

Some village Hampden, that with dauntless breast
  The little tyrant of his fields withstood,—
Some mute, inglorious Milton,—here may rest;
  Some Cromwell, guiltless of his country's blood.

The applause of listening senates to command,
  The threats of pain and ruin to despise,
To scatter plenty o'er a smiling land,
  And read their history in a nation's eyes.

Their lot forbade: nor circumscribed alone
  Their growing virtues, but their crimes confined;
Forbade to wade through slaughter to a throne,
  And shut the gates of mercy on mankind;

The struggling pangs of conscious truth to hide,
  To quench the blushes of ingenuous shame,
Or heap the shrine of luxury and pride
  With incense kindled at the Muse's flame.

Far from the madding crowd's ignoble strife,
  Their sober wishes never learned to stray;
Along the cool, sequestered vale of life
  They kept the noiseless tenor of their way.

Yet ev'n these bones from insult to protect,
  Some frail memorial still erected nigh,
With uncouth rhymes and shapeless sculpture decked,
  Implores the passing tribute of a sigh.

Their name, their years, spelt by the unlettered Muse,
  The place of fame and elegy supply;
And many a holy text around she strews,
  That teach the rustic moralist to die.

For who, to dumb forgetfulness a prey,
  This pleasing, anxious being e'er resigned,
Left the warm precincts of the cheerful day,
  Nor cast one longing, lingering look behind?

On some fond breast the parting soul relies,
  Some pious drops the closing eye requires;
Ev'n from the tomb the voice of nature cries,
  Ev'n in our ashes live their wonted fires.

For thee, who, mindful of the unhonored dead,
  Dost in these lines their artless tale relate,
If 'chance, by lonely contemplation led,
  Some kindred spirit shall inquire thy fate,—

Haply some hoary-headed swain may say,
  "Oft have we seen him at the peep of dawn
Brushing with hasty steps the dews away,
  To meet the sun upon the upland lawn.

"There, at the foot of yonder nodding beech
  That wreathes its old fantastic roots so high,
His listless length at noontide would he stretch,
  And pore upon the brook that babbles by.

"Hard by yon wood, now smiling as in scorn,
  Muttering his wayward fancies, would he rove;
Now drooping, woeful, wan, like one forlorn,
  Or crazed with care, or crossed in hopeless love.

"One morn I missed him on the 'customed hill,
  Along the heath, and near his favorite tree;
Another came,—nor yet beside the rill,
  Nor up the lawn, nor at the wood was he:

"The next, with dirges due, in sad array,
  Slow through the churchway path we saw him borne:
Approach and read (for thou canst read) the lay
  Graved on the stone beneath yon agèd thorn."

THE EPITAPH

Here rests his head upon the lap of Earth
  A youth to fortune and to fame unknown;
Fair Science frowned not on his humble birth,
  And Melancholy marked him for her own.

Large was his bounty, and his soul sincere,
  Heaven did a recompense as largely send:
He gave to misery (all he had) a tear,
  He gained from heaven ('twas all he wished) a friend.

No farther seek his merits to disclose,
  Or draw his frailties from their dread abode,
(There they alike in trembling hope repose,)
  The bosom of his Father and his God.

FITZ-GREENE HALLECK

JOSEPH RODMAN DRAKE

GREEN be the turf above thee,
  Friend of my better days!
None knew thee but to love thee,
  Nor named thee but to praise.

Tears fell, when thou wert dying,
  From eyes unused to weep,
And long, where thou art lying,
  Will tears the cold turf steep.

When hearts whose truth was proven,
  Like thine, are laid in earth,
There should a wreath be woven
  To tell the world their worth;

And I, who woke each morrow
  To clasp thy hand in mine,
Who shared thy joy and sorrow,
  Whose weal and woe were thine,—

It should be mine to braid it
  Around thy faded brow,
But I've in vain essayed it,
  And feel I cannot now.

While memory bids me weep thee,
  Nor thoughts nor words are free,
The grief is fixed too deeply
  That mourns a man like thee.

MARCO BOZZARIS

At midnight, in his guarded tent,
　The Turk was dreaming of the hour
When Greece, her knee in suppliance bent,
　Should tremble at his power.
In dreams, through camp and court, he bore
The trophies of a conqueror;
　In dreams his song of triumph heard;
Then wore his monarch's signet-ring;
Then pressed that monarch's throne—a king;
As wild his thoughts, and gay of wing
　As Eden's garden bird.

At midnight, in the forest shades,
　Bozzaris ranged his Suliote band,
True as the steel of their tried blades,
　Heroes in heart and hand.
There had the Persian's thousands stood,
There had the glad earth drunk their blood,
　On old Platæa's day;
And now there breathed that haunted air
The sons of sires who conquered there,
With arm to strike, and soul to dare,
　As quick, as far, as they.

An hour passed on—the Turk awoke;
　That bright dream was his last;
He woke—to hear his sentries shriek,
"To arms! they come! the Greek! the Greek!"
He woke—to die midst flame, and smoke,
And shout, and groan, and sabre-stroke.
　And death-shots falling thick and fast
As lightnings from the mountain-cloud;
And heard, with voice as trumpet loud,
　Bozzaris cheer his band:
"Strike—till the last armed foe expires;
Strike—for your altars and your fires;
Strike—for the green graves of your sires;
　God—and your native land!"

They fought—like brave men, long and well;
  They piled that ground with Moslem slain;
They conquered—but Bozzaris fell.
  Bleeding at every vein.
His few surviving comrades saw
His smile, when rang their proud hurrah,
  And the red field was won;
Then saw in death his eyelids close,
Calmly as to a night's repose,
  Like flowers at set of sun.

Come to the bridal chamber, Death!
  Come to the mother, when she feels,
For the first time, her first-born's breath!
  Come when the blessed seals
That close the pestilence are broke,
And crowded cities wail its stroke:
Come in consumption's ghastly form,
The earthquake's shock, the ocean-storm;
Come when the heart beats high and warm
  With banquet-song, and dance, and wine;
And thou art terrible!—The tear,
The groan, the knell, the pall, the bier;
And all we know, or dream, or fear
  Of agony, are thine.

But to the hero, when his sword
  Has won the battle for the free,
Thy voice sounds like a prophet's word;
And in its hollow tones are heard
  The thanks of millions yet to be.
Come, when his task of fame is wrought—
Come, with her laurel-leaf, blood-bought—
  Come in her crowning hour—and then
Thy sunken eye's unearthly light
To him is welcome as the sight
  Of sky and stars to prisoned men:
Thy grasp is welcome as the hand
Of brother in a foreign land;

Thy summons welcome as the cry
That told the Indian isles were nigh
  To the world-seeking Genoese,
When the land-wind from woods of palm,
And orange groves, and fields of balm,
  Blew o'er the Haytian seas.

Bozzaris! with the storied brave
  Greece nurtured in her glory's time,
Rest thee—there is no prouder grave,
  Even in her own proud clime.
She wore no funeral weeds for thee,
  Nor bade the dark hearse wave its plume,
Like torn branch from death's leafless tree,
In sorrow's pomp and pageantry,
  The heartless luxury of the tomb.
But she remembers thee as one
Long loved, and for a season gone.
For thee her poet's lyre is wreathed,
Her marble wrought, her music breathed;
For thee she rings the birthday bells;
Of thee her babe's first lisping tells;
For thine her evening prayer is said
At palace couch, and cottage bed;
Her soldier, closing with the foe,
Gives for thy sake a deadlier blow;
His plighted maiden, when she fears
For him, the joy of her young years,
Thinks of thy fate, and checks her tears.
  And she, the mother of thy boys,
Though in her eye and faded cheek
Is read the grief she will not speak,
  The memory of her buried joys—
And even she who gave thee birth,
Will, by her pilgrim-circled hearth,
Talk of thy doom without a sigh;
For thou art Freedom's now, and Fame's—
One of the few, the immortal names
  That were not born to die.

BRET HARTE

PLAIN LANGUAGE FROM TRUTHFUL JAMES

WHICH I wish to remark—
   And my language is plain—
That for ways that are dark
   And for tricks that are vain,
The heathen Chinee is peculiar:
   Which the same I would rise to explain.

Ah Sin was his name;
   And I shall not deny
In regard to the same
   What that name might imply;
But his smile it was pensive and childlike,
   As I frequent remarked to Bill Nye.

It was August the third,
   And quite soft was the skies,
Which it might be inferred
   That Ah Sin was likewise:
Yet he played it that day upon William
   And me in a way I despise.

Which we had a small game,
   And Ah Sin took a hand:
It was euchre. The same
   He did not understand;
But he smiled, as he sat by the table,
   With the smile that was childlike and bland.

Yet the cards they were stocked
   In a way that I grieve,
And my feelings were shocked
   At the state of Nye's sleeve,
Which was stuffed full of aces and bowers,
   And the same with intent to deceive.

But the hands that were played
   By that heathen Chinee,
And the points that he made,

BRET HARTE

Were quite frightful to see—
Till at last he put down a right bower,
    Which the same Nye had dealt unto me.

Then I looked up at Nye,
    And he gazed upon me;
And he rose with a sigh,
    And said, "Can this be!
We are ruined by Chinese cheap labor,"—
    And he went for that heathen Chinee.

In the scene that ensued
    I did not take a hand;
But the floor it was strewed
    Like the leaves on the strand
With the cards that Ah Sin had been hiding,
    In the game "he did not understand."

In his sleeves, which were long,
    He had twenty-four packs—
Which was coming it strong,
    Yet I state but the facts;
And we found on his nails, which were taper,
    What is frequent in tapers—that's wax.

Which is why I remark,
    And my language is plain,
That for ways that are dark,
    And for tricks that are vain,
The heathen Chinee is peculiar—
    Which the same I am free to maintain.

HER LETTER

I'M sitting alone by the fire,
    Dressed just as I came from the dance,
In a robe even *you* would admire,—
    It cost a cool thousand in France;
I'm bediamonded out of all reason,
    My hair is done up in a cue:
In short, sir, "the belle of the season"
    Is wasting an hour on you.

A dozen engagements I've broken;
　　I left in the midst of a set;
Likewise a proposal, half spoken,
　　That waits—on the stairs—for me yet.
They say he'll be rich—when he grows up,—
　　And then he adores me indeed.
And you, sir, are turning your nose up,
　　Three thousand miles off, as you read.

"And how do I like my position?"
　　"And what do I think of New York?"
"And now, in my higher ambition,
　　With whom do I waltz, flirt, or talk?"
"And isn't it nice to have riches,
　　And diamonds and silks, and all that?"
"And aren't it a change to the ditches
　　And tunnels of Poverty Flat?"

Well yes,—if you saw us out driving
　　Each day in the park, four-in-hand;
If you saw poor dear mamma contriving
　　To look supernaturally grand,—
If you saw papa's picture, as taken
　　By Brady, and tinted at that,—
You'd never suspect he sold bacon
　　And flour at Poverty Flat.

And yet, just this moment, when sitting
　　In the glare of the grand chandelier,
In the bustle and glitter befitting
　　The "finest soirée of the year,"—
In the mists of a gaze de chambéry
　　And the hum of the smallest of talk,—
Somehow, Joe, I thought of "The Ferry,"
　　And the dance that we had on "The Fork";

Of Harrison's barn, with its muster
　　Of flags festooned over the wall;
Of the candles that shed their soft lustre
　　And tallow on head-dress and shawl;

Of the steps that we took to one fiddle;
  Of the dress of my queer vis-a-vis;
And how I once went down the middle
  With the man that shot Sandy McGee;

Of the moon that was quietly sleeping
  On the hill, when the time came to go;
Of the few baby peaks that were peeping
  From under their bed-clothes of snow;
Of that ride,—that to me was the rarest;
  Of—the something you said at the gate:
Ah, Joe, then I wasn't an heiress
  To "the best-paying lead in the State."

Well, well, it's all past; yet it's funny
  To think, as I stood in the glare
Of fashion and beauty and money,
  That I should be thinking, right there,
Of some one who breasted highwater,
  And swam the North Fork, and all that,
Just to dance with old Folinsbee's daughter,
  The Lily of Poverty Flat.

But goodness! what nonsense I'm writing!
  (Mamma says my taste still is low,)
Instead of my triumphs reciting,
  I'm spooning on Joseph,—heigh-ho!
And I'm to be "finished" by travel,
  Whatever's the meaning of that,—
O, why did papa strike pay gravel
  In drifting on Poverty Flat?

Good-night,—here's the end of my paper;
  Good-night,—if the longitude please,—
For maybe, while wasting my taper,
  Your sun's climbing over the trees.
But know, if you haven't got riches,
  And are poor, dearest Joe, and all that,
That my heart's somewhere there in the ditches,
  And you've struck it,—on Poverty Flat.

HEINRICH HEINE

THE LORE-LEI

I KNOW not whence it rises,
    This thought so full of woe;—
But a tale of the times departed
    Haunts me—and will not go.

The air is cool, and it darkens,
    And calmly flows the Rhine;
The mountain peaks are sparkling
    In the sunny evening-shine.

And yonder sits a maiden,
    The fairest of the fair;
With gold is her garment glittering,
    And she combs her golden hair.

With a golden comb she combs it,
    And a wild song singeth she,
That melts the heart with a wondrous
    And powerful melody.

The boatman feels his bosom
    With a nameless longing move;
He sees not the gulfs before him,
    His gaze is fixed above.

Till over boat and boatman
    The Rhine's deep waters run;
And this with her magic singing
    The Lore-Lei hath done!

MRS. FELICIA HEMANS

LANDING OF THE PILGRIM FATHERS

THE breaking waves dashed high
    On a stern and rock-bound coast,
And the woods against a stormy sky
    Their giant branches tossed;

And the heavy night hung dark
　　The hills and waters o'er,
When a band of exiles moored their bark
　　On the wild New England shore.

Not as the conquerer comes,
　　They, the true-hearted, came;
Not with the roll of the stirring drums,
　　And the trumpet that sings of fame;
Not as the flying come,
　　In silence and in fear;—
They shook the depths of the desert's gloom
　　With their hymns of lofty cheer.

Amidst the storm they sang,
　　And the stars heard, and the sea;
And the sounding aisles of the dim woods rang
　　To the anthem of the free.
The ocean eagle soared
　　From his nest by the white wave's foam;
And the rocking pines of the forest roared—
　　This was their welcome home!

There were men with hoary hair,
　　Amidst that pilgrim-band:
Why had they come to wither there,
　　Away from their childhood's land?
There was woman's fearless eye,
　　Lit by her deep love's truth;
There was manhood's brow serenely high,
　　And the fiery heart of youth.

What sought they thus afar?
　　Bright jewels of the mine?
The wealth of seas? the spoils of war?—
　　They sought a faith's pure shrine!
Ay, call it holy ground,
　　The soil where first they trod:
They have left unstained what there they found—
　　Freedom to worship God!

OLIVER WENDELL HOLMES

CONTENTMENT

"Man wants but little here below."

LITTLE I ask; my wants are few;
　　I only wish a hut of stone,
(A *very plain* brown stone will do,)
　　That I may call my own;—
And close at hand is such a one,
In yonder street that fronts the sun.

Plain food is quite enough for me;
　　Three courses are as good as ten;—
If Nature can subsist on three,
　　Thank Heaven for three. Amen!
I always thought cold victual nice;—
My *choice* would be vanilla-ice.

I care not much for gold or land;—
　　Give me a mortgage here and there,—
Some good bank-stock,—some note of hand,
　　Or trifling railroad share,—
I only ask that Fortune send
A *little* more than I shall spend.

Honors are silly toys, I know,
　　And titles are but empty names;
I would, *perhaps,* be Plenipo,—
　　But only near St. James;
I'm very sure I should not care
To fill our Gubernator's chair.

Jewels are bawbles; 't is a sin
　　To care for such unfruitful things;—
One good-sized diamond in a pin,—
　　Some, *not so large,* in rings,—
A ruby, and a pearl, or so,
Will do for me;—I laugh at show.

My dame should dress in cheap attire;
  (Good, heavy silks are never dear;)—
I own perhaps I *might* desire
    Some shawls of true Cashmere,—
Some marrowy crapes of China silk,
Like wrinkled skins on scalded milk.

I would not have the horse I drive
  So fast that folks must stop and stare;
An easy gait—two, forty-five—
    Suits me; I do not care;—
Perhaps, for just a *single spurt,*
Some seconds less would do no hurt.

Of pictures, I should like to own
  Titians and Raphaels three or four,—
I love so much their style and tone,—
    One Turner, and no more,
(A landscape,—foreground golden dirt,—
The sunshine painted with a squirt.)

Of books but few,—some fifty score
  For daily use, and bound for wear;
The rest upon an upper floor;—
    Some *little* luxury *there*
Of red morocco's gilded gleam,
And vellum rich as country cream.

Busts, cameos, gems,—such things as these,
  Which others often show for pride,
I value for their power to please,
    And selfish churls deride;—
One Stradivarius, I confess,
Two Meerschaums, I would fain possess.

Wealth's wasteful tricks I will not learn,
  Nor ape the glittering upstart fool;—
Shall not carved tables serve my turn,
    But *all* must be of buhl?
Give grasping pomp its double share,—
I ask but *one* recumbent chair.

Thus humble let me live and die,
  Nor long for Midas' golden touch;
If Heaven more generous gifts deny,
  I shall not miss them *much,*—
Too grateful for the blessing lent
Of simple tastes and mind content!

THE DEACON'S MASTERPIECE;

OR, THE WONDERFUL "ONE-HOSS SHAY"

A LOGICAL STORY

HAVE you heard of the wonderful one-hoss shay,
That was built in such a logical way
It ran a hundred years to a day,
And then, of a sudden, it——ah, but stay,
I'll tell you what happened without delay,
Scaring the parson into fits,
Frightening people out of their wits,—
Have you ever heard of that, I say?

Seventeen hundred and fifty-five.
Georgius Secundus was then alive,—
Snuffy old drone from the German hive.
That was the year when Lisbon-town
Saw the earth open and gulp her down,
And Braddock's army was done so brown,
Left without a scalp to its crown.
It was on the terrible Earthquake-day
That the Deacon finished the one-hoss shay.

Now in building of chaises, I tell you what,
There is always *somewhere* a weakest spot,—
In hub, tire, felloe, in spring or thill,
In panel, or crossbar, or floor, or sill,
In screw, bolt, thoroughbrace,—lurking still,
Find it somewhere you must and will,—
Above or below, or within or without,—
And that's the reason, beyond a doubt,
That a chaise *breaks down,* but doesn't *wear out.*

But the Deacon swore, (as Deacons do,
With an "I dew vum," or an "I tell *yeou*,")
He would build one shay to beat the taown
'n' the keounty 'n' all the kentry raoun';
It should be so built that it *couldn'* break daown:
—"Fur," said the Deacon, " 't 's mighty plain
Thut the weakes' place mus' stan' the strain;
'n' the way t' fix it, uz I maintain,
Is only jest
T' make that place uz strong uz the rest."

So the Deacon inquired of the village folk
Where he could find the strongest oak,
That couldn't be split nor bent nor broke,—
That was for spokes and floor and sills;
He sent for lancewood to make the thills;
The crossbars were ash, from the straightest trees,
The panels of white-wood, that cuts like cheese,
But lasts like iron for things like these;
The hubs of logs from the "Settler's ellum,"—
Last of its timber,—they couldn't sell 'em,
Never an axe had seen their chips,
And the wedges flew from between their lips,
Their blunt ends frizzled like celery-tips;
Step and prop-iron, bolt and screw,
Spring, tire, axle, and linchpin too,
Steel of the finest, bright and blue;

Thoroughbrace bison-skin, thick and wide;
Boot, top, dasher, from tough old hide
Found in the pit when the tanner died.
That was the way he "put her through."—
"There!" said the Deacon, "naow she 'll dew!"
Do! I tell you, I rather guess
She was a wonder, and nothing less!
Colts grew horses, beards turned gray,
Deacon and deaconess dropped away,
Children and grandchildren—where were they?
But there stood the stout old one-hoss shay
As fresh as on Lisbon-earthquake-day!

EIGHTEEN HUNDRED;—it came and found
The Deacon's masterpiece strong and sound.
Eighteen hundred increased by ten;—
"Hahnsum kerridge" they called it then.
Eighteen hundred and twenty came;—
Running as usual; much the same.
Thirty and forty at last arrive,
And then came fifty, and FIFTY-FIVE.

Little of all we value here
Wakes on the morn of its hundredth year
Without both feeling and looking queer.
In fact, there's nothing that keeps its youth,
So far as I know, but a tree and truth.
(This is a moral that runs at large;
Take it.—You're welcome.—No extra charge.)

FIRST OF NOVEMBER,—the Earthquake-day—
There are traces of age in the one-hoss shay,
A general flavor of mild decay,
But nothing local, as one may say.
There couldn't be,—for the Deacon's art
Had made it so like in every part
That there wasn't a chance for one to start.
For the wheels were just as strong as the thills,
And the floor was just as strong as the sills,
And the panels just as strong as the floor,
And the whipple-tree neither less nor more,
And the back-crossbar as strong as the fore,
And spring and axle and hub *encore.*
And yet, *as a whole,* it is past a doubt
In another hour it will be *worn out!*

First of November, 'Fifty-five!
This morning the parson takes a drive.
Now, small boys, get out of the way!
Here comes the wonderful one-hoss shay,
Drawn by a rat-tailed, ewe-necked bay.
"Huddup!" said the parson.—Off went they.

The parson was working his Sunday's text,—
Had got to *fifthly,* and stopped perplexed
At what the—Moses—was coming next.
All at once the horse stood still,
Close by the meet'n'-house on the hill.
—First a shiver, and then a thrill,
Then something decidedly like a spill,—
And the parson was sitting upon a rock,
At half past nine by the meet'n'-house clock,—
Just the hour of the Earthquake shock!

—What do you think the parson found,
When he got up and stared around?
The poor old chaise in a heap or mound,
As if it had been to the mill and ground!
You see, of course, if you're not a dunce,
How it went to pieces all at once,—
All at once, and nothing first,—
Just as bubbles do when they burst.

End of the wonderful one-hoss shay—
Logic is logic. That's all I say.

THE HEIGHT OF THE RIDICULOUS

I wrote some lines once on a time
    In wondrous merry mood,
And thought, as usual, men would say
    They were exceeding good.

They were so queer, so very queer,
    I laughed as I would die;
Albeit, in the general way,
    A sober man am I.

I called my servant, and he came;
    How kind it was of him,
To mind a slender man like me,
    He of the mighty limb!

"These to the printer," I exclaimed,
   And, in my humorous way,
I added, (as a trifling jest,)
   "There 'll be the devil to pay."

He took the paper, and I watched,
   And saw him peep within;
At the first line he read, his face
   Was all upon the grin.

He read the next; the grin grew broad,
   And shot from ear to ear;
He read the third; a chuckling noise
   I now began to hear.

The fourth; he broke into a roar;
   The fifth; his waistband split;
The sixth; he burst five buttons off,
   And tumbled in a fit.

Ten days and nights, with sleepless eye,
   I watched that wretched man,
And since, I never dare to write
   As funny as I can.

THE LAST LEAF

I SAW him once before,
As he passed by the door,
   And again
The pavement stones resound,
As he totters o'er the ground
   With his cane.

They say that in his prime,
Ere the pruning-knife of Time
   Cut him down,
Not a better man was found
By the crier on his round
   Through the town.

But now he walks the streets.
And he looks at all he meets
   Sad and wan,
And he shakes his feeble head,
That it seems as if he said,
   "They are gone."

The mossy marbles rest
On the lips that he has pressed
   In their bloom;
And the names he loved to hear
Have been carved for many a year
   On the tomb.

My grandmama has said—
Poor old lady! she is dead
   Long ago—
That he had a Roman nose,
And his cheek was like a rose
   In the snow.

But now his nose is thin,
And it rests upon his chin
   Like a staff,
And a crook is in his back,
And a melancholy crack
   In his laugh.

I know it is a sin
For me to sit and grin
   At him here:
But the old three-cornered hat,
And the breeches, and all that,
   Are so queer!

And if I should live to be
The last leaf upon the tree
   In the spring—
Let them smile, as I do now,
At the old forsaken bough
   Where I cling.

THE CHAMBERED NAUTILUS

THIS is the ship of pearl which, poets feign,
   Sails the unshadowed main—
   The venturous bark that flings
On the sweet summer wind its purple wings
In gulfs enchanted, where the syren sings,
   And coral reefs lie bare,
Where the cold sea-maids rise to sun their streaming **hair.**

Its webs of living gauze no more unfurl:
   Wrecked is the ship of pearl!
   And every chambered cell
Where its dim-dreaming life was wont to dwell,
As the frail tenant shaped his growing shell,
   Before thee lies revealed—
Its irised ceiling rent, its sunless crypt unsealed.

Year after year beheld the silent toil
   That spread his lustrous coil:
   Still as the spiral grew,
He left the past year's dwelling for the new,
Stole with soft step its shining archway through,
   Built up its idle door,
Stretched in his last-found home, and knew the old no more.

Thanks for the heavenly message brought by thee,
   Child of the wandering sea,
   Cast from her lap, forlorn!
From thy dead lips a clearer note is born
Than ever Triton blew from wreathèd horn!
   While on mine ear it rings,
Through the deep caves of thought I hear a voice that **sings:**

Build thee more stately mansions, O my soul,
   As the swift seasons roll!
   Leave thy low-vaulted past!
Let each new temple, nobler than the last,
Shut thee from heaven with a dome more vast,
   Till thou at length art free,
Leaving thine outgrown shell by life's unresting sea!

OLD IRONSIDES

Ay, tear her tattered ensign down!
  Long has it waved on high,
And many an eye has danced to see
  The banner in the sky;
Beneath it rung the battle shout,
  And burst the cannon's roar;—
The meteor of the ocean air
  Shall sweep the clouds no more!

Her deck, once red with heroes' blood,
  Where knelt the vanquished foe,
When winds were hurrying o'er the flood,
  And waves were white below,
No more shall feel the victor's tread,
  Or know the conquered knee;—
The harpies of the shore shall pluck
  The eagle of the sea!

O better that her shattered hulk
  Should sink beneath the wave;
Her thunders shook the mighty deep,
  And there should be her grave;
Nail to the mast her holy flag,
  Set every threadbare sail,
And give her to the god of storms,
  The lightning and the gale!

THE LIVING TEMPLE

Not in the world of light alone,
Where God has built his blazing throne,
Nor yet alone in earth below,
With belted seas that come and go,
And endless isles of sunlit green,
Is all thy Maker's glory seen:
Look in upon thy wondrous frame,—
Eternal wisdom still the same!

The smooth, soft air with pulse-like waves
Flows murmuring through its hidden caves,
Whose streams of brightening purple rush,
Fired with a new and livelier blush,
While all their burden of decay
The ebbing current steals away,
And red with Nature's flame they start
From the warm fountains of the heart.

No rest that throbbing slave may ask,
Forever quivering o'er his task,
While far and wide a crimson jet
Leaps forth to fill the woven net
Which in unnumbered crossing tides
The flood of burning life divides,
Then, kindling each decaying part,
Creeps back to find the throbbing heart.

But warmed with that unchanging flame
Behold the outward moving frame,
Its living marbles jointed strong
With glistening band and silvery thong,
And linked to reason's guiding reins
By myriad rings in trembling chains,
Each graven with the threaded zone
Which claims it as the master's own.

See how yon beam of seeming white
Is braided out of seven-hued light,
Yet in those lucid globes no ray
By any chance shall break astray.
Hark how the rolling surge of sound,
Arches and spirals circling round,
Wakes the hushed spirit through thine ear
With music it is heaven to hear.

Then mark the cloven sphere that holds
All thought in its mysterious folds,
That feels sensation's faintest thrill,
And flashes forth the sovereign will;

Oliver Wendell Holmes

Samuel Johnson

Think on the stormy world that dwells
Locked in its dim and clustering cells!
The lightning gleams of power it sheds
Along its hollow glassy threads!

O Father! grant thy love divine
To make these mystic temples thine!
When wasting age and wearying strife
Have sapped the leaning walls of life,
When darkness gathers over all,
And the last tottering pillars fall,
Take the poor dust thy mercy warms,
And mould it into heavenly forms!

THOMAS HOOD

FAIR INES

OH, saw ye not fair Ines?
   She's gone into the west,
To dazzle when the sun is down,
   And rob the world of rest:
She took our daylight with her,
   The smiles that we love best,
With morning blushes on her cheek,
   And pearls upon her breast.

Oh turn again, fair Ines,
   Before the fall of night,
For fear the moon should shine alone,
   And stars unrivall'd bright;
And blessed will the lover be
   That walks beneath their light,
And breathes the love against thy cheek
   I dare not even write!

Would I had been, fair Ines,
   That gallant cavalier
Who rode so gayly by thy side,
   And whisper'd thee so near!—

Were there no bonny dames at home,
  Or no true lovers here,
That he should cross the seas to win
  The dearest of the dear?

I saw thee, lovely Ines,
  Descend along the shore,
With bands of noble gentlemen,
  And banners waved before;
And gentle youth and maidens gay,
  And snowy plumes they wore;
It would have been a beauteous dream,
  —If it had been no more!

Alas, alas, fair Ines,
  She went away with song,
With music waiting on her steps,
  And shoutings of the throng;
But some were sad and felt no mirth,
  But only music's wrong,
In sounds that sang Farewell, farewell,
  To her you've loved so long.

Farewell, farewell, fair Ines,
  That vessel never bore
So fair a lady on its deck,
  Nor danced so light before,—
Alas for pleasure on the sea,
  And sorrow on the shore!
The smile that blest one lover's heart
  Has broken many more!

SILENCE

THERE is a silence where hath been no sound,
  There is a silence where no sound may be,
  In the cold grave—under the deep, deep sea,
Or in wide desert where no life is found,
Which hath been mute, and still must sleep profound;
  No voice is hush'd—no life treads silently,
  But clouds and cloudy shadows wander free,

That never spoke, over the idle ground:
But in green ruins, in the desolate walls
  Of antique palaces, where man hath been,
Though the dun fox, or wild hyena, calls,
  And owls, that flit continually between,
Shriek to the echo, and the low winds moan,
There the true silence is, self-conscious and alone.

THE BRIDGE OF SIGHS

> One more unfortunate,
> Weary of breath,
> Rashly importunate,
> Gone to her death!
>
> Take her up tenderly,
> Lift her with care!
> Fashioned so slenderly—
> Young, and so fair!
>
> Look at her garments
> Clinging like cerements,
> Whilst the wave constantly
> Drips from her clothing;
> Take her up instantly,
> Loving, not loathing!
>
> Touch her not scornfully!
> Think of her mournfully
> Gently and humanly—
> Not of the stains of her
> All that remains of her
> Now is pure womanly.
>
> Make no deep scrutiny
> Into her mutiny,
> Rash and undutiful;

Past all dishonor,
Death has left on her
Only the beautiful.

Still, for all slips of hers,
One of Eve's family,
Wipe those poor lips of hers
Oozing so clammily.

Loop up her tresses
Escaped from the comb—
Her fair auburn tresses—
Whilst wonderment guesses
Where was her home?

Who was her father?
Who was her mother?
Had she a sister?
Had she a brother?
Or was there a dearer one
Still, and a nearer one
Yet, than all other?

Alas! for the rarity
Of Christian charity
Under the sun!
O! it was pitiful!
Near a whole city full,
Home she had none.

Sisterly, brotherly,
Fatherly, motherly
Feelings had changed—
Love, by harsh evidence,
Thrown from its eminence;
Even God's providence
Seeming estranged.

Where the lamps quiver
So far in the river,

With many a light
From window and casement,
From garret to basement,
She stood, with amazement,
Houseless by night.

The bleak wind of March
Made her tremble and shiver;
But not the dark arch,
Or the black flowing river;
Mad from life's history,
Glad to death's mystery
Swift to be hurled—
Anywhere, anywhere
Out of the world!

In she plunged boldly—
No matter how coldly
The rough river ran—
Over the brink of it!
Picture it—think of it!
Dissolute man!
Lave in it, drink of it,
Then, if you can!

Take her up tenderly—
Lift her with care!
Fashioned so slenderly—
Young, and so fair!

Ere her limbs, frigidly,
Stiffen too rigidly,
Decently, kindly,
Smoothe and compose them;
And her eyes, close them,
Staring so blindly!

Dreadfully staring
Through muddy impurity,
As when, with the daring
Last look of despairing,
Fixed on futurity.

Perishing gloomily,
Spurred by contumely,
Cold inhumanity,
Burning insanity,
Into her rest!
Cross her hands humbly,
As if praying dumbly,
Over her breast!

Owning her weakness,
Her evil behavior,
And leaving, with meekness,
Her sins to her Saviour!

THE SONG OF THE SHIRT

WITH fingers weary and worn,
  With eyelids heavy and red,
A woman sat in unwomanly rags,
  Plying her needle and thread,—
    Stitch! stitch! stitch!
  In poverty, hunger, and dirt,
And still with a voice of dolorous pitch
  She sang the "Song of the Shirt!"

"Work! work! work!
While the cock is crowing aloof!
  And work—work—work,
Till the stars shine through the roof!
It's, oh, to be a slave
  Along with the barbarous Turk,
Where woman has never a soul to save,
  If this is Christian work!

"Work—work—work
Till the brain begins to swim;

Work—work—work
Till the eyes are heavy and dim!
Seam, and gusset, and band,
  Band, and gusset, and seam,
Till over the buttons I fall asleep,
  And sew them on in a dream!

"O men with sisters dear!
  O men with mothers and wives!
It is not linen you 're wearing out,
  But human creatures' lives!
    Stitch—stitch—stitch,
  In poverty, hunger, and dirt,
Sewing at once, with a double thread,
  A shroud as well as a shirt!

"But why do I talk of Death,—
  That phantom of grisly bone?
I hardly fear his terrible shape,
  It seems so like my own,—
It seems so like my own,
  Because of the fasts I keep;
O God! that bread should be so dear,
  And flesh and blood so cheap!

"Work—work—work!
  My labor never flags;
And what are its wages? A bed of straw,
  A crust of bread—and rags,
That shattered roof—and this naked floor—
  A table—a broken chair—
And a wall so blank, my shadow I thank
  For sometimes falling there!

"Work—work—work
From weary chime to chime!
  Work—work—work
As prisoners work for crime!
Band, and gusset, and seam,
  Seam, and gusset, and band,

Till the heart is sick, and the brain benumbed,
  As well as the weary hand.

"Work—work—work
In the dull December light!
  And work—work—work
When the weather is warm and bright!
While underneath the eaves
  The brooding swallows cling,
As if to show me their sunny backs,
  And twit me with the spring.

"Oh, but to breathe the breath
Of the cowslip and primrose sweet,—
  With the sky above my head,
And the grass beneath my feet!
For only one short hour
  To feel as I used to feel,
Before I knew the woes of want
  And the walk that costs a meal!

"Oh, but for one short hour,—
  A respite, however brief!
No blessèd leisure for love or hope,
  But only time for grief!
A little weeping would ease my heart;
  But in their briny bed
My tears must stop, for every drop
  Hinders needle and thread!"

With fingers weary and worn,
  With eyelids heavy and red,
A woman sat in unwomanly rags,
  Plying her needle and thread,—
    Stitch! stitch! stitch!
  In poverty, hunger, and dirt,
And still in a voice of dolorous pitch,—
Would that its tone could reach the rich!—
  She sang this "Song of the Shirt!"

JOSEPH HOPKINSON

HAIL, COLUMBIA!

Hail, Columbia! happy land!
Hail, ye heroes! heaven-born band!
   Who fought and bled in Freedom's cause,
   Who fought and bled in Freedom's cause,
And when the storm of war was gone,
Enjoyed the peace your valor won.
   Let independence be our boast,
   Ever mindful what it cost;
   Ever grateful for the prize,
   Let its altar reach the skies.

      Firm, united, let us be,
      Rallying round our Liberty;
      As a band of brothers joined,
      Peace and safety we shall find.

Immortal patriots! rise once more:
Defend your rights, defend your shore;
   Let no rude foe, with impious hand,
   Let no rude foe, with impious hand,
Invade the shrine where sacred lies
Of toil and blood the well-earned prize.
   While offering peace sincere and just,
   In Heaven we place a manly trust,
   That truth and justice will prevail,
   And every scheme of bondage fail.

Sound, sound the trump of Fame!
Let Washington's great name
   Ring through the world with loud applause,
   Ring through the world with loud applause;
Let every clime to Freedom dear,
Listen with a joyful ear.
   With equal skill, and godlike power,
   He governed in the fearful hour
   Of horrid war; or guides, with ease,
   The happier times of honest peace.

Behold the chief who now commands,
Once more to serve his country, stands—
    The rock on which the storm will beat,
    The rock on which the storm will beat;
But, armed in virtue firm and true,
His hopes are fixed on Heaven and you.
    When hope was sinking in dismay,
    And glooms obscured Columbia's day,
    His steady mind, from changes free,
    Resolved on death or liberty.

    Firm united let us be,
    Rallying round our Liberty;
    As a band of brothers joined,
    Peace and safety we shall find.

LEIGH HUNT

ABOU BEN ADHEM AND THE ANGEL

ABOU BEN ADHEM (may his tribe increase!)
Awoke one night from a deep dream of peace,
And saw, within the moonlight in his room,
Making it rich, and like a lily in bloom,
An angel, writing in a book of gold;
Exceeding peace had made Ben Adhem bold:
And to the presence in the room he said,
"What writest thou?" The vision rais'd its head,
And with a look made of all sweet accord,
Answer'd, "The names of those who love the Lord."
"And is mine one?" said Abou. "Nay, not so,"
Replied the angel. Abou spoke more low,
But cheerily still; and said, "I pray thee, then,
Write me as one that loves his fellow-men."
    The angel wrote and vanish'd. The next night
It came again, with a great wakening light,
And show'd the names whom love of God had bless'd,
And, lo! Ben Adhem's name led all the rest.

THE GLOVE AND THE LIONS

KING FRANCIS was a hearty king, and loved a royal sport,
And one day, as his lions fought, sat looking on the court;
The nobles fill'd the benches, and the ladies in their pride,
And 'mongst them sat the Count de Lorge, with one for whom he
    sigh'd:
And truly 'twas a gallant thing to see that crowning show,
Valour and love, and a king above, and the royal beasts below.
Ramp'd and roar'd the lions, with horrid laughing jaws;
They bit, they glared, gave blows like beams, a wind went with their
    paws;
With wallowing might and stifled roar they roll'd on one another,
Till all the pit with sand and mane was in a thunderous smother;
The bloody foam above the bars came whisking through the air;
Said Francis then, "Faith, gentlemen, we're better here than there."
De Lorge's love o'erheard the king, a beauteous lively dame
With smiling lips and sharp bright eyes, which always seem'd the
    same;
She thought, the count my lover is brave as brave can be;
He surely would do wondrous things to show his love of me;
King, ladies, lovers, all look on; the occasion is divine;
I'll drop my glove to prove his love; great glory shall be mine.
She dropp'd her glove to prove his love, then look'd at him and
    smiled;
He bow'd, and in a moment leap'd among the lions wild:
The leap was quick, return was quick, he has regain'd the place,
Then threw the glove, but not with love, right in the lady's face.
"By God!" said Francis, "rightly done!" and he rose from where he
    sat;
"No love," quoth he, "but vanity, sets love a task like that."

JENNY KISSED ME

JENNY kiss'd me when we met,
    Jumping from the chair she sat in;
Time, you thief! who love to get
    Sweets into your list, put that in.
Say I'm weary, say I'm sad;
    Say that health and wealth have miss'd me;
Say I'm growing old, but add—
    Jenny kiss'd me!

SAMUEL JOHNSON

ONE-AND-TWENTY

LONG-EXPECTED one-and-twenty,
    Ling'ring year, at length is flown:
Pride and pleasure, pomp and plenty,
    Great * * * * * , are now your own.

Loosen'd from the minor's tether,
    Freed to mortgage or to sell,
Wild as wind, and light as feather,
    Bid the sons of thrift farewell.

Call the Betsies, Katies, and Jennies,
    All the names that banish care;
Lavish of your grandsires guineas,
    Show the spirit of an heir.

All that prey on vice and folly
    Joy to see their quarry fly:
There's the gamester, light and jolly,
    There's the lender, grave and sly.

Wealth, my lad, was made to wander,
    Let it wander as it will;
Call the jockey, call the pander,
    Bid them come and take their fill.

When the bonny blade carouses,
    Pockets full, and spirits high—
What are acres? what are houses?
    Only dirt, or wet or dry.

Should the guardian friend or mother
    Tell the woes of wilful waste,
Scorn their counsel, scorn their pother;—
    You can hang or drown at last!

BEN JONSON

TO CELIA

DRINK to me only with thine eyes,
    And I will pledge with mine;
Or leave a kiss but in the cup
    And I'll not look for wine.
The thirst that from the soul doth rise
    Doth ask a drink divine;
But might I of Jove's nectar sup,
    I would not change for thine.

I sent thee late a rosy wreath,
    Not so much honouring thee
As giving it a hope that there
    It could not wither'd be;
But thou thereon didst only breathe
    And sent'st it back to me;
Since when it grows, and smells, I swear,
    Not of itself but thee!

JOHN KEATS

TO AUTUMN

SEASON of mists and mellow fruitfulness!
    Close bosom-friend of the maturing sun!
Conspiring with him how to load and bless
    With fruit the vines that round the thatch-eaves run—
To bend with apples the mossed cottage trees,
    And fill all fruit with ripeness to the core—
        To swell the gourd, and plump the hazel shells
    With a sweet kernel—to set budding, more
And still more, later flowers for the bees,
Until they think warm days will never cease,
        For Summer has o'er-brimmed their clammy cells.

Who hath not seen thee oft amid thy store?
  Sometimes whoever seeks abroad may find
Thee sitting careless on a granary floor,
    Thy hair soft-lifted by the winnowing wind;
Or on a half-reaped furrow sound asleep,
  Drowsed with the fume of poppies, while thy hook
    Spares the next swath and all its twined flowers;
And sometime like a gleaner thou dost keep
  Steady thy laden head across a brook;
  Or by a cider-press, with patient look,
    Thou watchest the last oozings, hours by hours.

Where are the songs of Spring? Ay, where are they?
  Think not of them—thou hast thy music too:
While barred clouds bloom the soft-dying day,
  And touch the stubble-plains with rosy hue;
Then in a wailful choir the small gnats mourn
  Among the river sallows, borne aloft
    Or sinking, as the light wind lives or dies;
And full-grown lambs loud bleat from hilly bourn;
  Hedge-crickets sing; and now with treble soft
  The red-breast whistles from a garden-croft,
    And gathering swallows twitter in the skies.

ON FIRST LOOKING INTO CHAPMAN'S HOMER

MUCH have I travelled in the realms of gold,
And many goodly states and kingdoms seen;
Round many western islands have I been
Which bards in fealty to Apollo hold.
Oft of one wide expanse had I been told
That deep-browed Homer ruled as his demesne;
Yet did I never breathe its pure serene
Till I heard Chapman speak out loud and bold;
Then felt I like some watcher of the skies
When a new planet swims into his ken;
Or like stout Cortez, when with eagle eyes
He stared at the Pacific—and all his men
Looked at each other with a wild surmise—
Silent, upon a peak in Darien.

LA BELLE DAME SANS MERCI

'O what can ail thee, knight-at-arms,
    Alone and palely loitering?
The sedge has wither'd from the lake,
    And no birds sing.

'O what can ail thee, knight-at-arms!
    So haggard and so woe-begone?
The squirrel's granary is full,
    And the harvest's done.

'I see a lily on thy brow
    With anguish moist and fever-dew,
And on thy cheeks a fading rose
    Fast withereth too.'

'I met a lady in the meads,
    Full beautiful—a faery's child,
Her hair was long, her foot was light,
    And her eyes were wild.

'I made a garland for her head,
    And bracelets too, and fragrant zone;
She look'd at me as she did love,
    And made sweet moan.

'I set her on my pacing steed
    And nothing else saw all day long,
For sidelong would she bend, and sing
    A faery's song.

'She found me roots of relish sweet,
    And honey wild and manna-dew,
And sure in language strange she said
    "I love thee true."

'She took me to her elfin grot,
    And there she wept and sigh'd full sore;
And there I shut her wild wild eyes
    With kisses four.

'And there she lulléd me asleep,
   And there I dream'd—Ah! woe betide!
The latest dream I ever dream'd
   On the cold hill's side.

'I saw pale kings and princes too,
   Pale warriors, death-pale were they all:
They cried—"La belle Dame sans Merci
   Hath thee in thrall!"

'I saw their starved lips in the gloam
   With horrid warning gapéd wide,
And I awoke and found me here
   On the cold hill's side.

'And this is why I sojourn here
   Alone and palely loitering,
Though the sedge is wither'd from the lake,
   And no birds sing.'

ODE ON A GRECIAN URN

Thou still unravished bride of quietness!
   Thou foster-child of Silence and slow Time!
Sylvan historian, who canst thus express
   A flowery tale more sweetly than our rhyme!
What leaf-fringed legend haunts about thy shape
   Of deities or mortals, or of both,
     In Tempe or the dales of Arcady?
   What men or gods are these? what maidens loath?
What mad pursuit? What struggle to escape?
     What pipes and timbrels? What wild ecstasy?

Heard melodies are sweet, but those unheard
   Are sweeter; therefore, ye soft pipes, play on—
Not to the sensual ear, but, more endeared,
   Pipe to the spirit ditties of no tone!

Fair youth beneath the trees, thou canst not leave
   Thy song, nor ever can those trees be bare;
     Bold lover, never, never canst thou kiss,
Though winning near the goal; yet do not grieve—
     She cannot fade, though thou hast not thy bliss;
Forever wilt thou love, and she be fair!

Ah, happy, happy boughs! that cannot shed
   Your leaves, nor ever bid the Spring adieu;
And happy melodist, unwearied,
   Forever piping songs forever new;
More happy love! more happy, happy love!
   Forever warm and still to be enjoyed,
     Forever panting and forever young;
All breathing human passion far above,
     That leaves a heart high-sorrowful and cloyed,
     A burning forehead, and a parching tongue.

Who are these coming to the sacrifice?
   To what green altar, O mysterious priest,
Lead'st thou that heifer lowing at the skies,
   And all her silken flanks with garlands drest?
What little town by river or sea-shore,
   Or mountain-built with peaceful citadel,
     Is emptied of its folk, this pious morn?
And, little town, thy streets for evermore
   Will silent be; and not a soul, to tell
     Why thou art desolate, can e'er return.

O Attic shape! Fair attitude! with brede
   Of marble men and maidens overwrought,
With forest-branches and the trodden weed!
   Thou, silent form! dost tease us out of thought,
As doth eternity. Cold pastoral!
   When old age shall this generation waste,
     Thou shalt remain, in midst of other woe
   Than ours, a friend to man, to whom thou say'st,
"Beauty is truth, truth beauty,"—that is all
     Ye know on earth, and all ye need to know.

ODE TO A NIGHTINGALE

My heart aches, and a drowsy numbness pains
  My sense, as though of hemlock I had drunk;
Or emptied some dull opiate to the drains
  One minute past, and Lethe-ward had sunk.
'Tis not through envy of thy happy lot,
  But being too happy in thy happiness,
That thou, light-winged Dryad of the trees,
      In some melodious plot
Of beechen green, and shadows numberless,
Singest of Summer in full-throated ease.

Oh for a draught of vintage that hath been
  Cooled a long age in the deep-delved earth,
Tasting of Flora and the country green,
  Dance, and Provençal song, and sun-burned mirth!
Oh for a beaker full of the warm South,
  Full of the true, the blushful Hippocrene,
With beaded bubbles winking at the brim,
      And purple-stained mouth—
That I might drink, and leave the world unseen,
And with thee fade away into the forest dim!

Fade far away, dissolve, and quite forget
  What thou among the leaves hast never known—
The weariness, the fever, and the fret;
  Here, where men sit and hear each other groan—
Where palsy shakes a few sad, last grey hairs—
  Where youth grows pale, and spectre-thin, and dies—
Where but to think is to be full of sorrow,
      And leaden-eyed despairs—
Where beauty cannot keep her lustrous eyes,
Or new love pine at them beyond to-morrow!

Away! away! for I will fly to thee!
  Not charioted by Bacchus and his pards,
But on the viewless wings of poesy,
    Though the dull brain perplexes and retards;

Already with thee tender is the night,
　　And haply the queen-moon is on her throne,
Clustered around by all her starry fays;
　　　　But here there is no light,
　　Save what from heaven is with the breezes blown
Through verdurous glooms and winding mossy ways.

I can not see what flowers are at my feet,
　　Nor what soft incense hangs upon the boughs;
But, in embalmed darkness guess each sweet
　　Wherewith the seasonable month endows
The grass, the thicket, and the fruit-tree wild:
　　White hawthorn and the pastoral eglantine;
Fast-fading violets, covered up in leaves;
　　　　And mid-May's oldest child,
　　The coming musk-rose, full of dewy wine,
The murmurous haunt of bees on summer eves.

Darkling I listen; and for many a time
　　I have been half in love with easeful Death,
Called him soft names in many a mused rhyme,
　　To take into the air my quiet breath;
Now, more than ever, seems it rich to die,
　　To cease upon the midnight, with no pain,
While thou art pouring forth thy soul abroad,
　　　　In such an ecstasy!
　　Still wouldst thou sing, and I have ears in vain—
To thy high requiem become a sod.

Thou wast not born for death, immortal bird!
　　No hungry generations tread thee down;
The voice I hear this passing night was heard
　　In ancient days by emperor and clown:
Perhaps the self-same song that found a path
　　Through the sad heart of Ruth, when, sick for home,
She stood in tears amid the alien corn:
　　　　The same that oft-times hath
　　Charmed magic casements opening on the foam
Of perilous seas, in fairy lands forlorn.

Forlorn! the very word is like a bell,
   To toll me back from thee to my sole self!
Adieu! the Fancy cannot cheat so well
   As she is famed to do, deceiving elf!
Adieu! adieu! thy plaintive anthem fades
   Past the near meadows, over the still stream,
Up the hill-side; and now 'tis buried deep
   In the next valley-glades:
Was it a vision or a waking dream?
Fled is that music—do I wake or sleep?

FRANCIS SCOTT KEY

THE STAR SPANGLED BANNER

O say, can you see, by the dawn's early light,
   What so proudly we hailed at the twilight's last gleaming—
Whose broad stripes and bright stars, through the perilous fight,
   O'er the ramparts we watched were so gallantly streaming?
And the rocket's red glare, the bombs bursting in air,
Gave proof through the night that our flag was still there;
O! say, does that star-spangled banner yet wave
O'er the land of the free, and the home of the brave?

On that shore dimly seen through the mists of the deep,
   Where the foe's haughty host in dread silence reposes,
What is that which the breeze, o'er the towering steep,
   As it fitfully blows, now conceals, now discloses?
Now it catches the gleam of the morning's first beam,
In full glory reflected now shines on the stream;
'Tis the star-spangled banner; O long may it wave
O'er the land of the free, and the home of the brave!

And where is that band who so vauntingly swore
   That the havoc of war and the battle's confusion
A home and a country should leave us no more?
   Their blood has washed out their foul footsteps' pollution.
No refuge could save the hireling and slave
From the terror of flight, or the gloom of the grave;
And the star-spangled banner in triumph doth wave
O'er the land of the free, and the home of the brave.

O! Thus be it ever, when freemen shall stand
  Between their loved homes and the war's desolation!
Blest with victory and peace, may the heav'n-rescued land
  Praise the power that hath made and preserved us a nation.
Then conquer we must, when our cause it is just.
  And this be our motto—*"In God is our trust"*:
And the star-spangled banner in triumph shall wave
O'er the land of the free, and the home of the brave.

CHARLES KINGSLEY

THE SANDS O' DEE

"O MARY, go and call the cattle home,
  And call the cattle home,
  And call the cattle home,
  Across the sands o' Dee!"
The western wind was wild and dank wi' foam,
  And all alone went she.

The creeping tide came up along the sand,
  And o'er and o'er the sand,
  And round and round the sand,
  As far as eye could see;
The blinding mist came down and hid the land—
  And never home came she.

"Oh! is it weed, or fish, or floating hair—
  A tress o' golden hair—
  O' drownèd maiden's hair—
  Above the nets at sea?
Was never salmon yet that shone so fair
  Among the stakes on Dee."

They rowed her in across the rolling foam,
  The cruel, crawling foam,
  The cruel, hungry foam—
  To her grave beside the sea;
But still the boatmen hear her call the cattle home
  Across the sands o' Dee!

THE THREE FISHERS

THREE fishers went sailing away to the West,
  Away to the West as the sun went down;
Each thought on the woman who loved him the best,
  And the children stood watching them out of the town;
  For men must work, and women must weep,
  And there's little to earn, and many to keep,
    Though the harbor-bar be moaning.

Three wives sat up in the light-house tower,
  And they trimmed the lamps as the sun went down;
They looked at the squall, and they looked at the shower,
  And the night-rack came rolling up ragged and brown.
  But men must work, and women must weep,
  Though storms be sudden, and waters deep,
    And the harbor-bar be moaning.

Three corpses lay out on the shining sands
  In the morning gleam as the tide went down,
And the women are weeping and wringing their hands
  For those who will never come home to the town;
  For men must work, and women must weep,
  And the sooner it's over, the sooner to sleep:
    And good-bye to the bar and its moaning.

RUDYARD KIPLING

THE VAMPIRE

A FOOL there was and he made his prayer
  (Even as you and I!)
To a rag and a bone and a hank of hair
(We called her the woman who did not care),
But the fool he called her his lady fair
  (Even as you and I!)

Oh the years we waste and the tears we waste
And the work of our head and hand
Belong to the woman who did not know
(And now we know that she never could know)
And did not understand.

A fool there was and his goods he spent
(Even as you and I!)
Honor and faith and a sure intent
(And it wasn't the least what the lady meant),
But a fool must follow his natural bent
(Even as you and I!)

Oh the toil we lost and the spoil we lost
And the excellent things we planned
Belong to the woman who didn't know why
(And now we know she never knew why)
And did not understand.

The fool was stripped to his foolish hide
(Even as you and I!)
Which she might have seen when she threw him
aside—
(But it isn't on record the lady tried)
So some of him lived but the most of him died—
(Even as you and I!)

And it isn't the shame and it isn't the blame
That stings like a white-hot brand.
It's coming to know that she never knew why
(Seeing at last she could never know why)
And never could understand.

THE STORY OF URIAH

"Now there were two men in one city;
the one rich, and the other poor."

JACK BARRETT went to Quetta because they told him to.
He left his wife at Simla on three-fourths his monthly screw:
Jack Barrett died at Quetta ere the next month's pay he drew.

Jack Barrett went to Quetta. He didn't understand
The reason of his transfer from the pleasant mountain land:
The season was September, and it killed him out of hand.

Jack Barrett went to Quetta, and there gave up the ghost,
Attempting two men's duty in that very healthy post;
And Mrs. Barrett mourned for him five lively months at most.

Jack Barrett's bones at Quetta enjoy profound repose;
But I shouldn't be astonished if now his spirit knows
The reason of his transfer from the Himalayan snows.

And when the Last Great Bugle Call adown the Hurnai throbs,
When the last grim joke is entered in the big black Book of Jobs,
And Quetta graveyards give again their victims to the air,
I shouldn't like to be the man who sent Jack Barrett there.

THE BALLAD OF EAST AND WEST

Oh, East is East, and West is West, and never the twain shall meet,
Till Earth and Sky stand presently at God's great Judgment Seat;
But there is neither East nor West, Border, nor Breed, nor Birth,
When two strong men stand face to face, though they come from the
*   ends of the earth.*

Kamal is out with twenty men to raise the Border-side,
And he has lifted the Colonel's mare that is the Colonel's pride:
He has lifted her out of the stable-door between the dawn and the day,
And turned the calkins upon her feet, and ridden her far away.
Then up and spoke the Colonel's son that led a troop of the Guides:—
"Is there never a man of all my men can say where Kamal hides?"

Then up and spoke Mahommed Khan, the son of the Ressaldar:—
"If ye know the track of the morning-mist ye know where his pickets
    are.
At dusk he harries the Abazai—at dawn he is into Bonair;
But he must go by Fort Bukloh to his own place to fare.
So if ye gallop to Fort Bukloh as fast as a bird can fly,
By the favor of God, ye may cut him off ere he win to the Tongue of
    Jagai.

But if he be passed the Tongue of Jagai, right swiftly turn ye then—
For the length and the breadth of that grisly plain is sown with
    Kamal's men.
There is rock to the left, and rock to the right, and low lean thorn
    between,
And ye may hear a breech-bolt snick where never a man is seen."

The Colonel's son has taken a horse, and a raw rough dun was he,
With the mouth of a bell, and the heart of Hell, and the head of the
    gallows-tree.
The Colonel's son to the Fort has won; they bid him stay to eat—
Who rides at the tail of a Border thief, he sits not long at his meat.
He's up and away from Fort Bukloh as fast as he can fly,
Till he was aware of his father's mare in the gut of the Tongue of
    Jagai—
Till he was aware of his father's mare, with Kamal upon her back,
And when he could spy the white of her eye, he made the pistol crack.
He has fired once, he has fired twice, but the whistling ball went wide.
"Ye shoot like a soldier," Kamal said. "Show now if ye can ride."

It's up and over the Tongue of Jagai, as blown dust-devils go—
The dun he fled like a stag of ten, but the mare like a barren doe.
The dun he leaned against the bit and slugged his head above,
But the red mare played with the snaffle-bars as a maiden plays with a
    glove.
There was rock to the left, and rock to the right, and low lean thorn
    between,
And thrice he heard a breech-bolt snick, though never a man was seen.
They have ridden the low moon out of the sky, their hoofs drum up
    the dawn—
The dun he went like a wounded bull, but the mare like a new-roused
    fawn.
The dun he fell at a watercourse—in a woful heap fell he,
And Kamal has turned the red mare back, and pulled the rider free.

He has knocked the pistol out of his hand—small room was there to
    strive—
" 'Twas only by favor of mine," quoth he, "ye rode so long alive:
There was not a rock for twenty mile, there was not a clump of tree,
But covered a man of my own men with his rifle cocked on his knee.

If I had raised my bridle-hand, as I have held it low,
The little jackals that flee so fast were feasting all in a row:
If I had bowed my head on my breast, as I have held it high,
The kite that whistles above us now were gorged till she could not fly."

Lightly answered the Colonel's son: "Do good to bird and beast,
But count who come for the broken meats, before thou makest a feast.
If there should follow a thousand swords to carry my bones away,
Belike the price of a jackal's meal were more than a thief could pay.

They will feed their horse on the standing crop, their men on the
  garnered grain;
The thatch of the byres will serve their fires when all the cattle are
  slain.
But if thou thinkest the price be fair,—thy brethren wait to sup—
The hound is kin to the jackal-spawn,—howl, dog, and call them up!
And if thou thinkest the price be high, in steer and gear and stack,
Give me my father's mare again, and I'll fight my own way back!"

Kamal has gripped him by the hand and set him upon his feet.
"No talk shall be of dogs," said he, "when wolf and gray wolf meet.
May I eat dirt if thou hast hurt of me in deed or breath;
What dam of lances brought thee forth to jest at the dawn with
  Death?"

Lightly answered the Colonel's son: "I hold by the blood of my clan:
Take up the mare for my father's gift—by God, she has carried
  a man!"
The red mare ran to the Colonel's son and nuzzled against his breast.
"We be two strong men," said Kamal then, "but she loveth the
  younger best.
So shall she go with a lifter's dower, my turquoise-studded rein,
My broidered saddle and saddle-cloth, and silver stirrups twain."

The Colonel's son a pistol drew and held it muzzle-end.
"Ye have taken the one from a foe," said he; "will ye take the mate
  from a friend?"

"A gift for a gift," said Kamal straight; "a limb for the risk of a limb.
Thy father has sent his son to me—I'll send my son to him!"
With that he whistled his only son, that dropped from a mountain-
  crest—

He trod the ling like a buck in spring, and he looked like a lance in
  rest.

"Now, here is thy master," Kamal said, "who leads a troop of the
  Guides,
And thou must ride at his left side, as shield on shoulder rides.
Till death or I cut loose the tie, at camp and board and bed,
Thy life is his—thy fate it is to guard him with thy head.
So thou must eat the White Queen's meat, and all her foes are thine,
And thou must harry thy father's hold for the peace of the Border-
  line:
And thou must make a trooper tough, and hack thy way to power—
Belike they will raise thee to Ressaldar when I am hanged in Pesh-
  awur."

They have looked each other between the eyes, and there they found
  no fault;
They have taken the Oath of the Brother-in-Blood on leavened bread
  and salt;
They have taken the Oath of the Brother-in-Blood on fire and fresh-cut
  sod,
On the hilt and the haft of the Khyber knife, and the Wondrous
  Names of God.

The Colonel's son he rides the mare, and Kamal's boy the dun,
And two have come back to Fort Bukloh where there went forth but
  one.
And when they drew to the Quarter-Guard, full twenty swords flew
  clear—
There was not a man but carried his feud with the blood of the moun-
  taineer.
"Ha' done! ha' done!" said the Colonel's son. "Put up the steel at your
  sides!
Last night ye had struck at a Border thief—to-night 'tis a man of the
  Guides!"

Oh, East is East, and West is West, and never the two shall meet,
Till Earth and Sky stand presently at God's great Judgment Seat;
But there is neither East nor West, Border, nor Breed, nor Birth,
When two strong men stand face to face, though they come from the
  ends of the earth.

GUNGA DIN

The *bhisti*, or water-carrier, attached to regiments in India, is often one of the most devoted of the Queen's servants. He is also appreciated by the men.

You may talk o' gin an' beer
When you're quartered safe out 'ere,
An' you're sent to penny-fights an' Aldershot it;
But if it comes to slaughter
You will do your work on water,
An' you'll lick the bloomin' boots of 'im that's got it.
Now in Injia's sunny clime,
Where I used to spend my time
A-servin' of 'Er Majesty the Queen,
Of all them black-faced crew
The finest man I knew
Was our regimental *bhisti*, Gunga Din.
      He was "Din! Din! Din!
      You limping lump o' brick-dust, Gunga Din!
      Hi! *slippy hitherao!*
      Water, get it! *Panee loa!**
      You squidgy-nosed old idol, Gunga Din!"

The uniform 'e wore
Was nothin' much before,
An' rather less than 'arf o' that be'ind,
For a twisty piece o' rag
An' a goatskin water-bag
Was all the field-equipment 'e could find.
When the sweatin' troop-train lay
In a sidin' through the day,
Where the 'eat would make your bloomin' eye-brows crawl,
We shouted "Harry By!"†
Till our throats were bricky-dry,
Then we wopped 'im 'cause 'e couldn't serve us all.
      It was "Din! Din! Din!
      You 'eathen, where the mischief 'ave you been?
      You put some *juldee* in it,
      Or I'll *marrow* you this minute‡
      If you don't fill up my helmet, Gunga Din!"

*Bring water swiftly. †Mr. Atkins's equivalent for "O Brother!" ‡Hit you.

'E would dot an' carry one
Till the longest day was done,
An' 'e didn't seem to know the use o' fear.
If we charged or broke or cut,
You could bet your bloomin' nut,
'E'd be waitin' fifty paces right flank rear.
With 'is *mussick* on 'is back,
'E would skip with our attack,
An' watch us till the bugles made "Retire."
An' for all 'is dirty 'ide
'E was white, clear white, inside
When 'e went to tend the wounded under fire!
   It was "Din! Din! Din!"
  With the bullets kickin' dust-spots on the green.
  When the cartridges ran out,
  You could 'ear the front-files shout:
  "Hi! ammunition-mules an' Gunga Din!"

I sha'n't forgit the night
When I dropped be'ind the fight
With a bullet where my belt-plate should 'a' been.
I was chokin' mad with thirst,
An' the man that spied me first
Was our good old grinnin', gruntin' Gunga Din.
'E lifted up my 'ead,
An' 'e plugged me where I bled,
An' 'e guv me 'arf-a-pint o' water—green:
It was crawlin' and it stunk,
But of all the drinks I've drunk,
I'm gratefullest to one from Gunga Din.
   It was "Din! Din! Din!
  'Ere's a beggar with a bullet through 'is spleen;
  'E's chawin' up the ground an' 'e's kickin' all
   around:
  For Gawd's sake git the water, Gunga Din!"

'E carried me away
To where a *dooli* lay,
An' a bullet come an' drilled the beggar clean.

'E put me safe inside,
An' just before 'e died:
"I 'ope you liked your drink," sez Gunga Din.
So I'll meet 'im later on
In the place where 'e is gone—
Where it's always double drill and no canteen;
'E'll be squattin' on the coals
Givin' drink to pore damned souls,
An' I'll get a swig in Hell from Gunga Din!
    Din! Din! Din!
    You Lazarushian-leather Gunga Din!
    Tho' I've belted you an' flayed you,
    By the livin' Gawd that made you,
    You're a better man than I am, Gunga Din!

"TOMMY"

I WENT into a public-'ouse to get a pint o' beer,
The publican 'e up an' sez, "We serve no red-coats here."
The girls be'ind the bar they laughed an' giggled fit to die,
I outs into the street again, an' to myself sez I:
    O it's Tommy this, an' Tommy that, an' "Tommy go away;"
    But it's "Thank you, Mister Atkins," when the band begins to
        play,
    The band begins to play, my boys, the band begins to play,
    O it's "Thank you, Mister Atkins," when the band begins to
        play.

I went into a theatre as sober as could be,
They gave a drunk civilian room, but 'adn't none for me;
They sent me to the gallery or round the music-'alls,
But when it comes to fightin', Lord! they'll shove me in the stalls.
    For it's Tommy this, an' Tommy that, an' "Tommy wait out-
        side;"
    But it's "Special train for Atkins," when the trooper's on the
        tide,
    The troopship's on the tide, my boys, etc.

O makin' mock o' uniforms that guard you while you sleep
Is cheaper than them uniforms, an' they're starvation cheap;
An' hustlin' drunken sodgers when they're goin' large a bit
Is five times better business than paradin' in full kit.
    Then it's Tommy this, an' Tommy that, an' "Tommy, 'ow's yer
       soul?"'
    But it's "Thin red line of 'eroes" when the drums begin to roll,
    The drums begin to roll, my boys, etc.

We aren't no thin red 'eroes, nor we aren't no blackguards too,
But single men in barricks, most remarkable like you;
An' if sometimes our conduck isn't all your fancy paints,
Why, single men in barricks don't grow into plaster saints.
    While it's Tommy this, an' Tommy that, an' "Tommy fall
       be'ind;"
    But it's "Please to walk in front, sir," when there's trouble in
       the wind,
    There's trouble in the wind, my boys, etc.

You talk o' better food for us, an' schools, an' fires, an' all:
We'll wait for extry rations if you treat us rational.
Don't mess about the cook-room slops, but prove it to our face
The Widow's uniform is not the soldier-man's disgrace.
    For it's Tommy this, an' Tommy that, an' "Chuck him out,
       the brute!"
    But it's "Saviour of 'is country" when the guns begin to shoot;
    An' it's Tommy this, an' Tommy that, an' anything you please;
    An' Tommy ain't a bloomin' fool—you bet that Tommy sees!

"FUZZY WUZZY"

We've fought with many men acrost the seas,
    An' some of 'em was brave an' some was not:
The Paythan an' the Zulu an' Burmese;
    But the Fuzzy was the finest o' the lot.
We never got a ha'porth's change of 'im:
    'E squatted in the scrub an' 'ocked our 'orses,
'E cut our sentries up at Suakim.

An' 'e played the cat an' banjo with our forces.
So 'ere's *to* you, Fuzzy-Wuzzy, at your 'ome in the Sowdan;
You're a pore benighted 'eathen but a first-class fightin' man;
We gives you your certifikit, an' if you want it signed
We'll come an' 'ave a romp with you whenever you're in-
    clined.

We took our chanst among the Kyber 'ills,
    The Boers knocked us silly at a mile,
The Burman guv us Irriwaddy chills,
    An' a Zulu *impi* dished us up in style:
But all we ever got from such as they
    Was pop to what the Fuzzy made us swaller;
We 'eld our bloomin' own, the papers say,
    But man for man the Fuzzy knocked us 'oller.
        Then 'ere's *to* you, Fuzzy-Wuzzy, an' the missis and the kid;
        Our orders was to break you, an' of course we went an' did.
        We sloshed you with Martinis, an' it wasn't 'ardly fair;
        But for all the odds agin you, Fuzzy-Wuz, you bruk the
            square.

'E 'asn't got no papers of 'is own,
    'E 'asn't got no medals nor rewards,
So we must certify the skill 'e's shown
    In usin' of 'is long two-'anded swords:
When 'e's 'oppin' in an' out among the bush
    With 'is coffin-'eaded shield an' shovel-spear,
A 'appy day with Fuzzy on the rush
    Will last a 'ealthy Tommy for a year.
        So 'ere's *to* you, Fuzzy-Wuzzy, an' your friends which is no
            more,
        If we 'adn't lost some messmates we would 'elp you to de-
            plore;
        But give an' take's the gospel, an' we'll call the bargain fair,
        For if you 'ave lost more than us, you crumpled up the square!

'E rushes at the smoke when we let drive,
    An', before we know, 'e's 'ackin' at our 'ead,
'E's all 'ot sand an' ginger when alive,
    An' 'e's generally shammin' when 'e's dead.
'E's a daisy, 'e's a ducky, 'e's a lamb!

'E's a injia-rubber idiot on the spree,
'E's the on'y thing that doesn't care a damn
  For the Regiment o' British Infantree.
    So 'ere's *to* you, Fuzzy-Wuzzy, at your 'ome in the Sowdan;
    You're a pore benighted 'eathen but a first-class fightin' man;
    An' 'ere's *to* you, Fuzzy-Wuzzy, with your 'ayrick 'ead of
      'air—
    You big black boundin' beggar—for you bruk a British
    square.

DANNY DEEVER

"What are the bugles blowin' for?" said Files-on-Parade.
"To turn you out, to turn you out," the Color-Sergeant said.
"What makes you look so white, so white?" said Files-on-Parade.
"I'm dreadin' what I've got to watch," the Color-Sergeant said.
    For they're hangin' Danny Deever, you can 'ear the Dead
      March play,
    The regiment's in 'ollow square—they're hangin' him to-day;
    They've taken of his buttons off an' cut his stripes away,
    An' they're hangin' Danny Deever in the mornin'.

"What makes the rear-rank breathe so 'ard?" said Files-on-Parade.
"It's bitter cold, it's bitter cold," the Color-Sergeant said.
"What makes that front-rank man fall down?" says Files-on-Parade.
"A touch of sun, a touch of sun," the Color-Sergeant said.
    They are hangin' Danny Deever, they are marchin' of 'im
      round,
    They 'ave 'alted Danny Deever by 'is coffin on the ground;
    An' 'e'll swing in 'arf a minute for a sneakin', shootin' hound—
    O they're hangin' Danny Deever in the mornin'!

" 'Is cot was right-'and cot to mine," said Files-on-Parade.
" 'E's sleepin' out an' far to-night," the Color-Sergeant said.
"I've drunk 'is beer a score o' times," said Files-on-Parade.
" 'E's drinkin' bitter beer alone," the Color-Sergeant said.
    They are hangin' Danny Deever, you must mark 'im to 'is place,
    For 'e shot a comrade sleepin'—you must look 'im in the face;
    Nine 'undred of 'is county an' the regiment's disgrace,
    While they're hangin' Danny Deever in the mornin'.

"What's that so black agin the sun?" said Files-on-Parade.
"It's Danny fightin' 'ard for life," the Color-Sergeant said.
"What's that that whimpers over'ead?" said Files-on-Parade.
"It's Danny's soul that's passin' now," the Color-Sergeant said.
 For they're done with Danny Deever, you can 'ear the quick-
      step play,
 The regiment's in column, an' they're marchin' us away;
 Ho! the young recruits are shakin', an' they'll want their beer
      to-day,
 After hangin' Danny Deever in the mornin'.

OONTS!

Wot makes the soldier's 'eart to penk, wot makes 'im to perspire?
It isn't standin' up to charge or lyin' down to fire;
But it's everlastin' waitin' on a everlastin' road
For the commissariat camel an' 'is commissariat load.
    O the *oont*,* O the *oont*, O the commissariat *oont!*
    With 'is silly neck a-bobbin' like a basket full o' snakes;
    We packs 'im like a idol, an' you ought to 'ear 'im grunt,
    An' when we gets 'im loaded up 'is blessed girth-rope breaks.

Wot makes the rear-guard swear so 'ard when night is drorin' in,
An' every native follower is shiverin' for 'is skin?
It ain't the chanst o' bein' rushed by Paythans frum the 'ills,
It's the commissariat camel puttin' on 'is blessed frills!
    O the *oont*, O the *oont*, O the hairy scary *oont!*
    A-trippin' over tent-ropes when we've got the night alarm;
    We socks 'im with a stretcher-pole an' 'eads 'im off in front,
    An' when we've saved 'is bloomin' life 'e chaws our bloomin'
        arm.

The 'orse 'e knows above a bit, the bullock's but a fool,
The elephant's a gentleman, the baggage-mule's a mule;
But the commissariat cam-u-el, when all is said an' done,
'E's a devil an' a ostrich an' a orphan-child in one.

*Camel: *oo* is pronounced like *u* in "bull," but by Mr. Atkins to rhyme with "front."

O the *oont*, O the *oont*, O the Gawd-forsaken *oont!*
The 'umpy-lumpy, 'ummin'-bird a-singin' where 'e lies,
'E's blocked the 'ole division from the rear-guard to the front,
An' when we gets 'im up again—the beggar goes an' dies!

'E'll gall an' chafe an' lame an' fight; 'e smells most awful vile;
'E'll lose 'imself forever if you let 'im stray a mile;
'E's game to graze the 'ole day long 'an 'owl the 'ole night through,
An' when 'e comes to greasy ground 'e splits 'isself in two.
  O the *oont*, O the *oont*, O the floppin', droppin' *oont!*
  When 'is long legs give from under an' 'is meltin' eye is dim,
  The tribes is up be'ind us an' the tribes is out in front,
  It ain't no jam for Tommy, but it's kites and crows for 'im.

So when the cruel march is done an' when the roads is blind,
An' when we sees the camp in front an' 'ears the shots be'ind,
O then we strips 'is saddle off, and all 'is woes is past:
'E thinks on us that used 'im so, an' gets revenge at last.
  O the *oont*, O the *oont*, O the floatin', bloatin' *oont!*
  The late lamented camel in the water-cut he lies;
  We keeps a mile behind 'im an' we keeps a mile in front,
  But 'e gets into the drinkin' casks, and then o' course we dies.

RECESSIONAL

(A Victorian Ode.)

God of our fathers, known of old,—
Lord of our far-flung battle-line—
Beneath whose awful hand we hold
Dominion over palm and pine—
Lord God of Hosts, be with us yet,
Lest we forget—lest we forget!

The tumult and the shouting dies—
The Captains and the Kings depart—
Still stands Thine ancient sacrifice,
An humble and a contrite heart.
Lord God of Hosts, be with us yet,
Lest we forget—lest we forget!

Far-called our navies melt away—
On dune and headland sinks the fire—
Lo, all our pomp of yesterday
Is one with Nineveh and Tyre!
Judge of the Nations, spare us yet,
Lest we forget—lest we forget!

If, drunk with sight of power we loose
Wild tongues that have not Thee in awe—
Such boastings as the Gentiles use,
Or lesser breeds without the Law—
Lord God of Hosts, be with us yet,
Lest we forget—lest we forget!

For heathen heart that puts her trust
In reeking tube and iron shard—
All valiant dust that builds on dust,
And guarding calls not Thee to guard.
For frantic boast and foolish word,
Thy Mercy on Thy People, Lord!
Amen.

MANDALAY

By the old Moulmein Pagoda, lookin' eastward to the sea,
There's a Burma girl a-settin', an' I know she thinks o' me;
For the wind is in the palm-trees, an' the temple-bells they say:
"Come you back, you British soldier; come you back to Mandalay!"
　　Come you back to Mandalay,
　　Where the old Flotilla lay:
　　Can't you 'ear their paddles chunkin' from Rangoon to Mandalay?
　　O the road to Mandalay,
　　Where the flyin'-fishes play,
　　An' the dawn comes up like thunder outer China 'crost the Bay!

'Er petticut was yaller an' 'er little cap was green,
An' 'er name was Supi-yaw-lat—jes' the same as Theebaw's Queen,
An' I seed her fust a-smokin' of a whackin' white cheroot,
An' a-wastin' Christian kisses on an 'eathen idol's foot:

Bloomin' idol made o' mud—
Wot they called the Great Gawd Budd—
Plucky lot she cared for idols when I kissed 'er where she stud!
On the road to Mandalay—

When the mist was on the rice-fields an' the sun was droppin' slow,
She'd git 'er little banjo an' she'd sing "*Kullalo lo!*"
With 'er arm upon my shoulder an' her cheek agin my cheek
We useter watch the steamers an' the *hathis* pilin' teak.
 Elephints a-pilin' teak
 In the sludgy, squdgy creek,
 Where the silence 'ung that 'eavy you was 'arf afraid to speak!
 On the road to Mandalay—

But that's all shove be'ind me—long ago an' fur away,
An' there ain't no 'buses runnin' from the Benk to Mandalay;
An' I'm learnin' 'ere in London what the ten-year sodger tells:
"If you've 'eard the East a-callin', why, you won't 'eed nothin' else."
 No! you won't 'eed nothin' else
 But them spicy garlic smells
 An' the sunshine an' the palm-tree an' the tinkly temple-bells!
 On the road to Mandalay—

I am sick o' wastin' leather on these gutty pavin'-stones,
An' the blasted Henglish drizzle wakes the fever in my bones;
Tho' I walks with fifty 'ousemaids outer Chelsea to the Strand,
An' they talks a lot o' lovin', but wot do they understand?
 Beefy face an' grubby 'and—
 Law! wot *do* they understand?
 I've a neater, sweeter maiden in a cleaner, greener land!
 On the road to Mandalay—

Ship me somewheres east of Suez where the best is like the worst,
Where there aren't no Ten Commandments, an' a man can raise a
 thirst;
For the temple-bells are callin', an' it's there that I would be—
By the old Moulmein Pagoda, lookin' lazy at the sea—
 On the road to Mandalay,
 Where the old Flotilla lay,
 With our sick beneath the awnings when we went to Mandalay!
 Oh, the road to Mandalay,
 Where the flyin'-fishes play,
 An' the dawn comes up like thunder outer China 'crost the Bay!

CHARLES LAMB

THE OLD FAMILIAR FACES

I HAVE had playmates, I have had companions,
In my days of childhood, in my joyful school-days;
All, all are gone, the old familiar faces.

I have been laughing, I have been carousing,
Drinking late, sitting late, with my bosom cronies;
All, all are gone, the old familiar faces.

I loved a love once, fairest among women;
Closed are her doors on me, I must not see her—
All, all are gone, the old familiar faces.

I have a friend, a kinder friend has no man:
Like an ingrate, I left my friend abruptly;
Left him, to muse on the old familiar faces.

Ghost-like I paced round the haunts of my childhood,
Earth seemed a desert I was bound to traverse,
Seeking to find the old familiar faces.

Friend of my bosom, thou more than a brother,
Why wert thou not born in my father's dwelling?
So might we talk of the old familiar faces,—

How some they have died, and some they have left me,
And some are taken from me; all are departed;
All, all are gone, the old familiar faces.

HESTER

WHEN maidens such as Hester die,
Their place ye may not well supply,
Though ye among a thousand try,
    With vain endeavor.

A month or more has she been dead,
Yet cannot I by force be led
To think upon the wormy bed
    And her together.

A springy motion in her gait,
A rising step, did indicate
Of pride and joy no common rate,
    That flushed her spirit.

I know not by what name beside
I shall it call:—if 't was not pride,
It was a joy to that allied,
    She did inherit.

Her parents held the Quaker rule,
Which doth the human feeling cool,
But she was trained in Nature's school,
    Nature had blest her.

A waking eye, a prying mind,
A heart that stirs, is hard to bind,
A hawk's keen sight ye cannot blind,
    Ye could not Hester.

My sprightly neighbor, gone before
To that unknown and silent shore,
Shall we not meet, as heretofore,
    Some summer morning,

When from thy cheerful eyes a ray
Hath struck a bliss upon the day,
A bliss that would not go away,
    A sweet forewarning?

WALTER SAVAGE LANDOR
HOW MANY VOICES GAILY SING

How many voices gaily sing,
"O happy morn, O happy spring
Of life!" Meanwhile there comes o'er me
A softer voice from Memory,
And says, "If loves and hopes have flown
With years, think, too, what griefs are gone!"

EDWARD LEAR

THE OWL AND THE PUSSY-CAT

THE Owl and the Pussy-Cat went to sea
   In a beautiful pea-green boat:
They took some honey, and plenty of money
   Wrapped up in a five-pound note.
The Owl looked up to the stars above,
   And sang to a small guitar,
"O lovely Pussy, O Pussy, my love,
   What a beautiful Pussy you are,
         You are,
         You are!
   What a beautiful Pussy you are!"

Pussy said to the Owl, "You elegant fowl,
   How charmingly sweet you sing!
Oh! let us be married; too long we have tarried:
   But what shall we do for a ring?"
They sailed away, for a year and a day,
   To the land where the bong-tree grows;
And there in a wood a Piggy-wig stood,
   With a ring at the end of his nose,
         His nose,
         His nose,
   With a ring at the end of his nose.

"Dear Pig, are you willing to sell for one shilling
   Your ring?" Said the Piggy, "I will."
So they took it away, and were married next day
   By the Turkey who lives on the hill.
They dinèd on mince and slices of quince,
   Which they ate with a runcible spoon;
And hand in hand, on the edge of the sand
   They danced by the light of the moon,
         The moon,
         The moon,
   They danced by the light of the moon.

RUDYARD KIPLING

HENRY WADSWORTH LONGFELLOW

HENRY WADSWORTH LONGFELLOW

THE SKELETON IN ARMOR

SPEAK! speak! thou fearful guest!
Who, with thy hollow breast,
Still in rude armor drest,
 Comest to daunt me!
Wrapt not in eastern balms,
But with thy fleshless palms
Stretched, as if asking alms,
 Why dost thou haunt me?"

Then from those cavernous eyes
Pale flashes seemed to rise,
As when the northern skies
 Gleam in December;
And like the water's flow
Under December's snow,
Came a dull voice of woe
 From the heart's chamber:

"I was a Viking old!
My deeds, though manifold,
No Skald in song has told,
 No Saga taught thee!
Take heed that in thy verse
Thou dost the tale rehearse,
Else dread a dead man's curse!
 For this I sought thee.

"Far in the Northern land,
By the wide Baltic's strand,
I, with my childish hand,
 Tamed the ger-falcon;
And, with my skates fast bound,
Skimmed the half-frozen Sound,
That the poor whimpering hound
 Trembled to walk on.

"Oft to his frozen lair
Tracked I the grisly bear,
While from my path the hare
   Fled like a shadow;
Oft through the forest dark
Followed the were-wolf's bark,
Until the soaring lark
   Sang from the meadow.

"But when I older grew,
Joining a corsair's crew,
O'er the dark sea I flew
   With the marauders.
Wild was the life we led;
Many the souls that sped,
Many the hearts that bled,
   By our stern orders.

"Many a wassail bout
Wore the long winter out;
Often our midnight shout
   Set the cocks crowing,
As we the Bersek's tale
Measured in cups of ale,
Draining the oaken pail
   Filled to o'erflowing.

"Once, as I told in glee
Tales of the stormy sea,
Soft eyes did gaze on me,
   Burning, yet tender;
And, as the white stars shine
On the dark Norway pine,
On that dark heart of mine
   Fell their soft splendor.

"I wooed the blue-eyed maid,
Yielding, yet half afraid,
And in the forest's shade
   Our vows were plighted.

Under its loosened vest
Fluttered her little breast,
Like birds within their nest
  By the hawk frightened.

"Bright in her father's hall
Shields gleamed upon the wall,
Loud sang the minstrels all,
  Chanting his glory;
When of old Hildebrand
I asked his daughter's hand,
Mute did the minstrels stand
  To hear my story.

"While the brown ale he quaffed,
Loud then the champion laughed,
And, as the wind-gusts waft
  The sea-foam brightly,
So the loud laugh of scorn,
Out of those lips unshorn,
From the deep drinking-horn
  Blew the foam lightly.

"She was a Prince's child,
I but a Viking wild,
And though she blushed and smiled,
  I was discarded!
Should not the dove so white
Follow the sea-mew's flight?
Why did they leave that night
  Her nest unguarded?

"Scarce had I put to sea,
Bearing the maid with me—
Fairest of all was she
  Among the Norsemen!—
When, on the white sea-strand,
Waving his armed hand,
Saw we old Hildebrand,
  With twenty horsemen.

"Then launched they to the blast;
Bent like a reed each mast;
Yet we were gaining fast,
   When the wind failed us;
And with a sudden flaw
Came round the gusty skaw,
So that our foe we saw
   Laugh as he hailed us.

"And as, to catch the gale,
Round veered the flapping sail,
Death was the helmsman's hail—
   Death without quarter!
Mid-ships, with iron keel
Struck we her ribs of steel;
Down her black hulk did reel
   Through the black water!

"As with his wings aslant,
Sails the fierce cormorant,
Seeking some rocky haunt,
   With his prey laden,
So toward the open main,
Beating to sea again,
Through the wild hurricane
   Bore I the maiden.

"Three weeks we westward bore,
And when the storm was o'er,
Cloud-like we saw the shore
   Stretching to leeward;
There, for my lady's bower,
Built I the lofty tower
Which, to this very hour,
   Stands looking seaward.

"There lived we many years;
Time dried the maiden's tears;
She had forgot her fears,
   She was a mother.

Death closed her mild blue eyes;
Under that tower she lies;
Ne'er shall the sun arise
    On such another!

"Still grew my bosom then,
Still as a stagnant fen!
Hateful to me were men—
    The sunlight hateful!
In the vast forest here,
Clad in my warlike gear,
Fell I upon my spear;
    O, death was grateful!

"Thus, seamed with many scars,
Bursting its prison bars,
Up to its native stars
    My soul ascended!
There from the flowing bowl
Deep drinks the warrior's soul,
Skoal! to the Northland! *skoal!*"
    Thus the tale ended.

THE CHILDREN'S HOUR

BETWEEN the dark and the daylight,
    When the night is beginning to lower,
Comes a pause in the day's occupations,
    That is known as the children's hour.

I hear in the chamber above me
    The patter of little feet;
The sound of a door that is opened,
    And voices soft and sweet.

From my study I see in the lamplight,
    Descending the broad hall stair,
Grave Alice, and laughing Allegra,
    And Edith with golden hair.

A whisper and then a silence,
 Yet I know by their merry eyes
They are plotting and planning together
 To take me by surprise.

A sudden rush from the stairway;
 A sudden raid from the hall;
By three doors left unguarded
 They enter my castle-wall.

They climb up into my turret,
 O'er the arms and back of my chair;
If I try to escape they surround me,
 They seem to be everywhere.

They almost devour me with kisses,
 Their arms about me entwine,
Till I think of the Bishop of Bingen,
 In his Mouse-Tower on the Rhine.

Do you think, O blue-eyed banditti,
 Because you have scaled the wall,
Such an old mustache as I am
 Is not a match for you all?

I have you fast in my fortress,
 And will not let you depart,
But put you into the dungeon,
 In the round-tower of my heart.

And there will I keep you forever—
 Yes, forever and a day;
Till the walls shall crumble to ruin,
 And moulder in dust away.

A PSALM OF LIFE

TELL me not, in mournful numbers,
 "Life is but an empty dream;
For the soul is dead that slumbers,
 And things are not what they seem!"

Life is real! Life is earnest!
   And the grave is not its goal:
"Dust thou art, to dust returnest,"
   Was not spoken of the soul.

Not enjoyment, and not sorrow
   Is our destined end or way;
But to act that each to-morrow
   Finds us farther than to-day.

Art is long, and Time is fleeting,
   And our hearts, though stout and **brave,**
Still, like muffled drums, are beating
   Funeral marches to the grave.

In the world's broad field of battle,
   In the bivouac of Life,
Be not like dumb, driven cattle!
   Be a hero in the strife!

Trust no Future, howe'er pleasant!
   Let the dead Past bury its dead!
Act, act in the living Present,
   Heart within, and God o'erhead!

Lives of great men all remind us
   We can make our lives sublime,
And, departing, leave behind us
   Footprints on the sands of time:

Footprints, that perhaps another,
   Sailing o'er life's solemn main,
A forlorn and shipwrecked brother,
   Seeing, shall take heart again.

Let us, then, be up and doing,
   With a heart for any fate;
Still achieving, still pursuing,
   Learn to labor and to wait.

THE WRECK OF THE HESPERUS

IT was the schooner Hesperus,
  That sailed the wintry sea;
And the skipper had taken his little daughter,
  To bear him company.

Blue were her eyes as the fairy-flax,
  Her cheeks like the dawn of day,
And her bosom white as the hawthorn buds,
  That ope in the month of May.

The skipper he stood beside the helm,
  His pipe was in his mouth,
And he watched how the veering flaw did blow
  The smoke now West, now South.

Then up and spake an old Sailòr,
  Had sailed the Spanish Main,
"I pray thee, put into yonder port,
  For I fear a hurricane.

"Last night, the moon had a golden ring,
  And to-night no moon we see!"
The skipper, he blew a whiff from his pipe,
  And a scornful laugh laughed he.

Colder and louder blew the wind,
  A gale from the Northeast;
The snow fell hissing in the brine,
  And the billows frothed like yeast.

Down came the storm, and smote amain,
  The vessel in its strength;
She shuddered and paused, like a frightened steed,
  Then leaped her cable's length.

"Come hither! come hither! my little daughter,
  And do not tremble so;
For I can weather the roughest gale,
  That ever wind did blow."

He wrapped her warm in his seaman's coat
  Against the stinging blast;
He cut a rope from a broken spar,
  And bound her to the mast.

"O father! I hear the church-bells ring,
  O say, what may it be?"
" 'T is a fog-bell on a rock-bound coast!"—
  And he steered for the open sea.

"O father! I hear the sound of guns,
  O say, what may it be?"
"Some ship in distress, that cannot live
  In such an angry sea!"

"O father! I see a gleaming light,
  O say, what may it be?"
But the father answered never a word,
  A frozen corpse was he.

Lashed to the helm, all stiff and stark,
  With his face turned to the skies,
The lantern gleamed through the gleaming snow
  On his fixed and glassy eyes.

Then the maiden clasped her hands and prayed
  That savèd she might be;
And she thought of Christ, who stilled the wave,
  On the Lake of Galilee.

And fast through the midnight dark and drear,
  Through the whistling sleet and snow,
Like a sheeted ghost, the vessel swept
  Towards the reef of Norman's Woe.

And ever the fitful gusts between,
  A sound came from the land;
It was the sound of the trampling surf,
  On the rocks and the hard sea-sand.

The breakers were right beneath her bows,
    She drifted a dreary wreck,
And a whooping billow swept the crew
    Like icicles from her deck.

She struck where the white and fleecy waves
    Looked soft as carded wool,
But the cruel rocks, they gored her side
    Like horns of an angry bull.

Her rattling shrouds, all sheathed in ice,
    With the masts went by the board;
Like a vessel of glass, she stove and sank,
    Ho! ho! the breakers roared!

At daybreak on the bleak sea-beach,
    A fisherman stood aghast,
To see the form of a maiden fair,
    Lashed close to a drifting mast.

The salt-sea was frozen on her breast,
    The salt tears in her eyes;
And he saw her hair, like the brown sea-weed,
    On the billows fall and rise.

Such was the wreck of the Hesperus,
    In the midnight and the snow!
Christ save us all from a death like this,
    On the reef of Norman's Woe!

THE VILLAGE BLACKSMITH

UNDER a spreading chestnut tree
    The village smithy stands;
The smith, a mighty man is he,
    With large and sinewy hands;
And the muscles of his brawny arms
    Are strong as iron bands.

His hair is crisp, and black, and long,
  His face is like the tan;
His brow is wet with honest sweat,
  He earns whate'er he can,
And looks the whole world in the face,
  For he owes not any man.

Week in, week out, from morn till night,
  You can hear his bellows blow;
You can hear him swing his heavy sledge,
  With measured beat and slow,
Like a sexton ringing the village bell,
  When the evening sun is low.

And children coming home from school
  Look in at the open door;
They love to see the flaming forge,
  And hear the bellows roar,
And catch the burning sparks that fly
  Like chaff from a threshing floor.

He goes on Sunday to the church,
  And sits among his boys;
He hears the parson pray and preach,
  He hears his daughter's voice,
Singing in the village choir,
  And it makes his heart rejoice.

It sounds to him like her mother's voice,
  Singing in Paradise!
He needs must think of her once more,
  How in the grave she lies;
And with his hard, rough hand he wipes
  A tear out of his eyes.

Toiling,—rejoicing,—sorrowing,
  Onward through life he goes;
Each morning sees some task begun
  Each evening sees it close;
Something attempted, something done,
  Has earned a night's repose.

Thanks, thanks to thee, my worthy friend,
  For the lesson thou has taught!
Thus at the flaming forge of life
  Our fortunes must be wrought;
Thus on its sounding anvil shaped
  Each burning deed and thought!

RICHARD LOVELACE

TO ALTHEA, FROM PRISON

When Love with unconfinéd wings
  Hovers within my gates,
And my divine Althea brings
  To whisper at the grates;
When I lie tangled in her hair
  And fetter'd to her eye,
The Gods that wanton in the air
  Know no such liberty.

When flowing cups run swiftly round
  With no allaying Thames,
Our careless heads with roses bound,
  Our hearts with loyal flames;
When thirsty grief in wine we steep,
  When healths and draughts go free—
Fishes that tipple in the deep
  Know no such liberty.

When, (like committed linnets), I
  With shriller throat shall sing
The sweetness, mercy, majesty
  And glories of my King;
When I shall voice aloud how good
  He is, how great should be,
Enlargèd winds, that curl the flood,
  Know no such liberty.

Stone walls do not a prison make,
    Nor iron bars a cage;
Minds innocent and quiet take
    That for an hermitage;
If I have freedom in my love
    And in my soul am free,
Angels alone, that soar above,
    Enjoy such liberty.

JAMES RUSSELL LOWELL

SHE CAME AND WENT

As a twig trembles, which a bird
    Lights on to sing, then leaves unbent,
So is my memory thrilled and stirred;—
    I only know she came and went.

As clasps some lake, by gusts unriven,
    The blue dome's measureless content,
So my soul that moment's heaven;—
    I only know she came and went.

As, at one bound, our swift spring heaps
    The orchard's full of bloom and scent,
So clove her May my wintry sleeps;—
    I only know she came and went.

Oh, when the room grows slowly dim,
    And life's last oil is nearly spent,
One gush of light these eyes will brim,
    Only to think she came and went

THE COURTIN'

God makes sech nights, all white an' still
    Fur'z you can look or listen,
Moonshine an' snow on field an' hill,
    All silence an' all glisten.

Zekle crep' up quite unbeknown,
  An' peeked in thru' the winder,
An' there sot Huldy all alone,
  'Ith no one nigh to hender.

A fireplace filled the room's one side
  With half a cord o' wood in,—
There warn't no stoves (tell Comfort died)
  To bake ye to a puddin'.

The wa'nut logs shot sparkles out
  Towards the pootiest, bless her!
An' leetle flames danced all about
  The chiny on the dresser.

Agin the chimbley crook-necks hung,
  An' in amongst 'em rusted
The ole queen's arm thet Gran'ther Young
  Fetched back from Concord busted.

The very room, coz she was in,
  Seemed warm from floor to ceilin',
An' she looked full ez rosy agin
  Ez the apples she was peelin'.

'T was kin' o' kingdom-come to look
  On sech a blessèd cretur,
A dogrose blushin' to a brook
  Ain't modester nor sweeter.

He was six foot o' man, A 1,
  Clean grit an' human natur';
None couldn't quicker pitch a ton
  Nor dror a furrer straighter.

He'd sparked it with full twenty gals,
  He'd squired 'em, danced 'em, druv 'em,
Fust this one, an' then thet, by spells,—
  All is, he couldn't love 'em.

But long o' her his veins 'ould run
  All crinkly like curled maple,

The side she breshed felt full o' sun
   Ez a south slope in Ap'il.

She thought no v'ice hed sech a swing
   Ez hisn in the choir;
My! when he made Ole Hundred ring,
   She *knowed* the Lord was nigher.

An' she'd blush scarlit, right in prayer,
   When her new meetin'-bunnet
Felt somehow thru' its crown a pair
   O' blue eyes sot upon it.

Thet night, I tell ye, she looked *some!*
   She seemed to 've gut a new soul,
For she felt sartin-sure he 'd come,
   Down to her very shoe-sole.

She heered a foot, an' knowed it tu,
   A-raspin' on the scraper,—
All ways to once her feelin's flew
   Like sparks in burnt-up paper.

He kin' o' l'itered on the mat,
   Some doubtfle o' the sekle,
His heart kep' goin' pity-pat,
   But hern went pity Zekle.

An' yit she gin her cheer a jerk
   Ez though she wished him furder,
An' on her apples kep' to work,
   Parin' away like murder.

"You want to see my Pa, I s'pose?"
   "Wal . . . no . . . I come dasignin' "—
"To see my Ma? She 's sprinklin' clo'es
   Agin to-morrer's i'nin'."

To say why gals acts so or so,
   Or don't, 'ould be presumin';
Mebby to mean *yes* an' say *no*
   Comes nateral to women.

He stood a spell on one foot fust,
   Then stood a spell on t'other,
An' on which one he felt the wust
   He could n't ha' told ye nuther.

Says he, "I'd better call agin";
   Says she, "Think likely, Mister":
Thet last word pricked him like a pin,
   An' . . . Wal, he up an' kist her.

When Ma bimeby upon 'em slips,
   Huldy sot pale ez ashes,
All kin' o' smily roun' the lips
   An' teary roun' the lashes.

For she was jes' the quiet kind
   Whose naturs never vary,
Like streams that keep a summer mind
   Snowhid in Jenooary.

The blood clost roun' her heart felt glued
   Too tight for all expressin',
Tell mother see how metters stood,
   And gin 'em both her blessin'.

Then her red come back like the tide
   Down to the Bay o' Fundy,
An' all I know is, they was cried
   In meetin' come nex' Sunday.

AFTER THE BURIAL

Yes, Faith is a goodly anchor
   When skies are sweet as a psalm
It lolls at the bows so stalwart
   In bluff, broad-shouldered calm.

And when over breakers to leeward
   The tattered surges are hurled,
It may keep our head to the tempest,
   With its grip on the base of the world.

But, after the shipwreck, tell me
    What help in its iron thews,
Still true to the broken hawser,
    Deep down among seaweed and ooze?

In the breaking gulfs of sorrow,
    When the helpless feet stretch out,
And find in the deeps of darkness
    No footing so solid as doubt;

Then better one spar of memory,
    One broken plank of the Past,
That our human heart may cling to,
    Though hopeless of shore at last!

To the spirit its splendid conjectures,
    To the flesh its sweet despair,
Its tears o'er the thin worn locket
    With its anguish of deathless hair!

Immortal? I feel it and know it;
    Who doubts it of such as she?
But that is the pang's very secret—
    Immortal away from me!

There's a narrow ridge in the graveyard
    Would scarce stay a child in his race;
But to me and my thought it is wider
    Than the star-sown vague of space.

Your logic, my friend, is perfect,
    Your moral 's most drearily true;
But since the earth clashed on *her* coffin,
    I keep hearing that, and not you.

Console, if you will; I can bear it;
    'Tis a well-meant alms of breath;
But not all the preaching since Adam
    Has made Death other than Death.

It is pagan: but wait till you feel it,
    That jar of our earth, that dull shock,

When the ploughshare of deeper passion
　　Tears down to our primitive rock.

Communion in spirit? Forgive me,
　　But I, who am earthly and weak,
Would give all my incomes from dreamland
　　For her rose-leaf palm on my cheek!

That little shoe in the corner,
　　So worn and wrinkled and brown—
Its emptiness confutes you,
　　And argues your wisdom down.

MY LOVE

Not as all other women are
　　Is she that to my soul is dear;
Her glorious fancies come from far,
Beneath the silver evening star;
　　And yet her heart is ever near.

Great feelings hath she of her own,
　　Which lesser souls may never know;
God giveth them to her alone,
And sweet they are as any tone
　　Wherewith the wind may choose to blow,

Yet in herself she dwelleth not,
　　Although no home were half so fair;
No simplest duty is forgot;
Life hath no dim and lowly spot
　　That doth not in her sunshine share.

She doeth little kindnesses
　　Which most leave undone, or despise;
For naught that sets one heart at ease,
And giveth happiness or peace,
　　Is low esteemed in her eyes.

She hath no scorn of common things;
　　And though she seem of other birth,

Round us her heart entwines and clings,
And patiently she folds her wings
   To tread the humble paths of earth.

Blessing she is: God made her so;
   And deeds of week-day holiness
Fall from her noiseless as the snow;
Nor hath she ever chanced to know
   That aught were easier than to bless.

She is most fair, and thereunto
   Her life doth rightly harmonize;
Feeling or thought that was not true
Ne'er made less beautiful the blue
   Unclouded heaven of her eyes.

She is a woman; one in whom
   The spring-time of her childish years
Hath never lost its fresh perfume,
Though knowing well that life hath room
   For many blights and many tears.

I love her with a love as still
   As a broad river's peaceful might,
Which by high tower and lowly mill
Goes wandering at its own will,
   And yet doth ever flow aright.

And on its full, deep breast serene,
   Like quiet isles, my duties lie;
It flows around them and between,
And makes them fresh and fair and green,
   Sweet homes wherein to live and die.

ROBERT T. S. LOWELL

THE RELIEF OF LUCKNOW

Oh, that last day in Lucknow fort!
   We knew that it was the last;
That the enemy's lines crept surely on,
   And the end was coming fast.

To yield to that foe meant worse than death;
 And the men and we all worked on;
It was one day more of smoke and roar,
 And then it would all be done.

There was one of us, a corporal's wife,
 A fair, young, gentle thing,
Wasted with fever in the siege,
 And her mind was wandering.

She lay on the ground, in her Scottish plaid,
 And I took her head on my knee;
"When my father comes hame frae the pleugh," she said,
 "Oh! then please wauken me."

She slept like a child on her father's floor,
 In the flecking of woodbine-shade,
When the house-dog sprawls by the open door,
 And the mother's wheel is stayed.

It was smoke and roar and powder-stench,
 And hopeless waiting for death;
And the soldier's wife, like a full-tired child,
 Seemed scarce to draw her breath.

I sank to sleep; and I had my dream
 Of an English village-lane,
And wall and garden;—but one wild scream
 Brought me back to the roar again.

There Jessie Brown stood listening
 Till a sudden gladness broke
All over her face; and she caught my hand
 And drew me near as she spoke:—

"The Hielanders! Oh! dinna ye hear
 The slogan far awa?
The McGregors. Oh! I ken it weel;
 It's the grandest o' them a'!

"God bless the bonny Hielanders!
 We're saved! we're saved!" she cried;

And fell on her knees; and thanks to God
　　Flowed forth like a full flood-tide.

Along the battery-line her cry
　　Had fallen among the men,
And they started back;—they were there to die;
　　But was life so near them, then?

They listened for life; the rattling fire
　　Far off, and far-off roar,
Were all; and the colonel shook his head,
　　And they turned to their guns once more.

But Jessie said, "The slogan's done;
　　But winna ye hear it noo.
The Campbells are comin'? It's no a dream;
　　Our succors hae broken through!"

We heard the roar and the rattle afar,
　　But the pipes we could not hear;
So the men plied their work of hopeless war,
　　And knew that the end was near.

It was not long ere it made its way,—
　　A thrilling, ceaseless sound:
It was no noise from the strife afar,
　　Or the sappers under ground.

It *was* the pipes of the Highlanders!
　　And now they played *Auld Lang Syne*.
It came to our men like the voice of God,
　　And they shouted along the line.

And they wept, and shook one another's hands,
　　And the women sobbed in a crowd;
And every one knelt down where he stood,
　　And we all thanked God aloud.

That happy time, when we welcomed them,
　　Our men put Jessie first;

And the general gave her his hand, and cheers
Like a storm from the soldiers burst.

And the pipers' ribbons and tartan streamed,
   Marching round and round our line;
And our joyful cheers were broken with tears,
   As the pipes played *Auld Lang Syne*.

THOMAS BABINGTON MACAULAY

HORATIUS

A LAY MADE ABOUT THE YEAR OF ROME CCCLX

I.

LARS PORSENA of Clusium,
   By the Nine Gods he swore
That the great house of Tarquin
   Should suffer wrong no more.
By the Nine Gods he swore it,
   And named a trysting day,
And bade his messengers ride forth,
East and west and south and north,
   To summon his array.

II.

East and west and south and north
   The messengers ride fast,
And tower and town and cottage
   Have heard the trumpet's blast.
Shame on the false Etruscan
   Who lingers in his home,
When Porsena of Clusium
   Is on the march for Rome!

III.

The horsemen and the footmen
  Are pouring in amain
From many a stately market-place,
  From many a fruitful plain;
From many a lonely hamlet,
  Which, hid by beech and pine,
Like an eagle's nest, hangs on the crest
  Of purple Apennine;

IV.

From lordly Volaterrae,
  Where scowls the far-famed hold
Piled by the hands of giants
  For godlike kings of old;
From sea-girt Populonia,
  Whose sentinels descry
Sardinia's snowy mountain-tops
  Fringing the southern sky;

V.

From the proud mart of Pisae,
  Queen of the western waves,
Where ride Massilia's triremes,
  Heavy with fair-haired slaves;
From where sweet Clanis wanders
  Through corn and vines and flowers;
From where Cortona lifts to heaven,
  Her diadem of towers.

VI.

Tall are the oaks whose acorns
  Drop in dark Auser's rill:
Fat are the stags that champ the boughs
  Of the Ciminian hill;
Beyond all streams, Clitumnus
  Is to the herdsman dear,
Best of all pools the fowler loves
  The great Volsinian mere.

VII.

But now no stroke of woodman
  Is heard by Auser's rill;
No hunter tracks the stag's green path
  Up the Ciminian hill;
Unwatched along Clitumnus
  Grazes the milk-white steer;
Unharmed the water-fowl may dip
  In the Volsinian mere.

VIII.

The harvests of Arretium,
  This year, old men shall reap;
This year, young boys in Umbro
  Shall plunge the struggling sheep;
And in the vats of Luna,
  This year the must shall foam
Round the white feet of laughing girls
  Whose sires have marched to Rome.

IX.

There be thirty chosen prophets,
  The wisest of the land,
Who always by Lars Porsena
  Both morn and evening stand.
Evening and morn the thirty
  Have turned the verses o'er,
Traced from the right on linen white
  By mighty seers of yore;

X.

And with one voice the thirty
  Have their glad answer given:
"Go forth, go forth, Lars Porsena—
  Go forth, beloved of Heaven!
Go, and return in glory
  To Clusium's royal dome,
And hang round Nurscia's altars
  The golden shields of Rome!"

XI.

And now hath every city
Sent up her tale of men;
The foot are fourscore thousand,
The horse are thousands ten;
Before the gates of Sutrium
Is met the great array;
A proud man was Lars Porsena
Upon the trysting-day.

XII.

For all the Etruscan armies
Were ranged beneath his eye,
And many a banished Roman,
And many a stout ally;
And with a mighty following,
To join the muster, came
The Tusculan Mamilius,
Prince of the Latian name.

XIII.

But by the yellow Tiber
Was tumult and affright;
From all the spacious champaign
To Rome men took their flight.
A mile around the city
The throng stopped up the ways;
A fearful sight it was to see
Through two long nights and days.

XIV.

For aged folk on crutches,
And women great with child,
And mothers, sobbing over babes
That clung to them and smiled;
And sick men borne in litters
High on the necks of slaves,
And troops of sunburned husbandmen
With reaping-hooks and staves;

xv.

And droves of mules and asses
  Laden with skins of wine,
And endless flocks of goats and sheep,
  And endless herds of kine,
And endless trains of wagons,
  That creaked beneath the weight
Of corn-sacks and of household goods,
  Choked every roaring gate.

xvi.

Now, from the rock Tarpeian,
  Could the wan burghers spy
The line of blazing villages
  Red in the midnight sky.
The fathers of the city,
  They sat all night and day,
For every hour some horseman came
  With tidings of dismay.

xvii.

To eastward and to westward
  Have spread the Tuscan bands,
Nor house, nor fence, nor dovecot,
  In Crustumerium stands.
Verbenna down to Ostia
  Hath wasted all the plain;
Astur hath stormed Janiculum,
  And the stout guards are slain.

xviii.

I wis, in all the Senate
  There was no heart so bold
But sore it ached, and fast it beat,
  When that ill news was told.
Forthwith up rose the Consul,
  Up rose the fathers all;
In haste they girded up their gowns,
  And hied them to the wall.

XIX.

They held a council, standing
　Before the River-Gate;
Short time was there, ye well may guess,
　For musing or debate.
Out spake the Consul roundly:
　"The bridge must straight go down;
For, since Janiculum is lost,
　Nought else can save the town."

XX.

Just then a scout came flying,
　All wild with haste and fear:
"To arms! to arms! Sir Consul—
　Lars Porsena is here."
On the low hills to westward
　The Consul fixed his eye,
And saw the swarthy storm of dust
　Rise fast along the sky.

XXI.

And nearer fast and nearer
　Doth the red whirlwind come;
And louder still, and still more loud,
From underneath that rolling cloud,
Is heard the trumpets' war-note proud,
　The trampling and the hum.
And plainly and more plainly
　Now through the gloom appears,
Far to left and far to right,
In broken gleams of dark-blue light,
The long array of helmets bright,
　The long array of spears.

XXII.

And plainly and more plainly,
　Above that glimmering line,
Now might ye see the banners
　Of twelve fair cities shine;

But the banner of proud Clusium
    Was highest of them all—
The terror of the Umbrian,
    The terror of the Gaul.

XXIII.

And plainly and more plainly
    Now might the burghers know,
By port and vest, by horse and crest,
    Each warlike Lucumo:
There Cilnius of Arretium
    On his fleet roan was seen;
And Astur of the fourfold shield,
Girt with the brand none else may wield;
Tolumnius with the belt of gold,
And dark Verbenna from the hold
    By reedy Thrasymene.

XXIV.

Fast by the royal standard
    O'erlooking all the war,
Lars Porsena of Clusium
    Sat in his ivory car.
By the right wheel rode Mamilius,
    Prince of the Latian name;
And by the left false Sextus,
    That wrought the deed of shame.

XXV.

But when the face of Sextus
    Was seen among the foes,
A yell that rent the firmament
    From all the town arose.
On the housetops was no woman
    But spat towards him and hissed,
No child but screamed out curses,
    And shook its little fist.

XXVI.

But the Consul's brow was sad,
  And the Consul's speech was low,
And darkly looked he at the wall,
  And darkly at the foe:
"Their van will be upon us
  Before the bridge goes down;
And if they once may win the bridge,
  What hope to save the town?"

XXVII.

Then out spake brave Horatius,
  The Captain of the Gate:
"To every man upon this earth
  Death cometh soon or late.
And how can man die better
  Than facing fearful odds
For the ashes of his fathers,
  And the temples of his Gods?

XXVIII.

"And for the tender mother
  Who dandled him to rest,
And for the wife who nurses
  His baby at her breast,
And for the holy maidens
  Who feed the eternal flame—
To save them from false Sextus
  That wrought the deed of shame?

XXIX.

"Hew down the bridge, Sir Consul,
  With all the speed ye may;
I, with two more to help me,
  Will hold the foe in play—
In yon strait path a thousand
  May well be stopped by three.

Now who will stand on either hand,
And keep the bridge with me?"

XXX.

Then out spake Spurius Lartius—
A Ramnian proud was he:
"Lo, I will stand at thy right hand,
And keep the bridge with thee."
And out spake strong Herminius—
Of Titian blood was he:
"I will abide on thy left side,
And keep the bridge with thee."

XXXI.

"Horatius," quoth the Consul,
"As thou sayest, so let it be."
And straight against that great array
Forth went the dauntless Three.
For Romans in Rome's quarrel
Spared neither land nor gold,
Nor son nor wife, nor limb nor life,
In the brave days of old.

XXXII.

Then none was for a party—
Then all were for the State;
Then the great man helped the poor,
And the poor man loved the great;
Then lands were fairly portioned;
Then spoils were fairly sold:
The Romans were like brothers
In the brave days of old.

XXXIII.

Now Roman is to Roman
More hateful than a foe,
And the Tribunes beard the high,
And the Fathers grind the low.

As we wax hot in faction,
  In battle we wax cold:
Wherefore men fight not as they fought
  In the brave days of old.

XXXIV.

Now while the Three were tightening
  Their harness on their backs,
The Consul was the foremost man
  To take in hand an axe;
And Fathers, mixed with Commons,
  Seized hatchet, bar, and crow,
And smote upon the planks above,
  And loosed the props below.

XXXV.

Meanwhile the Tuscan army,
  Right glorious to behold,
Came flashing back the noonday light,
Rank behind rank, like surges bright
  Of a broad sea of gold.
Four hundred trumpets sounded
  A peal of warlike glee,
As that great host, with measured tread,
And spears advanced, and ensigns spread,
Rolled slowly towards the bridge's head,
  Where stood the dauntless Three.

XXXVI.

The Three stood calm and silent,
  And looked upon the foes,
And a great shout of laughter
  From all the vanguard rose;
And forth three chiefs came spurring
  Before that deep array;
To earth they sprang, their swords they drew,
And lifted high their shields, and flew
  To win the narrow way.

XXXVII.

Aunus, from green Tifernum,
　　Lord of the Hill of Vines;
And Seius, whose eight hundred slaves
　　Sicken in Ilva's mines;
And Picus, long to Clusium
　　Vassal in peace and war,
Who led to fight his Umbrian powers
From that gray crag where, girt with towers,
The fortress of Nequinum lowers
　　O'er the pale waves of Nar.

XXXVIII.

Stout Lartius hurled down Aunus
　　Into the stream beneath;
Herminius struck at Seius,
　　And clove him to the teeth;
At Picus brave Horatius
　　Darted one fiery thrust,
And the proud Umbrian's gilded arms
　　Clashed in the bloody dust.

XXXIX.

Then Ocnus of Falerii
　　Rushed on the Roman Three;
And Lausulus of Urgo,
　　The rover of the sea:
And Aruns of Volsinium,
　　Who slew the great wild boar—
The great wild boar that had his den
Amidst the reeds of Cosa's fen,
And wasted fields, and slaughtered men,
　　Along Albinia's shore.

XL.

Herminius smote down Aruns;
　　Lartius laid Ocnus low;

Right to the heart of Lausulus
  Horatius sent a blow:
"Lie there," he cried, "fell pirate!
  No more, aghast and pale,
From Ostia's walls the crowd shall mark
The track of thy destroying bark;
No more Campania's hinds shall fly
To woods and caverns, when they spy
  Thy thrice-accursed sail!"

XLI.

But now no sound of laughter
  Was heard among the foes;
A wild and wrathful clamor
  From all the vanguard rose.
Six spears' lengths from the entrance
  Halted that deep array,
And for a space no man came forth
  To win the narrow way.

XXLII.

But, hark! the cry is Astur:
  And lo! the ranks divide;
And the great Lord of Luna
  Comes with his stately stride.
Upon his ample shoulders
  Clangs loud the fourfold shield,
And in his hand he shakes the brand
  Which none but he can wield.

XLIII.

He smiled on those bold Romans,
  A smile serene and high;
He eyed the flinching Tuscans,
  And scorn was in his eye.

Quoth he, "The she-wolf's litter
  Stand savagely at bay;
But will ye dare to follow,
  If Astur clears the way?"

XLIV.

Then, whirling up his broadsword
  With both hands to the height,
He rushed against Horatius,
  And smote with all his might.
With shield and blade Horatius
  Right deftly turned the blow.
The blow, though turned, came yet too nigh,
It missed his helm, but gashed his thigh—
The Tuscans raised a joyful cry
  To see the red blood flow.

XLV.

He reeled, and on Herminius
  He leaned one breathing space
Then, like a wild-cat mad with wounds,
  Sprang right at Astur's face.
Through teeth, and skull, and helmet,
  So fierce a thrust he sped
The good sword stood a hand-breadth out
  Behind the Tuscan's head.

XLVI.

And the great Lord of Luna
  Fell at that deadly stroke,
As falls on Mount Avernus
  A thunder-smitten oak.
Far o'er the crashing forest
  The giant arms lie spread;
And the pale augers, muttering low,
  Gaze on the blasted head.

XLVII.

On Astur's throat Horatius
    Right firmly pressed his heel,
And thrice and four times tugged amain,
    Ere he wrenched out the steel.
"And see," he cried, "the welcome,
    Fair guests, that waits you here!
What noble Lucumo comes next
    To taste our Roman cheer?"

XLVIII.

But at his haughty challenge
    A sullen murmur ran,
Mingled with wrath, and shame, and dread,
    Along that glittering van.
There lacked not men of prowess,
    Nor men of lordly race;
For all Etruria's noblest
    Were round the fatal place.

XLIX.

But all Etruria's noblest
    Felt their hearts sink to see
On the earth the bloody corpses,
    In the path the dauntless Three!
And from the ghastly entrance,
    Where those bold Romans stood,
All shrank—like boys who, unaware,
Ranging a wood to start a hare,
Come to the mouth of the dark lair
Where, growling low, a fierce old bear
    Lies amidst bones and blood.

L.

Was none who would be foremost
    To lead such dire attack;

But those behind cried "Forward!"
   And those before cried "Back!"
And backward now, and forward,
   Wavers the deep array;
And on the tossing sea of steel
To and fro the standards reel,
And the victorious trumpet-peal
   Dies fitfully away.

LI.

Yet one man for one moment
   Strode out before the crowd;
Well known was he to all the Three,
   And they gave him greeting loud:
"Now welcome, welcome, Sextus!
   Now welcome to thy home!
Why dost thou stay, and turn away?
   Here lies the road to Rome."

LII.

Thrice looked he at the city;
   Thrice looked he at the dead;
And thrice came on in fury,
   And thrice turned back in dread;
And, white with fear and hatred,
   Scowled at the narrow way
Where, wallowing in a pool of blood,
   The bravest Tuscans lay.

LIII.

But meanwhile axe and lever
   Have manfully been plied;
And now the bridge hangs tottering
   Above the boiling tide.
"Come back, come back, Horatius!"
   Loud cried the Fathers all—
"Back, Lartius! back, Herminius!
   Back, ere the ruin fall!"

LXI.

But fiercely ran the current,
  Swollen high by months of rain;
And fast his blood was flowing;
  And he was sore in pain,
And heavy with his armor,
  And spent with changing blows;
And oft they thought him sinking,
  But still again he rose.

LXII.

Never, I ween, did swimmer,
  In such an evil case,
Struggle through such a raging flood
  Safe to the landing place;
But his limbs were borne up bravely
  By the brave heart within,
And our good Father Tiber
  Bare bravely up his chin.

LXIII.

"Curse on him!" quoth false Sextus,—
  "Will not the villain drown?
But for this stay, ere close of day
  We should have sacked the town!"
"Heaven help him!" quoth Lars Porsena,
  "And bring him safe to shore;
For such a gallant feat of arms
  Was never seen before."

LXIV.

And now he feels the bottom;
  Now on dry earth he stands;
Now round him throng the Fathers
  To press his gory hands;
And now, with shouts and clapping,
  And noise of weeping loud,

He enters through the River-Gate,
    Borne by the joyous crowd.

LXV.

They gave him of the corn-land,
    That was of public right,
As much as two strong oxen
    Could plough from morn till night;
And they made a molten image,
    And set it up on high—
And there it stands unto this day
    To witness if I lie.

LXVI.

It stands in the Comitium,
    Plain for all folk to see,—
Horatius in his harness,
    Halting upon one knee;
And underneath is written,
    In letters all of gold,
How valiantly he kept the bridge
    In the brave days of old.

LXVII.

And still his name sounds stirring
    Unto the men of Rome,
As the trumpet-blast that cries to them
    To charge the Volscian home;
And wives still pray to Juno
    For boys with hearts as bold
As his who kept the bridge so well
    In the brave days of old.

LXVIII.

And in the nights of winter,
    When the cold north winds blow,
And the long howling of the wolves
    Is heard amidst the snow;

When round the lonely cottage
　Roars loud the tempest's din,
And the good logs of Algidus
　Roar louder yet within;

LXIX.

When the oldest cask is opened,
　And the largest lamp is lit;
When the chestnuts glow in the embers,
　And the kid turns on the spit;
When young and old in circle
　Around the firebrands close;
When the girls are weaving baskets,
　And the lads are shaping bows;

LXX.

When the goodman mends his armor,
　And trims his helmet's plume;
When the goodwife's shuttle merrily
　Goes flashing through the loom;
With weeping and with laughter
　Still is the story told,
How well Horatius kept the bridge
　In the brave days of old.

CHRISTOPHER MARLOWE

THE PASSIONATE SHEPHERD TO HIS LOVE

Come live with me and be my Love,
And we will all the pleasures prove
That hills and valleys, dale and field,
And all the craggy mountains yield.

There will we sit upon the rocks
And see the shepherds feed their flocks,
By shallow rivers, to whose falls
Melodious birds sing madrigals.

There will I make thee beds of roses
And a thousand fragrant posies,
A cap of flowers, and a kirtle
Embroider'd all with leaves of myrtle.

A gown made of the finest wool,
Which from our pretty lambs we pull,
Fair linéd slippers for the cold,
With buckles of the purest gold.

A belt of straw and ivy buds
With coral clasps and amber studs:
And if these pleasures may thee move,
Come live with me and be my Love.

Thy silver dishes for thy meat
As precious as the gods do eat,
Shall on an ivory table be
Prepared each day for thee and me.

The shepherd swains shall dance and sing
For thy delight each May-morning:
If these delights thy mind may move,
Then live with me and be my Love.

JOHN MILTON

L'ALLEGRO

HENCE, loathed Melancholy,
  Of Cerberus and blackest Midnight born!
In Stygian cave forlorn,
  'Mongst horrid shapes, and shrieks, and sights unholy,
Find out some uncouth cell,
  Where brooding Darkness spreads his jealous wings,
And the night-raven sings;
  There, under ebon shades, and low-browed rocks,
As ragged as thy locks,
  In dark Cimmerian desert ever dwell.

But come, thou goddess fair and free,
In heaven ycleped Euphrosyne,
And by men, heart-easing Mirth;
Whom lovely Venus, at a birth,
With two sister Graces more,
To ivy-crowned Bacchus bore;
Or whether (as some sages sing)
The frolic wind that breathes the spring,
Zephyr, with Aurora playing—
As he met her once a-Maying—
There, on beds of violets blue,
And fresh-blown roses washed in dew,
Filled her with thee, a daughter fair,
So buxom, blithe, and debonair.

Haste thee, nymph, and bring with thee
Jest, and youthful Jollity;
Quips and cranks and wanton wiles,
Nods and becks and wreathed smiles,
Such as hang on Hebe's cheek,
And love to live in dimple sleek—
Sport, that wrinkled Care derides,
And laughter, holding both his sides.
Come! and trip it, as you go,
On the light fantastic toe;
And in thy right hand lead with thee
The mountain nymph, sweet Liberty;
And if I give thee honor due,
Mirth, admit me of thy crew,
To live with her, and live with thee,
In unreproved pleasures free;
To hear the lark begin his flight,
And singing startle the dull night
From his watch-tower in the skies,
Till the dappled dawn doth rise;
Then to come, in spite of sorrow,
And at my window bid good-morrow,
Through the sweet-brier, or the vine,
Or the twisted eglantine;
While the cock with lively din
Scatters the rear of darkness thin,

And to the stack, or the barn-door,
Stoutly struts his dames before;
Oft listening how the hounds and horn
Cheerily rouse the slumbering Morn,
From the side of some hoar hill
Through the high wood echoing shrill:
Sometime walking, not unseen,
By hedge-row elms, on hillocks green,
Right against the eastern gate,
Where the great sun begins his state,
Robed in flames, and amber light,
The clouds in thousand liveries dight;
While the ploughman near at hand
Whistles o'er the furrowed land,
And the milkmaid singeth blithe,
And the mower whets his scythe,
And every shepherd tells his tale
Under the hawthorn in the dale.

Straight mine eye hath caught new pleasures,
Whilst the landscape round it measures
Russet lawns, and fallows gray,
Where the nibbling flocks do stray—
Mountains, on whose barren breast
The laboring clouds do often rest—
Meadows trim with daisies pied,
Shallow brooks, and rivers wide;
Towers and battlements it sees
Bosomed high in tufted trees,
Where perhaps some beauty lies,
The cynosure of neighboring eyes.
Hard by, a cottage chimney smokes
From betwixt two aged oaks,
Where Corydon and Thyrsis met,
Are at their savory dinner set
Of herbs, and other country messes,
Which the neat-handed Phillis dresses;
And then in haste her bower she leaves,
With Thestylis to bind the sheaves;
Or, if the earlier season lead,
To the tanned haycock in the mead.

Sometimes with secure delight
The upland hamlets will invite,
When the merry bells ring round,
And the jocund rebecks sound
To many a youth, and many a maid,
Dancing in the chequered shade;
And young and old come forth to play
On a sunshine holiday,
Till the live-long daylight fail;
Then to the spicy nut-brown ale
With stories told of many a feat:
How fairy Mab the junkets eat:
She was pinched and pulled, she said,
And he, by friar's lantern led,
Tells how the drudging goblin sweat
To earn his cream-bowl duly set,
When in one night, ere glimpse of morn,
His shadowy flail hath threshed the corn
That ten day-laborers could not end;
Then lies him down the lubber fiend,
And stretched out all the chimney's length,
Basks at the fire his hairy strength,
And, crop-full, out of doors he flings,
Ere the first cock his matin rings.
Thus done the tales, to bed they creep,
By whispering winds soon lulled asleep.

Towered cities please us then,
And the busy hum of men,
Where throngs of knights and barons bold
In weeds of peace high triumphs hold,
With store of ladies, whose bright eyes
Rain influence, and judge the prize
Of wit or arms, while both contend
To win her grace whom all commend.
There let Hymen oft appear
In saffron robe, with taper clear,
And pomp and feast and revelry,
With mask, and antique pageantry;
Such sights as youthful poets dream
On summer eves by haunted stream:

Then to the well-trod stage anon,
If Jonson's learned sock be on,
Or sweetest Shakespeare, Fancy's child,
Warble his native wood-notes wild.

And ever, against eating cares,
Lap me in soft Lydian airs,
Married to immortal verse,
Such as the meeting soul may pierce,
In notes with many a winding bout
Of linked sweetness long drawn out,
With wanton heed and giddy cunning
The melting voice through mazes running,
Untwisting all the chains that tie
The hidden soul of harmony;
That Orpheus' self may heave his head
From golden slumber on a bed
Of heaped Elysian flowers, and hear
Such strains as would have won the ear
Of Pluto, to have quite set free
His half regained Eurydice.

These delights if thou canst give,
Mirth, with thee I mean to live.

ON HIS BLINDNESS

WHEN I consider how my light is spent
    Ere half my days, in this dark world and wide,
    And that one talent which is death to hide
Lodged with me useless, though my soul more bent
To serve therewith my Maker, and present
    My true account, lest he returning chide—
    "Doth God exact day-labor, light denied?"
I fondly ask; but Patience, to prevent
That murmur, soon replies: "God doth not need
Either man's work, or his own gifts; who best
Bear his mild yoke, they serve him best; his state
Is kingly: thousands at his bidding speed,
And post o'er land and ocean without rest;
They also serve who only stand and wait."

IL PENSEROSO

Hence, vain deluding joys,
The brood of folly without father bred!
How little you bestead,
    Or fill the fixed mind with all your toys!
Dwell in some idle brain,
    And fancies fond with gaudy shapes possess,
As thick and numberless
    As the gay motes that people the sunbeams;
Or likest hovering dreams,
    The fickle pensioners of Morpheus' train.
But hail, thou goddess, sage and holy!
Hail, divinest Melancholy!
Whose saintly visage is too bright
To hit the sense of human sight,
And therefore to our weaker view
O'erlaid with black, staid wisdom's hue—
Black, but such as in esteem
Prince Memnon's sister might beseem,
Or that starred Ethiop queen that strove
To set her beauty's praise above
The sea-nymphs, and their powers offended
Yet thou art higher far descended;
Thee bright-haired Vesta, long of yore
To solitary Saturn bore;
His daughter she; (in Saturn's reign
Such mixture was not held a stain).
Oft in glimmering bowers and glades
He met her, and in secret shades
Of woody Ida's inmost grove,
While yet there was no fear of Jove.

Come, pensive Nun, devout and pure,
Sober, steadfast, and demure,
All in a robe of darkest grain
Flowing with majestic train,
And sable stole of cypress lawn
Over thy decent shoulders drawn!
Come! but keep thy wonted state,
With even step and musing gait,

And looks commercing with the skies,
Thy rapt soul sitting in thine eyes;
There, held in holy passion still,
Forget thyself to marble, till
With a sad, leaden, downward cast
Thou fix them on the earth as fast;
And join with thee calm Peace, and Quiet;
Spare Fast, that oft with gods doth diet,
And hears the Muses in a ring
Aye round about Jove's altar sing:
And add to these retired Leisure,
That in trim gardens takes his pleasure;
But first, and chiefest, with thee bring
Him that yon soars on golden wing,
Guiding the fiery-wheeled throne—
The cherub Contemplation;
And the mute Silence hist along,
'Less Philomel will deign a song
In her sweetest, saddest plight,
Smoothing the rugged brow of night,
While Cynthia checks her dragon yoke
Gently o'er the accustomed oak.
Sweet bird! that shunn'st the noise of folly.
Most musical, most melancholy!
Thee, chauntress, oft the woods among
I woo, to hear thy even-song;
And, missing thee, I walk unseen
On the dry, smooth-shaven green,
To behold the wandering moon
Riding near her highest noon,
Like one that had been led astray
And oft, as if her head she bowed,
Through the heaven's wide pathless way;
Stooping through a fleecy cloud.
Oft, on a plat of rising ground,
I hear the far-off curfew sound
Over some wide-watered shore,
Swinging slow with sullen roar;
Or if the air will not permit,
Some still removed place will fit,

Where glowing emblems through the room
Teach light to counterfeit a gloom—
Far from all resort of mirth,
Save the cricket on the hearth,
Or the bellman's drowsy charm,
To bless the doors from nightly harm.
Or let my lamp at midnight hour
Be seen in some high lonely tower,
Where I may oft out-watch the Bear
With thrice-great Hermes, or unsphere
The spirit of Plato, to unfold
What worlds or what vast regions hold
The immortal mind that hath forsook
Her mansion in this fleshly nook;
And of those demons that are found
In fire, air, flood, or under ground,
Whose power hath a true consent
With planet or with element.
Sometime let gorgeous Tragedy
In sceptred pall come sweeping by,
Presenting Thebes, or Pelops' line,
Or the tale of Troy divine,
Or what (though rare) of later age
Ennobled hath the buskined stage.

But, O, sad virgin, that thy power
Might raise Musæus from his bower!
Or bid the soul of Orpheus sing
Such notes as, warbled to the string,
Drew iron tears down Pluto's cheek,
And made hell grant what love did seek!
Or call up him that left half told
The story of Cambuscan bold—
Of Camball, and of Algarsife—
And who had Canace to wife,
That owned the virtuous ring and glass—
And of the wondrous horse of brass,—
On which the Tartar king did ride!
And if aught else great bards beside
In sage and solemn tunes have sung,
Of tourneys and of trophies hung,

Of forests, and enchantments drear,
Where more is meant than meets the ear.

Thus, Night, oft see me in thy pale career,
Till civil-suited Morn appear;
Not tricked and flounced, as she was wont
With the Attic boy to hunt,
But kerchiefed in a comely cloud
While rocking winds are piping loud,
Or ushered with a shower still
When the gust hath blown his fill,
Ending on the rustling leaves,
With minute drops from off the eaves.
And when the sun begins to fling
His flaring beams, me, goddess, bring
To arched walks of twilight groves,
And shadows brown, that Sylvan loves,
Of pine or monumental oak,
Where the rude axe with heaved stroke
Was never heard the nymphs to daunt,
Or fright them from their hallowed haunt.
There in close covert by some brook,
Where no profaner eye may look,
Hide me from day's garish eye,
While the bee with honied thigh,
That at her flowery work doth sing,
And the waters murmuring
With such consort as they keep,
Entice the dewy-feathered sleep;
And let some strange mysterious dream
Wave at his wings, in airy stream
Of lively portraiture displayed,
Softly on my eyelids laid;
And, as I wake, sweet music breathe
Above, about, or underneath,
Sent by some spirit to mortals good,
Or the unseen genius of the wood.

But let my due feet never fail
To walk the studious cloisters pale,

And love the high embowered roof,
With antique pillars massy proof,
And storied windows, richly dight,
Casting a dim religious light.
There let the pealing organ blow
To the full voiced choir below,
In service high, and anthems clear,
As may with sweetness, through mine ear,
Dissolve me into ecstasies,
And bring all heaven before mine eyes.

And may at last my weary age
Find out the peaceful hermitage,
The hairy ground and mossy cell,
Where I may sit and rightly spell
Of every star that heaven doth shew,
And every herb that sips the dew,
Till old experience do attain
To something like prophetic strain.

These pleasures, Melancholy, give,
And I with thee will choose to live.

LYCIDAS

YET once more, O ye Laurels, and once more,
Ye Myrtles brown, with Ivy never sere,
I come to pluck your berries harsh and crude,
And with forced fingers rude
Shatter your leaves before the mellowing year.
Bitter constraint, and sad occasion dear
Compels me to disturb your season due;
For Lycidas is dead, dead ere his prime,
Young Lycidas, and hath not left his peer.
Who would not sing for Lycidas? he knew
Himself to sing, and build the lofty rhyme.
He must not float upon his watery bier
Unwept, and welter to the parching wind,
Without the meed of some melodious tear,

Begin, then, Sisters of the Sacred Well,
That from beneath the seat of Jove doth spring,
Begin, and somewhat loudly sweep the string.
Hence with denial vain, and coy excuse;
So may some gentle Muse
With lucky words favor my destined urn,
And as he passes turn,
And bid fair peace be to my sable shroud;
For we were nursed upon the self-same hill,
Fed the same flock by fountain, shade, and rill.
Together both, ere the high lawns appeared
Under the opening eyelids of the morn,
We drove a-field, and both together heard
What time the gray-fly winds her sultry horn,
Battening our flocks with the fresh dews of night,
Oft till the star that rose at evening bright
Toward Heaven's descent had sloped his westering wheel
Meanwhile the rural ditties were not mute,
Tempered to the oaten flute;
Rough Satyrs danced, and Fauns with cloven heel
From the glad sound would not be absent long,
And old Damætas loved to hear our song.

But O the heavy change, now thou art gone—
Now thou art gone, and never must return!
Thee, Shepherd, thee the woods, and desert caves,
With wild thyme and the gadding vine o'ergrown,
And all their echoes, mourn;
The willows, and the hazel copses green,
Shall now no more be seen,
Fanning their joyous leaves to thy soft lays.
As killing as the canker to the rose,
Or taint-worm to the weanling herds that graze,
Or frost to flowers that their gay wardrobe wear,
When first the white-thorn blows;
Such, Lycidas, thy loss to shepherd's ear.

Where were ye, Nymphs, when the remorseless deep
Closed o'er the head of your loved Lycidas?
For neither were ye playing on the steep,

Where your old bards, the famous Druids lie,
Nor on the shaggy top of Mona high,
Nor yet where Deva spreads her wizard stream—
Ah me! I fondly dream!
Had ye been there—for what could that have done?
What could the Muse herself that Orpheus bore,
The Muse herself for her enchanting son,
Whom universal Nature did lament,
When, by the rout that made the hideous roar,
His gory visage down the stream was sent,
Down the swift Hebrus to the Lesbian shore?

    Alas! what boots it with incessant care
To tend the homely, slighted shepherd's trade,
And strictly meditate the thankless muse?
Were it not better done, as others use,
To sport with Amaryllis in the shade,
Or with the tangles of Neæra's hair?
Fame is the spur that the clear spirit doth raise
(That last infirmity of noble minds)
To scorn delights, and live laborious days;
But the fair guerdon when we hope to find,
And think to burst out into sudden blaze,
Comes the blind Fury with the abhorred shears,
And slits the thin-spun life. But not the praise,
Phœbus replied, and touched my trembling ears;
Fame is no plant that grows on mortal soil,
Nor in the glistering foil
Set off to the world, nor in broad rumor lies;
But lives and spreads aloft by those pure eyes,
And perfect witness of all-judging Jove;
As he pronounces lastly on each deed,
Of so much fame in heaven expect thy meed.

    O fountain Arethuse, and thou honored flood,
Smooth-sliding Mincius, crowned with vocal reeds,
That strain I heard was of a higher mood;
But now my oat proceeds,
And listens to the herald of the sea
That came in Neptune's plea;

He asked the waves, and asked the felon winds,
What hard mishap hath doomed this gentle swain?
And questioned every gust of rugged winds
That blows from off each beakèd promontory;
They knew not of his story;
And sage Hippotades their answer brings,
That not a blast was from his dungeon strayed;
The air was calm, and on the level brine
Sleek Panope with all her sisters played.
It was that fatal and perfidious bark,
Built in the eclipse, and rigged with curses dark,
That sunk so low that sacred head of thine.

    Next Camus, reverend sire, went footing slow,
His mantle hairy, and his bonnet sedge,
Inwrought with figures dim, and on the edge,
Like to that sanguine flower, inscribed with woe.
Ah! who hath reft (quoth he) my dearest pledge?
Last came, and last did go,
The pilot of the Galilean Lake;
Two massy keys he bore of metals twain
(The golden opes, the iron shuts amain);
He shook his mitered locks, and stern bespake:
How well could I have spared for thee, young swain,
Enow of such as for their bellies' sake
Creep, and intrude, and climb into the fold!
Of other care they little reckoning make
Than how to scramble at the shearers' feast,
And shove away the worthy bidden guest;
Blind mouths! that scarce themselves know how to hold
A sheep-hook, or have learned aught else the least
That to the faithful herdsman's art belongs!
What recks it them? what need they? they are sped;
And when they list, their lean and flashy songs
Grate on their scrannel pipes of wretched straw;
The hungry sheep look up, and are not fed,
But, swollen with wind and the rank mist they draw,
Rot inwardly, and foul contagion spread;
Besides what the grim wolf with privy paw
Daily devours apace, and nothing said:—

But that two-handed engine at the door,
Stands ready to smite once, and smite no more.

Return, Alpheus, the dread voice is past,
That shrunk thy streams; return, Sicilian Muse,
And call the vales, and bid them hither cast
Their bells, and flowerets of a thousand hues.
Ye valleys low, where the mild whispers use
Of shades, and wanton winds, and gushing brooks,
On whose fresh lap the swart-star sparely looks,
Throw hither all your quaint enameled eyes,
That on the green turf suck the honeyed showers,
And purple all the ground with vernal flowers.
Bring the rathe primrose that forsaken dies,
The tufted crow-toe, and pale jessamine,
The white pink, and the pansy freaked with jet,
The glowing violet,
The musk-rose, and the well-attired woodbine,
With cowslips wan that hang the pensive head,
And every flower that sad embroidery wears;
Bid amaranthus all his beauty shed,
And daffodillies fill their cups with tears,
To strew the laureate hearse where Lycid lies.
For so to interpose a little ease,
Let our frail thoughts dally with false surmise.
Ah me! whilst thee the shores and sounding seas
Wash far away, where'er thy bones are hurled,
Whether beyond the stormy Hebrides,
Where thou, perhaps, under the whelming tide,
Visit'st the bottom of the monstrous world;
Or whether thou to our moist vows denied,
Sleep'st by the fable of Bellerus old,
Where the great vision of the guarded mount
Looks toward Namancos and Bayona's hold;
Look homeward, Angel, now, and melt with ruth!
And, O ye dolphins, waft the hapless youth!

Weep no more, woeful Shepherds, weep no more!
For Lycidas, your sorrow, is not dead,
Sunk though he be beneath the watery floor:
So sinks the day-star in the ocean bed,

And yet anon repairs his drooping head,
And tricks his beams, and with new-spangled ore
Flames in the forehead of the morning sky;
So Lycidas sunk low, but mounted high,
Through the dear might of Him that walked the waves,
Where, other groves and other streams along,
With nectar pure his oozy locks he laves,
And hears the unexpressive nuptial song,
In the blest kingdoms meek of Joy and Love.
There entertain him all the saints above,
In solemn troops and sweet societies,
That sing, and singing in their glory move,
And wipe the tears forever from his eyes.
Now, Lycidas, the shepherds weep no more;
Henceforth thou art the genius of the shore,
In thy large recompense, and shalt be good
To all that wander in that perilous flood.

Thus sang the uncouth swain to the oaks and rills,
While the still morn went out with sandals gray;
He touched the tender stops of various quills,
With eager thought warbling his Doric lay:
And now the sun had stretched out all the hills,
And now was dropt into the western bay;
At last he rose, and twitched his mantle blue:
To-morrow to fresh woods and pastures new.

JAMES MONTGOMERY

THE LORD THE GOOD SHEPHERD

THE Lord is my Shepherd, no want shall I know;
    I feed in green pastures, safe-folded I rest;
He leadeth my soul where the still waters flow,
    Restores me when wandering, redeems when oppressed.

Through the valley and shadow of death though I stray,
    Since thou art my guardian, no evil I fear;
Thy rod shall defend me, thy staff be my stay;
    No harm can befall with my Comforter near.

In the midst of affliction my table is spread;
  With blessings unmeasured my cup runneth o'er;
With perfume and oil thou anointest my head;
  O! what shall I ask of thy providence more?

Let goodness and mercy, my bountiful God!
  Still follow my steps till I meet thee above:
I seek, by the path which my forefathers trod
  Through the land of their sojourn, thy kingdom of love.

CLEMENT C. MOORE

THE NIGHT BEFORE CHRISTMAS

'Twas the night before Christmas, when all through the house
Not a creature was stirring, not even a mouse;
The stockings were hung by the chimney with care,
In hopes that St. Nicholas soon would be there;
The children were nestled all snug in their beds,
While visions of sugar-plums danced through their heads;
And mamma in her kerchief, and I in my cap,
Had just settled our brains for a long winter's nap,
When out on the lawn there rose such a clatter,
I sprang from my bed to see what was the matter.
Away to the window I flew like a flash,
Tore open the shutters and threw up the sash.
The moon, on the breast of the new-fallen snow,
Gave a lustre of mid-day to objects below;
When what to my wondering eyes should appear,
But a miniature sleigh, and eight tiny reindeer,
With a little old driver, so lively and quick,
I knew in a moment it must be St. Nick.
More rapid than eagles his coursers they came,
And he whistled, and shouted, and call'd them by name:
"Now, Dasher! now, Dancer! now, Prancer! now, Vixen!
On, Comet! on, Cupid! on, Donder and Blitzen!—
To the top of the porch, to the top of the wall!
Now, dash away, dash away, dash away all!"
As dry leaves that before the wild hurricane fly,
When they meet with an obstacle, mount to the sky,

So, up to the house-top the coursers they flew,
With the sleigh full of toys, and St. Nicholas too.
And then in a twinkling I heard on the roof
The prancing and pawing of each little hoof.
As I drew in my head, and was turning around,
Down the chimney St. Nicholas came with a bound.
He was dress'd all in fur from his head to his foot,
And his clothes were all tarnish'd with ashes and soot;
A bundle of toys he had flung on his back,
And he look'd like a peddler just opening his pack.
His eyes how they twinkled! his dimples how merry!
His cheeks were like roses, his nose like a cherry.
His droll little mouth was drawn up like a bow,
And the beard on his chin was as white as the snow.
The stump of a pipe he held tight in his teeth,
And the smoke, it encircled his head like a wreath.
He had a broad face and a little round belly
That shook, when he laugh'd, like a bowl full of jelly.
He was chubby and plump—a right jolly old elf—
And I laugh'd when I saw him, in spite of myself.
A wink of his eye, and a twist of his head,
Soon gave me to know I had nothing to dread.
He spake not a word, but went straight to his work,
And filled all the stockings; then turn'd with a jerk,
And laying his finger aside of his nose,
And giving a nod, up the chimney he rose.
He sprang to his sleigh, to his team gave a whistle,
And away they all flew like the down of a thistle;
But I heard him exclaim, ere he drove out of sight,
"Happy Christmas to all, and to all a good-night!"

THOMAS MOORE

THE HARP THAT ONCE THROUGH TARA'S HALLS

THE harp that once through Tara's halls
   The soul of music shed,
Now hangs as mute on Tara's walls
   As if that soul were fled.

So sleeps the pride of former days,
　So glory's thrill is o'er,
And hearts that once beat high for praise
　Now feel that pulse no more!

No more to chiefs and ladies bright
　The harp of Tara swells;
The chord alone, that breaks at night,
　Its tale of ruin tells.
Thus freedom now so seldom wakes,
　The only throb she gives,
Is when some heart indignant breaks,
　To show that still she lives!

"THE YOUNG MAY MOON"

The young May moon is beaming, love,
The glow-worm's lamp is gleaming, love;
　　How sweet to rove
　　Through Mona's grove
When the drowsy world is dreaming, love!

Then awake!—till rise of sun, my dear,
'Tis never too late for delight, my dear;
　　And the best of all ways
　　To lengthen our days
Is to steal a few hours from the night, my dear!

Now all the world is sleeping, love,
But the Sage, his star-watch keeping, love,
　　And I, whose star
　　More glorious far
Is the eye from that casement peeping, love.

Then awake!—till rise of sun, my dear,
The Sage's glass we'll shun, my dear,
　　Or in watching the flight
　　Of bodies of light
He might happen to take thee for one, my dear!

BELIEVE ME, IF ALL THOSE ENDEARING YOUNG CHARMS

BELIEVE me, if all those endearing young charms,
  Which I gaze on so fondly to-day,
Were to change by to-morrow, and fleet in my arms,
  Like fairy-gifts fading away,
Thou wouldst still be adored, as this moment thou art,
  Let thy loveliness fade as it will,
And around the dear ruin each wish of my heart
  Would entwine itself verdantly still.

It is not while beauty and youth are thine own,
  And thy cheeks unprofaned by a tear,
That the fervor and faith of a soul can be known,
  To which time will but make thee more dear;
No, the heart that has truly loved never forgets,
  But as truly loves on to the close,
As the sun-flower turns on her god, when he sets,
  The same look which she turned when he rose.

OFT, IN THE STILLY NIGHT

OFT, in the stilly night,
  Ere Slumber's chain has bound me,
Fond Memory brings the light
  Of other days around me;
    The smiles, the tears,
    Of boyhood's years,
  The words of love then spoken;
    The eyes that shone,
    Now dimmed and gone,
  The cheerful hearts now broken!
Thus, in the stilly night,
  Ere Slumber's chain hath bound me,
Sad Memory brings the light
  Of other days around me.

When I remember all
  The friends so linked together,
I've seen around me fall
  Like leaves in wintry weather;
    I feel like one
    Who treads alone
Some banquet-hall deserted,
    Whose lights are fled,
    Whose garlands dead,
And all but he departed!
Thus, in the stilly night,
  Ere Slumber's chain has bound me,
Sad Memory brings the light
  Of other days around me.

GEORGE POPE MORRIS

WOODMAN, SPARE THAT TREE

Woodman, spare that tree!
  Touch not a single bough!
In youth it sheltered me,
  And I'll protect it now.
'Twas my forefather's hand
  That placed it near his cot;
There, woodman, let it stand,
  Thy axe shall harm it not.

That old familiar tree,
  Whose glory and renown
Are spread, o'er land and sea—
  And wouldst thou hew it down?
Woodman, forebear thy stroke!
  Cut not its earth-bound ties;
Oh spare that aged oak
  Now towering to the skies!

When but an idle boy,
   I sought its grateful shade;
In all their gushing joy
   Here, too, my sisters played.
My mother kissed me here;
   My father pressed my hand—
Forgive this foolish tear,
   But let that old oak stand.

My heart-strings round thee cling,
   Close as thy bark, old friend!
Here shall the wild-bird sing,
   And still thy branches bend.
Old tree! the storm will brave!
   And, woodman, leave the spot;
While I've a hand to save,
   Thy axe shall harm it not.

MRS. CAROLINE E. NORTON

BINGEN ON THE RHINE

A soldier of the legion lay dying in Algiers,
There was lack of woman's nursing, there was dearth of woman's
   tears;
But a comrade stood beside him, while his life-blood ebbed away,
And bent, with pitying glances, to hear what he might say.
The dying soldier faltered, as he took that comrade's hand,
And he said, "I never more shall see my own, my native land:
Take a message and a token to some distant friends of mine;
For I was born at Bingen,—at Bingen on the Rhine.

"Tell my brothers and companions, when they meet and crowd
   around,
To hear my mournful story, in the pleasant vineyard ground
That we fought the battle bravely, and, when the day was done,
Full many a corse lay ghastly pale beneath the setting sun:
And 'mid the dead and dying were some grown old in wars,—
The death-wound on their gallant breasts, the last of many scars;
And some were young, and suddenly beheld life's morn decline,—
And one had come from Bingen,—fair Bingen on the Rhine.

"Tell my mother that her other son shall comfort her old age;
For I was still a truant bird, that thought his home a cage.
For my father was a soldier, and even as a child
My heart leaped forth to hear him tell of struggles fierce and wild;
And when he died, and left us to divide his scanty hoard,
I let them take whate'er they would,—but kept my father's sword;
And with boyish love I hung it where the bright light used to shine,
On the cottage wall at Bingen,—calm Bingen on the Rhine.

"Tell my sister not to weep for me, and sob with drooping head,
When the troops come marching home again, with glad and gallant
    tread,
But to look upon them proudly, with a calm and steadfast eye,
For her brother was a soldier, too, and not afraid to die;
And if a comrade seek her love, I ask her in my name,
To listen to him kindly, without regret or shame,
And to hang the old sword in its place (my father's sword and mine),
For the honor of old Bingen,—dear Bingen on the Rhine.

"There's another—not a sister; in the happy days gone by,
You'd have known her by the merriment that sparkled in her eye;
Too innocent for coquetry,—too fond for idle scorning,—
O, friend! I fear the lightest heart makes sometimes heaviest mourn-
    ing!
Tell her the last night of my life (for ere the moon be risen,
My body will be out of pain, my soul be out of prison),—
I dreamed I stood with *her,* and saw the yellow sunlight shine
On the vine-clad hills of Bingen,—sweet Bingen on the Rhine.

"I saw the blue Rhine sweep along,—I heard, or seemed to hear,
The German songs we used to sing in chorus sweet and clear;
And down the pleasant river, and up the slanting hill,
The echoing chorus sounded through the evening calm and still;
And her glad blue eyes were on me, as we passed with friendly talk,
Down many a path beloved of yore, and well-remembered walk!
And her little hand lay lightly, confidingly in mine,—
But we meet no more at Bingen,—loved Bingen on the Rhine."

His trembling voice grew faint and hoarse,—his grasp was childish
    weak,—

His eyes put on a dying look,—he sighed and ceased to speak;
His comrade bent to lift him, but the spark of life had fled,—
The soldier of the Legion in a foreign land is dead!
And the soft moon rose up slowly, and calmly she looked down
On the red sand of the battle-field, with bloody corses strewn;
Yes, calmly on that dreadful scene her pale light seemed to shine,
As it shone on distant Bingen,—fair Bingen on the Rhine.

LADY NAIRN

THE LAND O' THE LEAL

I'm wearing awa', Jean,
Like snaw when its thaw, Jean,
I'm wearing awa'
    To the land o' the leal.
There's nae sorrow there, Jean,
There's neither cauld nor care, Jean,
The day is aye fair
    In the land o' the leal.

Ye were aye leal and true, Jean,
Your task's ended noo, Jean,
And I'll welcome you
    To the land o' the leal!
Our bonnie bairn's there, Jean,
She was baith guid and fair, Jean;
O we grudged her right sair
    To the land o' the leal!

Then dry that tearfu' e'e, Jean,
My soul langs to be free, Jean,
And angels wait on me
    To the land o' the leal.
Now fare ye weel, my ain Jean,
This warld's care is vain, Jean;
We'll meet and aye be fain
    In the land o' the leal.

JOHN HOWARD PAYNE

HOME, SWEET HOME

'MID pleasures and palaces though we may roam,
Be it ever so humble, there's no place like home!
A charm from the sky seems to hallow us there,
Which, seek through the world, is ne'er met with elsewhere.
 Home, home, sweet, sweet home!
 There's no place like home!

An exile from home, splendor dazzles in vain;
Oh! give me my lowly thatch'd cottage again!
The birds, singing gayly, that came at my call—
Give me them!—and the peace of mind dearer than all.
 Home, home, sweet, sweet home!
 There's no place like home!

EDGAR ALLAN POE

THE BELLS

 HEAR the sledges with the bells—
  Silver bells—
What a world of merriment their melody foretells!
 How they tinkle, tinkle, tinkle,
  In the icy air of night!
 While the stars that oversprinkle
 All the heavens, seem to twinkle
  With a crystalline delight;
 Keeping time, time, time,
 In a sort of Runic rhyme,
To the tintinnabulation that so musically wells
 From the bells, bells, bells, bells,
  Bells, bells, bells—
From the jingling and the tinkling of the bells.

Hear the mellow wedding-bells,
Golden bells!
What a world of happiness their harmony foretells!
Through the balmy air of night
How they ring out their delight
From the molten-golden notes!
And all in tune,
What a liquid ditty floats
To the turtle-dove that listens, while she gloats
On the moon!
Oh, from out the sounding cells,
What a gush of euphony voluminously wells!
How it swells!
How it dwells
On the Future! how it tells
Of the rapture that impels
To the swinging and the ringing
Of the bells, bells, bells—
Of the bells, bells, bells, bells,
Bells, bells, bells—
To the rhyming and the chiming of the bells!

Hear the loud alarum bells—
Brazen bells!
What a tale of terror, now, their turbulency tells!
In the startled ear of night
How they scream out their affright!
Too much horrified to speak,
They can only shriek, shriek,
Out of tune,
In a clamorous appealing to the mercy of the fire,
In a mad expostulation with the deaf and frantic fire
Leaping higher, higher, higher,
With a desperate desire,
And a resolute endeavor,
Now—now to sit or never,
By the side of the pale-faced moon.
Oh, the bells, bells, bells!
What a tale their terror tells
Of despair!

How they clang, and clash, and roar!
What a horror they outpour
On the bosom of the palpitating air!
Yet the ear, it fully knows,
By the twanging
And the clanging,
How the danger ebbs and flows;
Yet the ear distinctly tells,
In the jangling
And the wrangling,
How the danger sinks and swells,
By the sinking or the swelling in the anger of the bells—
Of the bells—
Of the bells, bells, bells, bells,
Bells, bells, bells—
In the clamor and the clangor of the bells!

Hear the tolling of the bells—
Iron bells!
What a world of solemn thought their monody compels!
In the silence of the night
How we shiver with affright
At the melancholy menace of their tone!
For every sound that floats
From the rust within their throats,
Is a groan:
And the people—ah, the people—
They that dwell up in the steeple,
All alone,
And who, tolling, tolling, tolling,
In that muffled monotone,
Feel a glory in so rolling
On the human heart a stone—
They are neither man nor woman—
They are neither brute nor human—
They are Ghouls!
And their king it is who tolls;
And he rolls, rolls, rolls, rolls,
A pæan from the bells!
And his merry bosom swells
With the pæan of the bells!

And he dances and he yells;
Keeping time, time, time,
In a sort of Runic rhyme,
To the pæan of the bells—
Of the bells;
Keeping time, time, time,
In a sort of Runic rhyme,
To the throbbing of the bells—
Of the bells, bells, bells,
To the sobbing of the bells;
Keeping time, time, time,
As he knells, knells, knells,
In a happy Runic rhyme,
To the rolling of the bells—
Of the bells, bells, bells—
To the tolling of the bells,
Of the bells, bells, bells, bells,
Bells, bells, bells,—
To the moaning and the groaning of the bells.

THE RAVEN

ONCE upon a midnight dreary, while I pondered, weak and weary,
Over many a quaint and curious volume of forgotten lore,—
While I nodded, nearly napping, suddenly there came a tapping,
As of some one gently rapping, rapping at my chamber door.
" 'T is some visitor," I muttered, "tapping at my chamber door:
Only this, and nothing more."

Ah, distinctly I remember, it was in the bleak December,
And each separate dying ember wrought its ghost upon the floor.
Eagerly I wished the morrow; vainly I had sought to borrow
From my books surcease of sorrow—sorrow for the lost Lenore—
For the rare and radiant maiden whom the angels name Lenore—
Nameless here for evermore.

And the silken, sad, uncertain rustling of each purple curtain,
Thrilled me—filled me with fantastic terrors never felt before;
So that now, to still the beating of my heart, I stood repeating,
" 'T is some visitor entreating entrance at my chamber door,—
Some late visitor entreating entrance at my chamber door;
   This it is, and nothing more."

Presently my soul grew stronger: hesitating then no longer,
"Sir," said I, "or Madam, truly your forgiveness I implore;
But the fact is, I was napping, and so gently you came rapping,
And so faintly you came tapping, tapping at my chamber door,
That I scarce was sure I heard you"—here I opened wide the door;—
   Darkness there, and nothing more!

Deep into that darkness peering, long I stood there, wondering, fear-
  ing,
Doubting, dreaming dreams no mortal ever dared to dream before;
But the silence was unbroken, and the darkness gave no token,
And the only word there spoken was the whispered word "Lenore!"
This I whispered, and an echo murmured back the word "Lenore!"
   Merely this, and nothing more.

Back into the chamber turning, all my soul within me burning,
Soon again I heard a tapping, somewhat louder than before.
"Surely," said I, "surely that is something at my window-lattice;
Let me see then what thereat is, and this mystery explore,—
Let my heart be still a moment, and this mystery explore;—
   'T is the wind, and nothing more!"

Open then I flung the shutter, when, with many a flirt and flutter,
In there stepped a stately raven of the saintly days of yore.
Not the least obeisance made he; not an instant stopped or stayed he;
But, with mien of lord or lady, perched above my chamber door,—
Perched upon a bust of Pallas, just above my chamber door,—
   Perched, and sat, and nothing more.

Then this ebony bird beguiling my sad fancy into smiling,
By the grave and stern decorum of the countenance it wore,
"Though thy crest be shorn and shaven, thou," I said, "art sure no
  craven;
Ghastly, grim, and ancient raven, wandering from the nightly shore!

Tell me what thy lordly name is on the night's Plutonian shore!"
        Quoth the raven, "Nevermore!"

Much I marveled this ungainly fowl to hear discourse so plainly,
Though its answer little meaning—little relevancy bore;
For we cannot help agreeing that no living human being
Ever yet was blessed with seeing bird above his chamber door—
Bird or beast upon the sculptured bust above his chamber door,
        With such name as "Nevermore!"

But the raven sitting lonely on the placid bust, spoke only
That one word, as if his soul in that one word he did outpour.
Nothing further then he uttered—not a feather then he fluttered—
Till I scarcely more than muttered, "Other friends have flown before—
On the morrow *he* will leave me, as my hopes have flown before."
        Then the bird said, "Nevermore!"

Startled at the stillness broken by reply so aptly spoken,
"Doubtless," said I, "what it utters is its only stock and store,
Caught from some unhappy master, whom unmerciful disaster
Followed fast and followed faster, till his songs one burden bore,—
Till the dirges of his hope one melancholy burden bore,
        Of—"Never—nevermore!"

But—the raven still beguiling all my sad soul into smiling,—
Straight I wheeled a cushioned seat in front of bird, and bust, and
    door;
Then, upon the velvet sinking, I betook myself to linking
Fancy unto fancy, thinking what this ominous bird of yore—
What this grim, ungainly, ghastly, gaunt, and ominous bird of yore
        Meant in croaking, "Nevermore!"

This I sat engaged in guessing, but no syllable expressing
To the fowl, whose fiery eyes now burned into my bosom's core;
This and more I sat divining, with my head at ease reclining
On the cushion's velvet lining that the lamp-light gloated o'er,
But whose velvet violet lining, with the lamp-light gloating o'er,
        She shall press—ah! nevermore!

Then methought the air grew denser, perfumed from an unseen
    censer,
Swung by seraphim whose foot-falls tinkled on the tufted floor.

"Wretch," I cried, "thy God hath lent thee—by these angels he hath
   sent thee
Respite—respite and nepenthe from the memories of Lenore!
Quaff, oh quaff this kind nepenthe, and forget this lost Lenore!"
       Quoth the raven, "Nevermore!"

"Prophet!" said I, "thing of evil!—prophet still, if bird or devil!
Whether tempter sent, or whether tempest tossed thee here ashore,
Desolate yet all undaunted, on this desert land enchanted—
In this home by horror haunted—tell me truly, I implore—
Is there—is there balm in Gilead?—tell me—tell me, I implore!"
       Quoth the raven, "Nevermore!"

"Prophet!" said I, "thing of evil!—prophet still, if bird or devil!
By that heaven that bends above us—by that God we both adore,
Tell this soul with sorrow laden, if, within the distant Aidenn,
It shall clasp a sainted maiden, whom the angels name Lenore;
Clasp a rare and radiant maiden, whom the angels name Lenore!"
       Quoth the raven, "Nevermore!"

ANNABEL LEE

It was many and many a year ago,
   In a Kingdom by the sea,
That a maiden there lived whom you may know
   By the name of Annabel Lee;
And this maiden she lived with no other thought
   Than to love and be loved by me.

I was a child and she was a child,
   In this Kingdom by the sea,
But we loved with a love that was more than love,
   I and my Annabel Lee;
With a love that the winged seraphs of heaven
   Coveted her and me.

And this was the reason that, long ago,
　In this Kingdom by the sea,
A wind blew out of a cloud, chilling
　My beautiful Annabel Lee;
So that her highborn kinsman came
　And bore her away from me,
To shut her up in a sepulcher
　In this Kingdom by the sea.

The angels not half so happy in heaven,
　Went envying her and me;
Yes that was the reason (as all men know,
　In this Kingdom by the sea)
That the wind came out of the cloud by night,
　Chilling and killing my Annabel Lee.

But our love it was stronger by far than the love
　Of those that were older than we,
　Of many far wiser than we;
And neither the angels in heaven above,
　Nor the demons down under the sea,
Can ever dissever my soul from the soul
　Of the beautiful Annabel Lee:
For the moon never beams, without bringing me dreams
　Of the beautiful Annabel Lee;

And the stars never rise, but I feel the bright eyes
　Of the beautiful Annabel Lee;
And so, all the night-tide, I lie down by the side
Of my darling—my darling—my life and my bride,
　In her sepulcher there by the sea,
　In her tomb by the sounding sea.

ALEXANDER POPE

From "THE RAPE OF THE LOCK"

And now, unveiled, the toilet stands displayed,
Each silver vase in mystic order laid:
First, robed in white, the nymph intent adores,
With head uncovered, the cosmetic powers.

A heavenly image in the glass appears,
To that she bends, to that her eye she rears,
The inferior priestess, at her altar's side,
Trembling begins the sacred rites of pride.
Unnumbered treasures ope at once, and here
The various offerings of the world appear;
From each she nicely culls with curious toil,
And decks the goddess with the glittering spoil.
This casket India's glowing gems unlocks,
And all Arabia breathes from yonder box:
The tortoise here and elephant unite,
Transformed to combs, the speckled and the white.
Here files of pins extend their shining rows,
Puffs, powders, patches, bibles, billet-doux.
Now awful beauty puts on all its arms;
The fair each moment rises in her charms.
Repairs her smiles, awakens every grace,
And calls forth all the wonders of her face;
Sees by degrees a purer blush arise,
And keener lightnings quicken in her eyes.
The busy sylphs surround their darling care,
These set the head and those divide the hair;
Some fold the sleeve, whilst others plait the gown,
And Betty's praised for labors not her own.

THE DYING CHRISTIAN TO HIS SOUL

Vital spark of heavenly flame,
Quit, O quit, this mortal frame!
Trembling, hoping, lingering, flying—
O the pain, the bliss of dying!
Cease, fond nature, cease thy strife,
And let me languish into life!

Hark! they whisper: angels say,
Sister spirit, come away!
What is this absorbs me quite,
Steals my senses, shuts my sight,
Drowns my spirit, draws my breath?
Tell me, my soul! can this be death?

The world recedes—it disappears;
Heaven opens on my eyes, my ears
With sounds seraphic ring;
Lend, lend your wings! I mount, I fly!
O Grave! where is thy victory?
O Death! where is thy sting?

SIR WALTER RALEIGH

THE FÆRIE QUEEN

(To Spenser)

Methought I saw the grave where Laura lay,
Within that temple where the vestal flame
Was wont to burn: and, passing by that way
To see that buried dust of living flame,
Whose tomb fair love and fairer Virtue kept,
All suddenly I saw the Færie Queen,
At whose approach the soul of Petrarch wept;
And from henceforth those graces were not seen,
For they this Queen attended; in whose stead
Oblivion laid him down on Laura's hearse.
Hereat the hardest stones were seen to bleed
And groans of buried ghosts the heavens did pierce:
Where Homer's spright did tremble all for grief,
And curse the access of that celestial thief.

THOMAS BUCHANAN READ

DRIFTING

My soul to-day
Is far away,
Sailing the Vesuvian Bay;
My winged boat,
A bird afloat,
Swims round the purple peaks remote;—

Round purple peaks
It sails and seeks
Blue inlets and their crystal creeks,
Where high rocks throw,
Through deeps below,
A duplicate golden glow.

Far, vague, and dim
The mountains swim;
While on Vesuvius' misty brim,
With outstretched hands,
The gray smoke stands,
O'erlooking the volcanic lands.

Here Ischia smiles
O'er liquid miles;
And yonder, bluest of the isles,
Calm Capri waits,
Her sapphire gates
Beguiling to her bright estates.

I heed not, if
My rippling skiff
Float swift or slow from cliff to cliff:—
With dreamful eyes
My spirt lies
Under the walls of Paradise.

Under the walls
Where swells and falls
The Bay's deep breast at intervals,
At peace I lie,
Blown softly by,
A cloud upon this liquid sky.

The day, so mild,
Is Heaven's own child,
With Earth and Ocean reconciled;—
The airs I feel
Around me steal
Are murmuring to the murmuring keel.

Over the rail
My hand I trail
Within the shadow of the sail,
A joy intense;
The cooling sense
Glides down my drowsy indolence.

With dreamful eyes
My spirit lies
Where Summer sings and never dies,—
O'erveiled with vines,
She glows and shines
Among her future oil and wines.

Her children, hid
The cliffs amid,
Are gambolling with the gambolling kid,
Or down the walls,
With tipsy calls,
Laugh on the rocks like waterfalls.

The fisher's child,
With tresses wild,
Unto the smooth, bright sand beguiled,
With glowing lips
Sings as he skips,
Or gazes at the far-off ships.

Yon deep bark goes
Where Traffic blows
From lands of sun to lands of snows:—
This happier one,
Its course is run
From lands of snow to lands of sun.

O happy ship,
To rise and dip,
With the blue crystal at your lip!
O happy crew,
My heart with you
Sails, and sails, and sings anew!

No more, no more
The worldly shore
Upbraids me with its loud uproar!
With dreamful eyes
My spirits lies
Under the walls of Paradise!

SHERIDAN'S RIDE

Up from the South at break of day,
Bringing to Winchester fresh dismay,
The affrighted air with a shudder bore,
Like a herald in haste, to the chieftain's door,
The terrible grumble and rumble and roar,
Telling the battle was on once more,
And Sheridan twenty miles away.

And wider still those billows of war
Thundered along the horizon's bar,
And louder yet into Winchester rolled
The roar of that red sea uncontrolled,
Making the blood of the listener cold
As he thought of the stake in that fiery fray,
With Sheridan twenty miles away.

But there is a road from Winchester town,
A good, broad highway leading down;
And there, through the flash of the morning light,
A steed as black as the steeds of night,
Was seen to pass as with eagle flight.
As if he knew the terrible need,
He stretched away with the utmost speed;
Hills rose and fell,—but his heart was gay,
With Sheridan fifteen miles away.

Still sprung from those swift hoofs, thundering south,
The dust, like smoke from the cannon's mouth,

Or the trail of a comet sweeping faster and faster,
Foreboding to traitors the doom of disaster.
The heart of the steed and the heart of the master
Were beating like prisoners assaulting their walls,
Impatient to be where the battle-field calls;
Every nerve of the charger was strained to full play,
With Sheridan only ten miles away.

Under his spurning feet the road
Like an arrowy Alpine river flowed,
And the landscape sped away behind
Like an ocean flying before the wind;
And the steed, like a bark fed with furnace ire,
Swept on with his wild eyes full of fire;
But, lo! he is nearing his heart's desire,
He is snuffing the smoke of the roaring fray,
With Sheridan only five miles away.

The first that the General saw were the groups
Of stragglers, and then the retreating troops;
What was done,—what to do,—a glance told him both,
And, striking his spurs with a terrible oath,
He dashed down the line 'mid a storm of huzzas,
And the wave of retreat checked its course there because
The sight of the master compelled it to pause.
With foam and with dust the black charger was gray,
By the flash of his eye and his nostril's play
He seemed to the whole great army to say,
"I have brought you Sheridan all the way
From Winchester, down to save the day!"

Hurrah, hurrah for Sheridan!
Hurrah, hurrah for horse and man!
And when their statues are placed on high,
Under the dome of the Union sky,—
The American soldier's Temple of Fame,—
There with the glorious General's name
Be it said in letters both bold and bright:
"Here is the steed that saved the day
By carrying Sheridan into the fight,
From Winchester,—twenty miles away!"

JAMES RUSSELL LOWELL

Sir Walter Scott

SIR WALTER SCOTT

HUNTING SONG

Waken, lords and ladies gay,
On the mountain dawns the day;
All the jolly chase is here
With hawk and horse and hunting-spear;
Hounds are in their couples yelling,
Hawks are whistling, horns are knelling,
Merrily merrily mingle they,
'Waken, lords and ladies gay.'

Waken, lords and ladies gay,
The mist has left the mountain gray,
Springlets in the dawn are steaming,
Diamonds on the brake are gleaming;
And foresters have busy been
To track the buck in thicket green;
Now we come to chant our lay
'Waken, lords and ladies gay.'

Waken, lords and ladies gay,
To the greenwood haste away;
We can show you where he lies,
Fleet of foot and tall of size;
We can show the marks he made
When 'gainst the oak his antlers fray'd;
You shall see him brought to bay;
'Waken, lords and ladies gay.'

Louder, louder chant the lay
Waken, lords and ladies gay!
Tell them youth and mirth and glee
Run a course as well as we;
Time, stern huntsman! who can baulk,
Stanch as hound and fleet as hawk;
Think of this, and rise with day,
Gentle lords and ladies gay!

THE LAST MINSTREL

THE way was long, the wind was cold.
The minstrel was infirm and old;
His wither'd cheek and tresses gray
Seem'd to have known a better day;
The harp, his sole remaining joy,
Was carried by an orphan boy.
The last of all the bards was he,
Who sung of border chivalry.
For, well-a-day! their date was fled,
His tuneful brethren all were dead;
And he, neglected and oppress'd,
Wish'd to be with them, and at rest.
No more, on prancing palfrey borne,
He caroll'd, light as lark at morn;
No longer, courted and caress'd,
High placed in hall, a welcome guest,
He pour'd, to lord and lady gay,
The unpremeditated lay:
Old times were changed, old manners gone;
A stranger fill'd the Stuarts' throne;
The bigots of the iron time
Had call'd his harmless art a crime.
A wandering harper, scorn'd and poor,
He begg'd his bread from door to door;
And tuned, to please a peasant's ear,
The harp a king had loved to hear.

He pass'd where Newark's stately tower
Looks out from Yarrow's birchen bower:
The minstrel gazed with wistful eye—
No humbler resting-place was nigh.
With hesitating step, at last,
The embattled portal-arch he pass'd,
Whose ponderous grate and massy bar
Had oft roll'd back the tide of war,
But never closed the iron door
Against the desolate and poor.
The duchess marked his weary pace,
His timid mien, and reverend face,

And bade her page the menials tell,
That they should tend the old man well:
For she had known adversity,
Though born in such a high degree;
In pride of power, in beauty's bloom,
Had wept o'er Monmouth's bloody tomb.

When kindness had his wants supplied,
And the old man was gratified,
Began to rise his minstrel pride;
And he began to talk anon
Of good Earl Francis, dead and gone,
And of Earl Walter, rest him God!
A braver ne'er to battle rode;
And how full many a tale he knew,
Of the old warriors of Buccleuch;
And, would the noble duchess deign
To listen to an old man's strain,
Though stiff his hand, his voice though weak;
He thought, even yet, the sooth to speak,
That if she loved the harp to hear,
He could make music to her ear.

The humble boon was soon obtain'd;
The aged minstrel audience gained.
But, when he reach'd the room of state,
Where she with all her ladies sate,
Perchance he wished his boon denied;
For, when to tune his harp he tried,
His trembling hand had lost the ease,
Which marks security to please;
And scenes, long past, of joy and pain,
Came wildering o'er his aged brain—
He tried to tune his harp in vain.
The pitying duchess praised its chime,
And gave him heart, and gave him time,
Till every string's according glee
Was blended into harmony.
And then, he said, he would full fain
He could recall an ancient strain,

He never thought to sing again.
It was not framed for village churls,
But for high dames and mighty earls;
He had play'd it to King Charles the good,
When he kept court in Holyrood;
And much he wish'd, yet fear'd, to try,
The long-forgotten melody.
Amid the strings his fingers stray'd,
And an uncertain warbling made,
And oft he shook his hoary head.
But when he caught the measure wild,
The old man raised his face, and smiled;
And lighten'd up his faded eye,
With all a poet's ecstasy!
In varying cadence, soft or strong,
He swept the sounding chords along:
The present scene, the future lot,
His toils, his wants, were all forgot:
Cold diffidence and age's frost,
In the full tide of song were lost;
Each blank, in faithless memory void,
The poet's glowing thought supplied;
And while his harp responsive rung,
'Twas thus the latest minstrel sung.

LOCHINVAR

O, YOUNG Lochinvar is come out of the west;
Through all the wide border his steed was the best;
And save his good broad-sword he weapon had none;
He rode all unarmed, and he rode all alone.
So faithful in love, and so dauntless in war,
There never was knight like the young Lochinvar.

He staid not for brake, and he stopped not for stone;
He swam the Eske river, where ford there was none;
But, ere he alighted at Netherby gate,
The bride had consented, the gallant came late:
For a laggard in love, and a dastard in war,
Was to wed the fair Ellen of brave Lochinvar.

So boldly he entered the Netherby Hall,
'Mong bridesmen, and kinsmen, and brothers, and all;
Then spoke the bride's father, his hand on his sword,
(For the poor craven bridegroom said never a word,)
"O come ye in peace here, or come ye in war,
Or to dance at our bridal, young Lord Lochinvar?"

"I long wooed your daughter, my suit you denied—
Love swells like the Solway, but ebbs like its tide—
And now I am come, with this lost love of mine,
To lead but one measure, drink one cup of wine;
There are maidens in Scotland more lovely by far,
That would gladly be bride to the young Lochinvar."

The bride kissed the goblet—the knight took it up;
He quaffed off the wine, and he threw down the cup.
She looked down to blush, and she looked up to sigh,
With a smile on her lips, and a tear in her eye.
He took her soft hand, ere her mother could bar—
"Now, tread we a measure!" said young Lochinvar.

So stately his form, and so lovely her face,
That never a hall such a galliard did grace;
While her mother did fret and her father did fume,
And the bridegroom stood dangling his bonnet and plume;
And the bride-maidens whispered, " 'T were better by far
To have matched our fair cousin with young Lochinvar."

One touch to her hand, and one word in her ear,
When they reached the hall door, and the charger stood near
So light to the croup the fair lady he swung,
So light to the saddle before her he sprung!
"She is won! we are gone, over bank, bush, and scaur;
They'll have fleet steeds that follow," quoth young Lochinvar

There was mounting 'mong Græmes of the Netherby clan;
Forsters, Fenwicks, and Musgraves, they rode and they ran
There was racing and chasing on Cannobie Lea,
But the lost bride of Netherby ne'er did they see.
So daring in love, and so dauntless in war,
Have ye e'er heard of gallant like young Lochinvar?

JOCK OF HAZELDEAN

'Why weep ye by the tide, ladie?
   Why weep ye by the tide?
I'll wed ye to my youngest son,
   And ye sall be his bride:
And ye sall be his bride, ladie,
   Sae comely to be seen'—
But aye she loot the tears down fa'
   For Jock of Hazeldean.

'Now let this wilfu' grief be done,
   And dry that cheek so pale;
Young Frank is chief of Errington
   And lord of Langley-dale;
His step is first in peaceful ha',
   His sword in battle keen'—
But aye she loot the tears down fa'
   For Jock of Hazeldean.

'A chain of gold ye sall not lack,
   Nor braid to bind your hair,
Nor mettled hound, nor managed hawk,
   Nor palfrey fresh and fair;
And you the foremost o' them a'
   Shall ride our forest-queen'—
But aye she loot the tears down fa'
   For Jock of Hazeldean.

The kirk was deck'd at morning-tide,
   The tapers glimmer'd fair;
The priest and bridegroom wait the bride,
   And dame and knight are there:
They sought her baith by bower and ha';
   The ladie was not seen!
She's o'er the Border, and awa'
   Wi' Jock of Hazeldean.

THE TEVIOT

Sweet Teviot, by thy silver tide,
  The glaring bale-fires blaze no more!
No longer steel-clad warriors ride
  Along thy wild and willow'd shore;
Where'er thou wind'st, by dale or hill,
All, all is peaceful, all is still,
  As if thy waves, since Time was born,
Since first they roll'd their way to Tweed,
Had only heard the shepherd's reed,
  Nor started at the bugle-horn!
Unlike the tide of human time,
  Which, though it change in ceaseless flow,
Retains each grief, retains each crime,
  Its earliest course was doom'd to know;
And, darker as it downward bears,
Is stain'd with past and present tears!
  Low as that tide has ebb'd with me,
It still reflects to Memory's eye
The hour, my brave, my only boy,
  Fell by the side of great Dundee.
Why, when the volleying musket play'd
Against the bloody Highland blade,
Why was not I beside him laid!—
Enough—he died the death of fame;
Enough—he died with conquering Græme.

FITZ-JAMES AND RODERICK DHU

Then each at once his falchion drew,
Each on the ground his scabbard threw,
Each look'd to sun, and stream, and plain,
As what he ne'er might see again;
Then, foot, and point, and eye opposed,
In dubious strife they darkly closed.—
Ill fared it now with Roderick Dhu,
That on the field his targe he threw,
Whose brazen studs, and tough bull-hide,
Had death so often turn'd aside;

For, train'd abroad his arms to wield,
Fitz-James's blade was sword and shield:
He practised every pass and ward,
To feint, to thrust, to strike, to guard:
While, less expert, though stronger far,
The Gael maintain'd unequal war.
Three times in closing strife they stood,
And thrice the Saxon sword drank blood;
No stinted draught—no scanty tide!
The gushing flood the tartans dyed:
Fierce Roderick felt the fatal drain,
And shower'd his blows like wintry rain;
And as firm tower, or castle-roof,
Against the winter shower is proof,
The foe, invulnerable still,
Foil'd his wild rage by steady skill;
Till, at advantage ta'en, his brand
Forced Roderick's weapon from his hand,
And backwards borne upon the lea,
Brought the proud chieftain to his knee.
"Now yield thee, or by him who made
The world! thy heart-blood dyes my blade."—
"Thy threats, thy mercy, I defy;
Let recreant yield, who fears to die."—
Like adder darting from his coil—
Like wolf that dashes through the toil—
Like mountain-cat that guards her young,
Full at Fitz-James's throat he sprung:
Received, but reck'd not of a wound,
And lock'd his arms his foeman round.
Now, gallant Saxon! hold thy own;
No maiden's hand is round thee thrown!
That desperate grasp thy frame might feel
Through bars of brass and triple steel.
They tug, they strain—down, down they go,—
The Gael above, Fitz-James below!
The chieftain's gripe his throat compress'd,
His knee was planted in his breast;
His clotted locks he backward threw,
Across his brow his hand he drew,
From blood and mist to clear his sight—

Then gleam'd aloft his dagger bright;
But hate and fury ill supplied
The stream of life's exhausted tide;
And all too late the advantage came
To turn the odds of deadly game;
For while the dagger gleam'd on high,
Reel'd soul and sense, reel'd brain and eye.
Down came the blow—but in the heath
The erring blade found bloodless sheath.—
The struggling foe may now unclasp
The fainting chief's relaxing grasp.
Unwounded from the dreadful close,
But breathless all, Fitz-James arose.

WILLIAM SHAKESPEARE

SONNETS

I

WHEN I do count the clock that tells the time,
And see the brave day sunk in hideous night;
When I behold the violet past prime,
And sable curls all silver'd o'er with white;
When lofty trees I see barren of leaves,
Which erst from heat did canopy the herd,
And summer's green, all girded up in sheaves,
Borne on the bier with white and bristly beard;
Then of thy beauty do I question make,
That thou among the wastes of time must go,
Since sweets and beauties do themselves forsake,
And die as fast as they see others grow;
   And nothing 'gainst Time's scythe can make defence
   Save breed, to brave him when he takes thee hence.

II

When I consider every thing that grows
Holds in perfection but a little moment,
That this huge stage presenteth naught but shows,

Whereon the stars in secret influence comment;
When I perceive that men as plants increase,
Cheered and check'd even by the selfsame sky,
Vaunt in their youthful sap, at height decrease,
And wear their brave state out of memory;
Then the conceit of this inconstant stay
Sets you most rich in youth before my sight,
Where wasteful time debateth with decay,
To change your day of youth to sullied night;
   And, all in war with Time, for love of you,
   As he takes from you, I engraft you new.

III

Shall I compare thee to a summer's day?
Thou art more lovely and more temperate:
Rough winds do shake the darling buds of May,
And summer's lease hath all too short a date:
Sometime too hot the eye of heaven shines,
And often is his gold complexion dimm'd;
And every fair from fair sometime declines,
By chance, or nature's changing course, untrimm'd;
But thy eternal summer shall not fade,
Nor lose possession of that fair thou owest;
Nor shall Death brag thou wander'st in his shade,
When in eternal lines to time thou growest:
   So long as men can breathe, or eyes can see,
   So long lives this, and this gives life to thee.

IV

As an unperfect actor on the stage,
Who with his fear is put besides his part,
Or some fierce thing replete with too much rage,
Whose strength's abundance weakens his own heart;
So I, for fear of trust, forget to say
The perfect ceremony of love's rite,
And in mine own love's strength seem to decay,
O'ercharg'd with burden of mine own love's might.

O, let my books be, then, the eloquence
And dumb presagers of my speaking breast;
Who plead for love, and look for recompence,
More than that tongue that more hath more express'd.
   O, learn to read what silent love hath writ:
   To hear with eyes belongs to love's fine wit.

V

When in disgrace with fortune and men's eyes,
I all alone beweep my outcast state,
And trouble deaf Heaven with my bootless cries,
And look upon myself, and curse my fate,
Wishing me like to one more rich in hope,
Featur'd like him, like him with friends possess'd,
Desiring this man's art, and that man's scope,
With what I most enjoy contented least;
Yet in these thoughts myself almost despising,
Haply I think on thee,—and then my state
(Like to the lark at break of day arising
From sullen earth) sings hymns at heaven's gate;
   For thy sweet love remember'd such wealth brings,
   That then I scorn to change my state with kings.

VI

When to the sessions of sweet silent thought
I summon up remembrance of things past,
I sigh the lack of many a thing I sought,
And with old woes new wail my dear time's waste:
Then can I drown an eye, unus'd to flow,
For precious friends hid in death's dateless night,
And weep afresh love's long-since cancell'd woe,
And moan the expense of many a vanish'd sight:
Then can I grieve at grievances foregone,
And heavily from woe to woe tell o'er
The sad account of fore-bemoaned moan,
Which I new pay as if not paid before.
   But if the while I think on thee, dear friend,
   All losses are restor'd, and sorrows end.

VII

If thou survive my well-contented day,
When that churl Death my bones with dust shall cover,
And shalt by fortune once more re-survey
These poor rude lines of thy deceased lover,—
Compare them with the bettering of the time;
And though they be outstripp'd by every pen,
Reserve them for my love, not for their rhyme,
Exceeded by the height of happier men.
O, then vouchsafe me but this loving thought,—
"Had my friend's muse grown with this growing age,
A dearer birth than this his love had brought,
To march in ranks of better equipage:
   But since he died, and poets better prove,
   Theirs for their style I'll read, his for his love."

VIII

So am I as the rich, whose blessed key
Can bring him to his sweet up-locked treasure,
The which he will not every hour survey,
For blunting the fine point of seldom pleasure.
Therefore are feasts so solemn and so rare,
Since, seldom coming, in the long year set,
Like stones of worth they thinly placed are,
Or captain jewels in the carkanet.
So is the time that keeps you, as my chest,
Or as the wardrobe which the robe doth hide,
To make some special instant special-blest,
By new unfolding his imprison'd pride.
   Blessed are you, whose worthiness gives scope,
   Being had, to triumph, being lack'd, to hope.

IX

Being your slave, what should I do but tend
Upon the hours and times of your desire?
I have no precious time at all to spend,
Nor services to do, till you require.

Nor dare I chide the world-without-end hour,
Whilst I, my sovereign, watch the clock for you,
Nor think the bitterness of absence sour,
When you have bid your servant once adieu;
Nor dare I question with my jealous thought
Where you may be, or your affairs suppose,
But, like a sad slave, stay and think of naught,
Save, where you are, how happy you make those.
   So true a fool is love, that in your will,
   Though you do anything, he thinks no ill.

Like as the waves make towards the pebbled shore,
So do our minutes hasten to their end;
Each changing place with that which goes before,
In sequent toil all forwards do contend.
Nativity, once in the main of light,
Crawls to maturity, wherewith being crown'd,
Crooked eclipses 'gainst his glory fight,
And Time, that gave, doth now his gift confound.
Time doth transfix the flourish set on youth,
And delves the parallels in beauty's brow;
Feeds on the rarities of nature's truth,
And nothing stands but for his scythe to mow:
   And yet, to times in hope my verse shall stand,
   Praising thy worth, despite his cruel hand.

XI

When I have seen by Time's fell hand defac'd
The rich-proud cost of outworn buried age;
When sometime lofty towers I see down-raz'd,
And brass eternal, slave to mortal rage;
When I have seen the hungry ocean gain
Advantage on the kingdom of the shore,
And the firm soil win of the watery main,
Increasing store with loss, and loss with store;

When I have seen such interchange of state,
Or state itself confounded to decay;
Ruin hath taught me thus to ruminate,—
That Time will come and take my love away.
  This thought is as a death, which cannot choose
  But weep to have that which it fears to lose.

XII

Since brass, nor stone, nor earth, nor boundless sea,
But sad mortality o'ersways their power,
How with this rage shall beauty hold a plea,
Whose action is no stronger than a flower?
O, how shall summer's honey breath hold out
Against the wreckful siege of battering days,
When rocks impregnable are not so stout,
Nor gates of steel so strong, but Time decays?
O fearful meditation! where alack,
Shall Time's best jewel from Time's chest lie hid?
Or what strong hand can hold his swift foot back?
Or who his spoil of beauty can forbid?
  O, none, unless this miracle have might,
  That in black ink my love may still shine bright.

XIII

Tir'd with all these, for restful death I cry,—
As, to behold desert a beggar born,
And needy nothing trimm'd in jollity,
And purest faith unhappily forsworn,
And gilded honour shamefully misplac'd,
And maiden virtue rudely strumpeted,
And right perfection wrongfully disgrac'd,
And strength by limping sway disabled,
And art made tongue-tied by authority,
And folly, doctor-like, controlling skill,
And simple truth miscall'd simplicity,
And captive good attending captain ill:—
  Tir'd with all these, from these would I be gone,
  Save that, to die, I leave my love alone.

XIV

No longer mourn for me when I am dead,
Than you shall hear the surly sullen bell
Give warning to the world that I am fled
From this vile world, with vilest worms to dwell:
Nay, if you read this line, remember not
The hand that writ it; for I love you so,
That I in your sweet thoughts would be forgot,
If thinking on me then should make you woe.
O, if, I say, you look upon this verse,
When I perhaps compounded am with clay,
Do not so much as my poor name rehearse;
But let your love even with my life decay;
   Lest the wise world should look into your moan,
   And mock you with me after I am gone.

XV

That time of year thou may'st in me behold
When yellow leaves, or none, or few, do hang
Upon those boughs which shake against the cold,
Bare ruin'd choirs, where late the sweet birds sang.
In me thou seest the twilight of such day
As after sunset fadeth in the west;
Which by and by black night doth take away,
Death's second self, that seals up all in rest.
In me thou seest the glowing of such fire,
That on the ashes of his youth doth lie,
As the death-bed whereon it must expire,
Consum'd with that which it was nourish'd by.
   This thou perceiv'st, which makes thy love more strong,
   To love that well which thou must leave ere long:

XVI

Farewell! thou art too dear for my possessing,
And like enough thou know'st thy estimate:
The charter of thy worth gives thee releasing;
My bonds in thee are all determinate.

For how do I hold thee but by thy granting?
And for that riches where is my deserving?
The cause of this fair gift in me is wanting,
And so my patient back again is swerving.
Thyself thou gav'st, thy own worth then not knowing,
Or me, to whom thou gav'st it, else mistaking;
So thy great gift, upon misprision growing,
Comes home again, on better judgment making.
   Thus have I had thee, as a dream doth flatter,
   In sleep a king, but, waking, no such matter.

XVII

They that have power to hurt and will do none,
That do not do the thing they most do show,
Who, moving others, are themselves as stone,
Unmoved, cold, and to temptation slow;
They rightly do inherit heaven's graces,
And husband nature's riches from expense;
They are the lords and owners of their faces,
Others but stewards of their excellence.
The summer's flower is to the summer sweet,
Though to itself it only live and die;
But if that flower with base infection meet,
The basest weed outbraves his dignity:
   For sweetest things turn sourest by their deeds;
   Lilies that fester smell far worse than weeds.

XVIII

How like a winter hath my absence been
From thee, the pleasure of the fleeting year!
What freezings have I felt, what dark days seen!
What old December's bareness everywhere!
And yet this time remov'd was summer's time;
The teeming autumn, big with rich increase,
Bearing the wanton burden of the prime,
Like widow'd wombs after their lords' decease:
Yet this abundant issue seem'd to me
But hope of orphans, and unfather'd fruit;
For summer and his pleasures wait on thee,
And, thou away, the very birds are mute;

Of, if they sing, 'tis with so dull a cheer,
That leaves look pale, dreading the winter's near.

XIX

To me, fair friend, you never can be old,
For as you were when first your eye I ey'd,
Such seems your beauty still. Three winters' cold
Have from the forests shook three summers' pride,
Three beauteous springs to yellow autumn turn'd
In process of the seasons have I seen,
Three April perfumes in three hot Junes burn'd,
Since first I saw you fresh, which yet are green.
Ah, yet doth beauty, like a dial-hand,
Steal from his figure, and no pace perceiv'd;
So your sweet hue, which methinks still doth stand,
Hath motion, and mine eye may be deceiv'd:
  For fear of which, hear this, thou age unbred,—
  Ere you were born, was beauty's summer dead.

XX

When in the chronicle of wasted time
I see descriptions of the fairest wights,
And beauty making beautiful old rhyme,
In praise of ladies dead, and lovely knights;
Then in the blazon of sweet beauty's best,
Of hand, of foot, of lip, of eye, of brow,
I see their antique pen would have express'd
Even such a beauty as you master now.
So all their praises are but prophecies
Of this our time, all you prefiguring;
And, for they look'd but with divining eyes,
They had not skill enough your worth to sing:
  For we, which now behold these present days,
  Have eyes to wonder, but lack tongues to praise.

XXI

O, never say that I was false of heart,
Though absence seem'd my flame to qualify.

As easy might I from myself depart,
As from my soul, which in thy breast doth lie:
That is my home of love: if I have rang'd,
Like him that travels, I return again;
Just to the time, not with the time exchang'd,—
So that myself bring water for my stain.
Never believe, though in my nature reign'd
All frailties that besiege all kinds of blood,
That it could so preposterously be stain'd,
To leave for nothing all thy sum of good;
   For nothing this wide universe I call,
   Save thou, my rose; in it thou art my all.

XXII

Let me not to the marriage of true minds
Admit impediments. Love is not love
Which alters when it alteration finds,
Or bends with the remover to remove:
O, no! it is an ever-fixed mark,
That looks on tempests, and is never shaken;
It is the star to every wandering bark,
Whose worth's unknown, although his height be taken.
Love's not Time's fool, though rosy lips and cheeks
Within his bending sickle's compass come;
Love alters not with his brief hours and weeks,
But bears it out even to the edge of doom.
   If this be error, and upon me prov'd,
   I never writ, nor no man ever lov'd.

XXIII

When my love swears that she is made of truth,
I do believe her, though I know she lies,
That she might think me some untutor'd youth,
Unlearned in the world's false subtleties.
Thus vainly thinking that she thinks me young,
Although she knows my days are past the best,
Simply I credit her false-speaking tongue:
On both sides thus is simple truth supprest.

But wherefore says she not she is unjust?
And wherefore say not I that I am old?
O, love's best habit is in seeming trust,
And age in love loves not to have years told:
   Therefore I lie with her, and she with me,
   And in our faults by lies we flatter'd be.

XXIV

In faith, I do not love thee with mine eyes,
For they in thee a thousand errors note;
But 'tis my heart that loves what they despise,
Who, in despite of view, is pleas'd to dote;
Nor are mine ears with thy tongue's tune delighted;
Nor tender feeling, to base touches prone,
Nor taste, nor smell, desire to be invited
To any sensual feast with thee alone:
But my five wits, nor my five senses can
Dissuade one foolish heart from serving thee,
Who leaves unsway'd the likeness of a man,
Thy proud heart's slave and vassal wretch to be:
   Only my plague thus far I count my gain,
   That she that makes me sin, awards me pain.

XXV

O me, what eyes hath Love put in my head,
Which have no correspondence with true sight!
Or, if they have, where is my judgment fled,
That censures falsely what they see aright?
If that be fair whereon my false eyes dote,
What means the world to say it is not so?
If it be not, then love doth well denote
Love's eye is not so true as all men's: no,
How can it? O, how can Love's eye be true,
That is so vex'd with watching and with tears?
No marvel, then, though I mistake my view;
The sun itself sees not, till heaven clears.
   O cunning Love! with tears thou keep'st me blind,
   Lest eyes well-seeing thy foul faults should find.

PERCY BYSSHE SHELLEY

TO THE SKYLARK

Hail to thee, blithe spirit!—
Bird thou never wert,—
That from heaven, or near it,
Pourest thy full heart
In profuse strains of unpremeditated art.

Higher still and higher,
From the earth thou springest,
Like a cloud of fire,
The blue deep thou wingest,
And singing still dost soar, and soaring ever singest.

In the golden lightning
Of the sunken sun,
O'er which clouds are brightening,
Thou dost float and run;
Like an embodied joy whose race is just begun.

The pale, purple even
Melts around thy flight;
Like a star of heaven,
In the broad daylight
Thou art unseen, but yet I hear thy shrill delight,

Keen as are the arrows
Of the silver sphere,
Whose intense lamp narrows
In the white dawn clear,
Until we hardly see, we feel that it is there.

All the earth and air
With thy voice is loud,
As, when night is bare,
From one lonely cloud
The moon rains out her beams, and heaven is overflowed.

What thou art we know not;—
　　What is most like thee?
From rainbow-clouds there flow not
　　Drops so bright to see,
As from thy presence showers a rain of melody.

Like a poet hidden
　　In the light of thought,
Singing hymns unbidden,
　　Till the world is wrought
To sympathy with hopes and fears it heeded not:

Like a high-born maiden,
　　In a palace tower,
Soothing her love-laden
　　Soul in secret hour
With music sweet as love, which overflows her bower:

Like a glow-worm golden
　　In a dell of dew,
Scattering unbeholden
　　Its aërial hue
Among the flowers and grass, which screen it from the view:

Like a rose embowered
　　In its own green leaves,
By warm winds deflowered,
　　Till the scent it gives
Makes faint with too much sweet these heavy-wingéd thieves

Sound of vernal showers
　　On the twinkling grass,
Rain-awakened flowers,—
　　All that ever was
Joyous, and clear, and fresh, thy music doth surpass.

Teach us, sprite or bird,
　　What sweet thoughts are thine:
I have never heard
　　Praise of love or wine,
That panted forth a flood of rapture so divine.

Chorus hymeneal,
   Or triumphal chant,
Matched with thine would be all
   But an empty vaunt—
A thing wherein we feel there is some hidden want.

What objects are the fountains
   Of thy happy strain?
What fields, or waves, or mountains?
   What shapes of sky or plain?
What love of thine own kind? what ignorance of pain?

With thy clear, keen joyance
   Languor cannot be:
Shadow of annoyance
   Never came near thee:
Thou lovest, but ne'er knew love's sad satiety.

Waking or asleep,
   Thou of death must deem
Things more true and deep
   Than we mortals dream;
Or how could thy notes flow in such a crystal stream?

We look before and after,
   And pine for what is not:
Our sincerest laughter
   With some pain is fraught;
Our sweetest songs are those that tell of saddest thought.

Yet if we could scorn
   Hate, and pride, and fear;
If we were things born
   Not to shed a tear,
I know not how thy joy we ever should come near.

Better than all measures
   Of delightful sound;
Better than all treasures
   That in books are found,
Thy skill to poet were, thou scorner of the ground!

Teach me half the gladness
That thy brain must know,
Such harmonious madness
From my lips would flow,
The world should listen then, as I am listening now.

TO NIGHT

Swiftly walk over the western wave,
Spirit of Night!
Out of the misty eastern cave,
Where, all the long and lone daylight,
Thou wovest dreams of joy and fear,
Which make thee terrible and dear,—
Swift be thy flight!

Wrap thy form in a mantle gray,
Star-inwrought!
Blind with thine hair the eyes of Day,
Kiss her until she be wearied out;
Then wander o'er city, and sea, and land,
Touching all with thine opiate wand—
Come, long-sought!

When I arose and saw the dawn,
I sighed for thee;
When night rode high, and the dew was gone,
And noon lay heavy on flower and tree,
And the weary Day turned to her rest,
Lingering like an unloved guest,
I sighed for thee.

Thy brother Death came, and cried,
Wouldst thou me?
Thy sweet child Sleep, the filmy-eyed,
Murmured like a noontide bee,
Shall I nestle near thy side?
Wouldst thou me?—and I replied,
"No, not thee!"

Death will come when thou art dead,
     Soon, too soon—
Sleep will come when thou art fled;
Of neither would I ask the boon
I ask of thee, belovèd Night—
Swift be thine approaching flight,
     Come soon, soon!

THE CLOUD

I bring fresh showers for the thirsting flowers,
     From the seas and the streams;
I bear light shade for the leaves when laid
     In their noonday dreams.
From my wings are shaken the dews that waken
     The sweet buds every one,
When rocked to rest on their mother's breast,
     As she dances about the sun.
I wield the flail of the lashing hail,
     And whiten the green plains under;
And then again I dissolve it in rain,
     And laugh as I pass in thunder.

I sift the snow on the mountains below,
     And their great pines groan aghast;
And all the night 'tis my pillow white,
     While I sleep in the arms of the blast.
Sublime on the towers of my skiey bowers
     Lightning, my pilot, sits;
In a cavern under is fettered the thunder;
     It struggles and howls at fits.

Over earth and ocean, with gentle motion,
     This pilot is guiding me,
Lured by the love of the genii that move
     In the depths of the purple sea;
Over the rills, and the crags, and the hills,
     Over the lakes and the plains,
Wherever he dream, under mountain or stream,
     The Spirit he loves remains;
And I all the while bask in heaven's blue smile,
     Whilst he is dissolving in rains.

The sanguine sunrise, with his meteor eyes,
    And his burning plumes outspread,
Leaps on the back of my sailing rack,
    When the morning star shines dead.
As, on the jag of a mountain crag
    Which an earthquake rocks and swings,
An eagle, alit, one moment may sit
    In the light of its golden wings.
And when sunset may breathe, from the lit sea beneath
    Its ardors of rest and of love,
And the crimson pall of eve may fall
    From the depth of heaven above,
With wings folded I rest on mine airy nest,
    As still as a brooding dove.

That orbéd maiden with white fire laden,
    Whom mortals call the moon,
Glides glimmering o'er my fleece-like floor,
    By the midnight breezes strewn;
And wherever the beat of her unseen feet,
    Which only the angels hear,
May have broken the woof of my tent's thin roof,
    The stars peep behind her and peer:
And I laugh to see them whirl and flee,
    Like a swarm of golden bees,
When I widen the rent in my wind-built tent,
    Till the calm rivers, lakes, and seas,
Like strips of the sky fallen through me on high,
    Are each paved with the moon and these.

I bind the sun's throne with a burning zone,
    And the moon's with a girdle of pearl;
The volcanoes are dim, and the stars reel and swim,
    When the whirlwinds my banner unfurl.
From cape to cape, with a bridge-like shape,
    Over a torrent sea,
Sunbeam proof, I hang like a roof,
    The mountain its columns be.
The triumphal arch, through which I march
    With hurricane, fire, and snow,

When the powers of the air are chained to my chair,
  Is the million-colored bow;
The sphere-fire above, its soft colors wove,
  While the moist earth was laughing below.

I am the daughter of earth and water,
  And the nursling of the sky;
I pass through the pores of the ocean and shores;
  I change, but I cannot die.
For after the rain, when, with never a stain,
  The pavilion of heaven is bare,
And the winds and sunbeams, with their convex gleams,
  Build up the blue dome of air—
I silently laugh at my own cenotaph,
  And out of the caverns of rain,
Like a child from the womb, like a ghost from the tomb,
  I arise and upbuild it again.

LINES TO AN INDIAN AIR

I ARISE from dreams of thee
  In the first sweet sleep of night,
When the winds are breathing low,
  And the stars are shining bright.
I arise from dreams of thee,
  And a spirit in my feet
Has led me—who knows how?—
  To thy chamber-window, sweet!

The wandering airs, they faint
  On the dark, the silent stream—
The champak odors fail
  Like sweet thoughts in a dream;
The nightingale's complaint,
  It dies upon her heart,
As I must die on thine,
  O beloved as thou art!

O lift me from the grass!
  I die, I faint, I fail!
Let thy love in kisses rain
  On my lips and eyelids pale.
My cheek is cold and white, alas!
  My heart beats loud and fast;
Oh! press it close to thine again,
  Where it will break at last.

ODE TO THE WEST WIND

O WILD West Wind, thou breath of Autumn's being,
Thou, from whose unseen presence the leaves dead
Are driven, like ghosts from an enchanter fleeing,
Yellow, and black, and pale, and hectic red,
Pestilence-stricken multitudes! O thou
Who chariotest to their dark wintry bed
The wingéd seeds, where they lie cold and low,
Each like a corpse within its grave, until
Thine azure sister of the Spring shall blow
Her clarion o'er the dreaming earth, and fill
(Driving sweet buds like flocks to feed in air)
With living hues and odours plain and hill:
Wild Spirit, which art moving everywhere;
Destroyer and Preserver; Hear, oh hear!

Thou on whose stream, 'mid the steep sky's commotion,
Loose clouds like earth's decaying leaves are shed,
Shook from the tangled boughs of heaven and ocean,
Angels of rain and lightning! there are spread
On the blue surface of thine airy surge,
Like the bright hair uplifted from the head
Of some fierce Maenad, ev'n from the dim verge
Of the horizon to the zenith's height—
The locks of the approaching storm. Thou dirge
Of the dying year, to which this closing night
Will be the dome of a vast sepulchre,
Vaulted with all thy congregated might
Of vapours, from whose solid atmosphere
Black rain, and fire, and hail, will burst: Oh hear!

Thou who didst waken from his summer-dreams
The blue Mediterranean, where he lay,
Lull'd by the coil of his crystalline streams,
Beside a pumice isle in Baiae's bay,
And saw in sleep old palaces and towers
Quivering within the wave's intenser day,
All overgrown with azure moss, and flowers
So sweet, the sense faints picturing them! Thou
For whose path the Atlantic's level powers
Cleave themselves into chasms, while far below
The sea-blooms and the oozy woods which wear
The sapless foliage of the ocean, know
Thy voice, and suddenly grow gray with fear
And tremble and despoil themselves: Oh hear!

If I were a dead leaf thou mightest bear;
If I were a swift cloud to fly with thee;
A wave to pant beneath thy power, and share
The impulse of thy strength, only less free
Than Thou, O uncontrollable! If even
I were as in my boyhood, and could be
The comrade of thy wanderings over heaven,
As then, when to outstrip thy skiey speed
Scarce seem'd a vision,—I would ne'er have striven
As thus with thee in prayer in my sore need.
Oh! lift me as a wave, a leaf, a cloud!
I fall upon the thorns of life! I bleed!
A heavy weight of hours has chain'd and bow'd
One too like thee—tameless, and swift, and proud.

Make me thy lyre, ev'n as the forest is:
What if my leaves are falling like its own!
The tumult of thy mighty harmonies
Will take from both a deep autumnal tone,
Sweet though in sadness. Be thou, Spirit fierce,
My spirit! be thou me, impetuous one!
Drive my dead thoughts over the universe,
Like wither'd leaves, to quicken a new birth;
And, by the incantation of this verse,

Scatter, as from an unextinguish'd hearth
Ashes and sparks, my words among mankind!
Be through my lips to unawaken'd earth
The trumpet of a prophecy! O Wind,
If Winter comes, can Spring be far behind?

ADONAIS

[ON THE DEATH OF KEATS]

I WEEP for ADONAIS—he is dead!
Oh, weep for Adonais! though our tears
Thaw not the frost which binds so dear a head!
And thou, sad Hour, selected from all years
To mourn our loss, rouse thy obscure compeers,
And teach them thine own sorrow; say: With me
Died Adonais: till the Future dares
Forget the Past, his fate and fame shall be
An echo and a light unto eternity!

Where wert thou, mighty Mother, when he lay,
When thy son lay, pierced by the shaft which flies
In darkness? where was lorn Urania
When Adonais died? With veiled eyes,
'Mid listening Echoes, in her Paradise
She sate, while one, with soft enamored breath,
Rekindled all the fading melodies,
With which, like flowers that mock the corse beneath,
He had adorned and hid the coming bulk of death.

Oh, weep for Adonais—he is dead!
Wake, melancholy Mother, wake and weep!
Yet wherefore? Quench within their burning bed
Thy fiery tears, and let thy loud heart keep,
Like his, a mute and uncomplaining sleep;
For he is gone, where all things wise and fair
Descend:—oh, dream not that the amorous Deep
Will yet restore him to the vital air;
Death feeds on his mute voice, and laughs at our despair.

Most musical of mourners, weep again!
Lament anew, Urania!—He died,
Who was the Sire of an immortal strain,
Blind, old, and lonely, when his country's pride,
The priest, the slave, and the liberticide
Trampled and mocked with many a loathed rite
Of lust and blood; he went, unterrified
Into the gulf of death; but his clear Sprite
Yet reigns o'er earth, the third among the sons of light.

Most musical of mourners, weep anew!
Not all to that bright station dared to climb:
And happier they their happiness who knew,
Whose tapers yet burn through that night of time
In which suns perished; others more sublime,
Struck by the envious wrath of man or God,
Have sunk, extinct in their refulgent prime;
And some yet live, treading the thorny road,
Which leads, through toil and hate, to Fame's serene abode.

But now, thy youngest, dearest one, has perished,
The nursling of thy widowhood, who grew
Like a pale flower by some sad maiden cherished,
And fed with true love tears instead of dew;
Most musical of mourners, weep anew!
Thy extreme hope, the loveliest and the last,
The bloom, whose petals, nipt before they blew,
Died on the promise of the fruit, is waste:
The broken lily lies—the storm is overpast.

To that high Capital, where kingly Death
Keeps his pale court in beauty and decay,
He came; and bought, with price of purest breath
A grave among the eternal.—Come away!
Haste, while the vault of blue Italian day
Is yet his fitting charnel-roof! while still
He lies, as if in dewy sleep he lay;
Awake him not, surely he takes his fill
Of deep and liquid rest, forgetful of all ill.

He will awake no more, oh, never more!
Within the twilight chamber spreads apace
Tl e shadow of white Death, and at the door
Invisible Corruption waits to trace
Hi extreme way to her dim dwelling-place;
Tl e eternal Hunger sits, but pity and awe
Soothe her pale rage, nor dares she to deface
So fair a prey, till darkness and the law
Of change shall o'er his sleep the mortal curtain draw.

Oh, weep for Adonais!—The quick Dreams,
The passion-winged Ministers of thought,
Who were his flocks, whom near the living streams
Of his young spirit he fed, and whom he taught
The love which was its music, wander not,—
Wander no more, from kindling brain to brain,
But droop there, whence they sprung; and mourn their lot
Round the cold heart, where, after their sweet pain,
They ne'er will gather strength, nor find a home again.

And one with trembling hand clasps his cold head,
And fans him with her moonlight wings, and cries,
"Our love, our hope, our sorrow, is not dead;
See, on the silken fringe of his faint eyes,
Like dew upon a sleeping flower, there lies
A tear some Dream hath loosened from his brain."
Lost Angel of a ruined Paradise!
She knew not 'twas her own, as with no stain
She faded, like a cloud which had outwept its rain.

One from a lucid urn of starry dew
Washed his light limbs, as if embalming them;
Another clipt her profuse locks, and threw
The wreath upon him, like an anadem,
Which frozen tears instead of pearls begem;
Another in her wilful grief would break
Her bow and winged reeds, as if to stem
A greater loss with one which was more weak;
And dull the barbed fire against his frozen cheek.

Another Splendor on his mouth alit,
That mouth whence it was wont to draw the breath
Which gave it strength to pierce the guarded wit,
And pass into the panting heart beneath
With lightning and with music; the damp death
Quenched its caress upon its icy lips;
And, as a dying meteor stains a wreath
Of moonlight vapor, which the cold night clips,
It flushed through his pale limbs, and passed to its eclipse.

And others came,—Desires and Adorations,
Winged Persuasions, and veiled Destinies,
Splendors and Glooms and glimmering Incarnations
Of hopes and fears, and twilight Phantasies;
And Sorrow, with her family of Sighs,
And Pleasure, blind with tears, led by the gleam
Of her own dying smile instead of eyes,
Came in slow pomp;—the moving pomp might seem
Like pageantry of mist on an autumnal stream.

All he had loved and moulded into thought,
From shape, and hue, and odor, and sweet sound,
Lamented Adonais. Morning sought
Her eastern watch-tower, and her hair unbound,
Wet with the tears which should adorn the ground,
Dimmed the aerial eyes that kindle day;
Afar the melancholy thunder moaned,
Pale Ocean in unquiet slumber lay,
And the wild winds flew round, sobbing in their dismay.

Lost Echo sits amid the voiceless mountains,
And feeds her grief with his remembered lay,
And will no more reply to winds or fountains,
Or amorous birds perched on the young green spray,
Or herdsman's horn, or bell at closing day;
Since she can mimic not his lips, more dear
Than those for whose disdain she pined away
Into a shadow of all sounds:—a drear
Murmur between their songs, is all the woodmen hear.

Grief made the young Spring wild, and she threw down
Her kindling buds, as if she Autumn were,
Or they dead leaves; since her delight is flown,
For whom should she have waked the sullen year?
To Phœbus was not Hyacinth so dear,
Nor to himself Narcissus, as to both
Thou, Adonais; wan they stand and sere,
Amid the faint companions of their youth,
With dew all turned to tears, odor to sighing ruth.

Thy spirit's sister, the lorn nightingale,
Mourns not her mate with such melodious pain;
Not so the eagle, who like thee could scale
Heaven, and could nourish in the sun's domain
Her mighty youth with morning, doth complain,
Soaring and screaming round her empty nest,
As Albion wails for thee; the curse of Cain
Light on his head who pierced thy innocent breast,
And scared the angel soul that was its earthly guest!

Ah, woe is me! Winter is come and gone,
But grief returns with the revolving year;
The airs and streams renew their joyous tone;
The ants, the bees, the swallows, re-appear;
Fresh leaves and flowers deck the dead Seasons' bier;
The amorous birds now pair in every brake,
And build their mossy homes in field and brere;
And the green lizard and the golden snake,
Like unimprisoned flames, out of their trance awake.

Through wood and stream and field and hill and ocean
A quickening life from the Earth's heart has burst,
As it has ever done with change and motion,
From the great morning of the world, when first
God dawned on Chaos; in its stream immersed,
The lamps of Heaven flash with a softer light;
All baser things pant with life's sacred thirst,
Diffuse themselves, and spend in love's delight
The beauty and the joy of their renewed might.

The leprous corpse, touched by this spirit tender,
Exhales itself in flowers of gentle breath;
Like incarnations of the stars, when splendor
Is changed to fragrance, they illumine death,
And mock the merry worm that wakes beneath;
Nought we know dies. Shall that alone which knows
Be as a sword consumed before the sheath
By sightless lightning? th' intense atom glows
A moment, then is quenched in a most cold repose.

Alas! that all we loved of him should be,
But for our grief, as if it had not been,
And grief itself be mortal! Woe is me!
Whence are we, and why are we? of what scene
The actors or spectators? Great and mean
Meet massed in death, who lends what life must borrow.
As long as skies are blue, and fields are green,
Evening must usher night, night urge the morrow,
Month follow month with woe, and year wake year to sorrow.

He will awake no more, oh, never more!
"Wake thou," cried Misery, "childless Mother, rise
Out of thy sleep, and slake, in thy heart's core,
A wound more fierce than his with tears and sighs."
And all the Dreams that watched Urania's eyes,
And all the Echoes whom their sister's song
Had held in holy silence, cried: "Arise!"
Swift as a Thought by the snake Memory stung,
From her ambrosial rest the fading Splendor sprung.

She rose like an autumnal Night that springs
Out of the East, and follows wild and drear
The golden Day, which, on eternal wings,
Even as a ghost abandoning a bier,
Has left the Earth a corpse. Sorrow and fear
So struck, so roused, so rapt Urania,
So saddened round her like an atmosphere
Of stormy mist, so swept her on her way,
Even to the mournful place where Adonais lay.

Out of her secret Paradise she sped,
Through camps and cities rough with stone and steel,
And human hearts, which to her aery tread
Yielding not, wounded the invisible
Palms of her tender feet where'er they fell;
And barbed tongues, and thoughts more sharp than they,
Rent the soft Form they never could repel,
Whose sacred blood, like the young tears of May,
Paved with eternal flowers that undeserving way.

In the death-chamber for a moment, Death,
Shamed by the presence of that living Might,
Blushed to annihilation, and the breath
Revisited those lips, and life's pale light
Flashed through those limbs, so late her dear delight.
"Leave me not wild and drear and comfortless,
As silent lightning leaves the starless night!
Leave me not!" cried Urania: her distress
Roused Death; Death rose and smiled, and met her vain caress.

"Stay yet awhile! speak to me once again;
Kiss me, so long but as a kiss may live;
And in my heartless breast and burning brain
That word, that kiss shall all thoughts else survive,
With food of saddest memory kept alive,
Now thou art dead, as if it were a part
Of thee, my Adonais! I will give
All that I am to be as thou now art!
But I am chained to Time, and cannot thence depart!

"O gentle child, beautiful as thou wert,
Why didst thou leave the trodden paths of men
Too soon, and with weak hands, though mighty heart,
Dare the unpastured dragon in his den?
Defenceless as thou wert, oh! where was then
Wisdom the mirrored shield, or scorn the spear?
Or hadst thou waited the full cycle, when
Thy spirit should have filled its crescent sphere,
The monsters of life's waste had fled from thee like deer.

"The herded wolves, bold only to pursue,
The obscene ravens clamorous o'er the dead,
The vultures, to the conqueror's banner true,
Who feed where Desolation first has fed,
And whose wings rain contagion,—how they fled,
When, like Apollo, from his golden bow,
The Pythan of the age one arrow sped
And smiled!—The spoilers tempt no second blow;
They fawn on the proud feet that spurn them lying low.

"The sun comes forth, and many reptiles spawn;
He sets, and each ephemeral insect then
Is gathered into death without a dawn,
And the immortal stars awake again;
So it is in the world of living men;
A god-like mind soars forth in its delight,
Making earth bare and veiling Heaven, and when
It sinks, the swarms that dimmed or shared its light,
Leave to its kindred lamps the spirit's awful night."

Thus ceased she; and the mountain shepherds came,
Their garlands sere, their magic mantles rent;
The Pilgrim of Eternity, whose fame
Over his living head like Heaven is bent,
An early but enduring monument,
Came, veiling all the lightnings of his song
In sorrow; from her wilds Ierne sent
The sweetest lyrist of her saddest wrong,
And love taught grief to fall like music from his tongue.

'Midst others of less note, came one frail Form,
A phantom among men, companionless
As the last cloud of an expiring storm,
Whose thunder is its knell; he, as I guess,
Had gazed on nature's naked loveliness,
Actæon-like, and now he fled astray
With feeble steps o'er the world's wilderness,
And his own thoughts, along that rugged way,
Pursued, like raging hounds, their father and their prey.

A pard-like Spirit, beautiful and swift—
A love in desolation masked—a Power
Girt round with weakness—it can scarce uplift
The weight of the superincumbent hour;
It is a dying lamp, a falling shower,
A breaking billow;—even whilst we speak
Is it not broken? On the withering flower
The killing sun smiles brightly; on a cheek
The life can burn in blood, even while the heart may break.

His head was bound with pansies over-blown,
And faded violets, white, and pied, and blue;
And a light spear topped with a cypress cone,
Round whose rude shaft dark ivy tresses grew
Yet dripping with the forest's noon-day dew,
Vibrated as the ever-beating heart
Shook the weak hand that grasped it; of that crew
He came the last, neglected and apart;
A herd-abandoned deer, struck by the hunter's dart.

All stood aloof, and at his partial moan
Smiled through their tears; well knew that gentle band
Who in another's fate now wept his own;
As in the accents of an unknown land
He sang new sorrow; sad Urania scanned
The Stranger's mien, and murmured: "Who art thou?"
He answered not, but with a sudden hand
Made bare his branded and ensanguined brow,
Which was like Cain's or Christ's. Oh! that it should be so!

What softer voice is hushed over the dead?
Athwart what brow is that dark mantle thrown?
What form leans sadly o'er the white death-bed,
In mockery of monumental stone,
The heavy heart heaving without a moan?
If it be he who, gentlest of the wise,
Taught, soothed, loved, honored the departed one;
Let me not vex, with inharmonious sighs,
The silence of that heart's accepted sacrifice.

Our Adonais has drunk poison—oh!
What deaf and viperous murderer could crown
Life's early cup with such a draught of woe?
The nameless worm would now itself disown;
It felt, yet could escape the magic tone
Whose prelude held all envy, hate, and wrong,
But what was howling in one breast alone,
Silent with expectation of the song,
Whose master's hand is cold, whose silver lyre unstrung.

Live thou, whose infamy is not thy fame!
Live! fear no heavier chastisement from me,
Thou noteless blot on a remembered name!
But be thyself, and know thyself to be!
And ever at thy season be thou free
To spill the venom when thy fangs o'erflow;
Remorse and Self-contempt shall cling to thee;
Hot Shame shall burn upon thy secret brow,
And like a beaten hound tremble thou shalt—as now.

Nor let us weep that our delight is fled
For from these carrion-kites that scream below;
He wakes or sleeps with the enduring dead;
Thou canst not soar where he is sitting now.
Dust to the dust! but the pure spirit shall flow
Back to the burning fountain whence it came,
A portion of the Eternal, which must glow
Through time and change, unquenchably the same,
Whilst thy cold embers choke the sordid hearth of shame.

Peace, peace! he is not dead, he doth not sleep—
He hath awakened from the dream of life—
'Tis we, who, lost in stormy visions, keep
With phantoms an unprofitable strife,
And in mad trance strike with our spirit's knife
Invulnerable nothings—*We* decay
Like corpses in a charnel; fear and grief
Convulse us and consume us day by day,
And cold hopes swarm like worms within our living clay.

He has out-soared the shadow of our night;
Envy and calumny, and hate and pain,
And that unrest which men miscall delight,
Can touch him not, and torture not again;
From the contagion of the world's slow stain
He is secure, and now can never mourn
A heart grown cold, a head grown grey in vain;
Nor when the spirit's self has ceased to burn,
With sparkless ashes load an unlamented urn!

He lives, he wakes—'tis Death is dead, not he;
Mourn not for Adonais.—Thou young Dawn,
Turn all thy dew to splendor, for from thee
The spirit thou lamentest is not gone;
Ye caverns and ye forests, cease to moan!
Cease, ye faint flowers and fountains, and thou Air,
Which like a mourning veil thy scarf hadst thrown
O'er the abandoned Earth, now leave it bare
Even to the joyous stars which smile on its despair!

He is made one with Nature: there is heard
His voice in all her music, from the moan
Of thunder to the song of night's sweet bird;
He is a presence to be felt and known
In darkness and in light, from herb and stone,
Spreading itself where'er that Power may move
Which has withdrawn his being to its own;
Which wields the world with never wearied love
Sustains it from beneath, and kindles it above.

He is a portion of the loveliness
Which once he made more lovely: he doth bear
His part, while the one Spirit's plastic stress
Sweeps through the dull dense world, compelling there
All new successions to the forms they wear,
Torturing the unwilling dross that checks its flight
To its own likeness, as each mass may bear;
And bursting in its beauty and its might
From trees and beasts and men into the Heaven's light.

The splendors of the firmament of time
May be eclipsed, but are extinguished not;
Like stars to their appointed height they climb,
And death is a low mist which cannot blot
The brightness it may veil. When lofty thought
Lifts a young heart above its mortal lair,
And love and life contend in it, for what
Shall be its earthly doom, the dead live there,
And move like wings of light on dark and stormy air.

The inheritors of unfulfilled renown
Rose from their thrones, built beyond mortal thought
Far in the Unapparent. Chatterton
Rose pale, his solemn agony had not
Yet faded from him; Sidney, as he fought
And as he fell, and as he lived and loved,
Sublimely mild, a Spirit without spot,
Arose; and Lucan by his death approved;
Oblivion as they rose shrank like a thing reproved.

And many more, whose names on Earth are dark,
But whose transmitted effluence cannot die
So long as fire outlives the parent spark,
Rose, robed in dazzling immortality.
"Thou art become as one of us," they cry;
"It was for thee yon kingless sphere has long
Swung blind in unascended majesty,
Silent alone amid a Heaven of song.
Assume thy winged throne, thou Vesper of our throng!"

Who mourns for Adonais? oh, come forth,
Fond wretch! and know thyself and him aright.
Clasp with thy panting soul the pendulous Earth;
As from a centre, dart thy spirit's light
Beyond all worlds, until its spacious might
Satiate the void circumference: then shrink
Even to a point within our day and night;
And keep thy heart light, lest it make thee sink
When hope has kindled hope, and lured thee to the brink.

Or go to Rome, which is the sepulchre,
Oh, not of him, but of our joy: 'tis nought
That ages, empires, and religions, there
Lie buried in the ravage they have wrought;
For such as he can lend,—they borrow not
Glory from those who made the world their prey;
And he is gathered to the kings of thought
Who waged contention with their time's decay,
And of the past are all that cannot pass away.

Go thou to Rome,—at once the Paradise,
The grave, the city, and the wilderness;
And where its wrecks like shattered mountains rise,
And flowering weeds and fragrant copses dress
The bones of Desolation's nakedness,
Pass, till the Spirit of the spot shall lead
Thy footsteps to a slope of green access,
Where, like an infant's smile, over the dead
A light of laughing flowers along the grass is spread.

And grey walls moulder round on which dull Time
Feeds, like slow fire upon a hoary brand:
And one keen pyramid with wedge sublime,
Pavilioning the dust of him who planned
This refuge for his memory, doth stand
Like flame transformed to marble; and beneath
A field is spread on which a newer band
Have pitched in Heaven's smile their camp of death,
Welcoming him we lose with scarce extinguished breath.

Here pause: these graves are all too young as yet
To have outgrown the sorrow which consigned
Its charge to each: and if the seal is set,
Here, on one fountain of a mourning mind,
Break it not thou! too surely shalt thou find
Thine own well full, if thou returnest home,
Of tears and gall. From the world's bitter wind
Seek shelter in the shadow of the tomb.
What Adonais is, why fear we to become?

The One remains, the many change and pass;
Heaven's light for ever shines, Earth's shadows fly;
Life, like a dome of many colored glass,
Stains the white radiance of Eternity,
Until Death tramples it to fragments.—Die,
If thou wouldst be with that which thou dost seek!
Follow where all is fled!—Rome's azure sky,
Flowers, ruins, statutes, music, words are weak
The glory they transfuse with fitting truth to speak.

Why linger, why turn back, why shrink, my Heart?
Thy hopes are gone before: from all things here
They have departed; thou shouldst now depart!
A light is passed from the revolving year,
And man, and woman; and what still is dear
Attracts to crush, repels to make thee wither.
The soft sky smiles,—the low wind whispers near:
'Tis Adonais calls! oh, hasten thither,
No more let Life divide what Death can join together.

That Light whose smile kindles the Universe,
That Beauty in which all things work and move,
That Benediction which the eclipsing curse
Of birth can quench not, that sustaining Love
Which, through the web of being blindly wove
By man and beast and earth and air and sea,
Burns bright or dim, as each are mirrors of
The fire for which all thirst, now beams on me,
Consuming the last clouds of cold mortality.

The breath whose might I have invoked in song
Descends on me; my spirit's bark is driven
Far from the shore, far from the trembling throng
Whose sails were never to the tempest given;
The massy earth and sphered skies are riven!
I am borne darkly, fearfully afar,
Whilst, burning through the inmost veil of Heaven,
The soul of Adonais, like a star,
Beacons from the abode where the Eternal are.

PERCY BYSSHE SHELLEY

WILLIAM WORDSWORTH

ROBERT SOUTHEY

AFTER BLENHEIM

It was a summer evening,
　Old Kaspar's work was done,
And he before his cottage door
　Was sitting in the sun;
And by him sported on the green
His little grandchild Wilhelmine.

She saw her brother Peterkin
　Roll something large and round
Which he beside the rivulet
　In playing there had found;
He came to ask what he had found
That was so large and smooth and round.

Old Kaspar took it from the boy
　Who stood expectant by;
And then the old man shook his head,
　And with a natural sigh
' 'Tis some poor fellow's skull,' said he,
'Who fell in the great victory.

'I find them in the garden,
　For there's many here about;
And often when I go to plough
　The ploughshare turns them out.
For many thousand men,' said he,
'Were slain in that great victory.'

'Now tell us what 'twas all about,'
　Young Peterkin he cries;
And little Wilhelmine looks up
　With wonder-waiting eyes;
'Now tell us all about the war,
And what they fought each other for.'

'It was the English,' Kaspar cried,
   'Who put the French to rout;
But what they fought each other for
   I could not well make out.
But everybody said,' quoth he,
'That 'twas a famous victory.

'My father lived at Blenheim then,
   Yon little stream hard by;
They burnt his dwelling to the ground,
   And he was forced to fly:
So with his wife and child he fled,
Nor had he where to rest his head.

'With fire and sword the country round
   Was wasted far and wide
And many a childing mother then
   And newborn baby died:
But things like that, you know, must be
At every famous victory.

'They say it was a shocking sight
   After the field was won;
For many thousand bodies here
   Lay rotting in the sun:
But things like that, you know, must be
After a famous victory.

'Great praise the Duke of Marlbro' won
   And our good Prince Eugene;'
'Why 'twas a very wicked thing!'
   Said little Wilhelmine;
'Nay .. nay .. my little girl,' quoth he,
'It was a famous victory.

'And everybody praised the Duke
   Who this great fight did win.'
'But what good came of it at last?
   Quoth little Peterkin:—
'Why that I cannot tell,' said he,
'But 'twas a famous victory.'

EDMUND SPENSER

PROTHALAMION

Calm was the day, and through the trembling air
Sweet-breathing Zephyrus did softly play—
A gentle spirit, that lightly did delay
Hot Titan's beams, which then did glister fair;
When I, (whom sullen care,
Through discontent of my long fruitless stay
In princes' court, and expectation vain
Of idle hopes, which still do fly away
Like empty shadows, did afflict my brain)
Walk'd forth to ease my pain
Along the shore of silver-streaming Thames;
Whose rutty bank, the which his river hems,
Was painted all with variable flowers,
And all the meads adorn'd with dainty gems
Fit to deck maidens' bowers,
And crown their paramours
Against the bridal day, which is not long:
   Sweet Thames! run softly, till I end my song.

There in a meadow by the river's side
A flock of nymphs I chancèd to espy,
All lovely daughters of the flood thereby,
With goodly greenish locks all loose untied
As each had been a bride;
And each one had a little wicker basket
Made of fine twigs, entrailèd curiously.
In which they gather'd flowers to fill their flasket,
And with fine fingers cropt full feateously
The tender stalks on high.
Of every sort which in that meadow grew
They gather'd some; the violet, pallid blue
The little daisy that at evening closes,
The virgin lily and the primrose true,
With store of vermeil roses,
To deck their bridegrooms' posies
Against the bridal day, which was not long:
   Sweet Thames! run softly, till I end my song.

With that I saw two Swans of goodly hue
Come softly swimming down along the Lee;
Two fairer birds I yet did never see;
The snow which doth the top of Pindus strow
Did never whiter show,
Nor Jove himself, when he a swan would be
For love of Leda, whiter did appear;
Yet Leda was (they say) as white as he,
Yet not so white as these, nor nothing near;
So purely white they were
That even the gentle stream, the which them bare,
Seem'd foul to them, and bade his billows spare
To wet their silken feathers, lest they might
Soil their fair plumes with water not so fair,
And mar their beauties bright
That shone as Heaven's light
Against their bridal day, which was not long:
    Sweet Thames! run softly, till I end my song.

Eftsoons the nymphs, which now had flowers their fill,
Ran all in haste to see that silver brood
As they came floating on the crystal flood;
Whom when they saw, they stood amazéd still
Their wondering eyes to fill;
Them seem'd they never saw a sight so fair
Of fowls, so lovely, that they sure did deem
Them heavenly born, or to be that same pair
Which through the sky draw Venus' silver team;
For sure they did not seem
To be begot of any earthly seed,
But rather Angels, or of Angels' breed;
Yet were they bred of summer's heat, they say,
In sweetest season, when each flower and weed
The earth did fresh array;
So fresh they seem'd as day,
Ev'n as their bridal day, which was not long:
    Sweet Thames! run softly, till I end my song.

Then forth they all out of their baskets drew
Great store of flowers, the honour of the field,
That to the sense did fragrant odours yield,

All which upon those goodly birds they threw
And all the waves did strew,
That like old Peneus' waters they did seem
When down along by pleasant Tempe's shore
Scatter'd with flowers, through Thessaly they stream,
That they appear, through lilies' plenteous store,
Like a bride's chamber-floor.
Two of those nymphs meanwhile two garlands bound
Of freshest flowers which in that mead they found,
The which presenting all in trim array,
Their snowy foreheads therewithal they crown'd;
Whilst one did sing this lay
Prepared against that day,
Against their bridal day, which was not long:
    Sweet Thames! run softly, till I end my song.

'Ye gentle birds! the world's fair ornament,
And Heaven's glory, whom this happy hour
Doth lead unto your lovers' blissful bower,
Joy may you have, and gentle heart's content
Of your love's couplement;
And let fair Venus, that is queen of love,
With her heart-quelling son upon you smile,
Whose smile, they say, hath virtue to remove
All love's dislike, and friendship's faulty guile
For ever to assoil.
Let endless peace your steadfast hearts accord,
And blessèd plenty wait upon your board;
And let your bed with pleasures chaste abound,
That fruitful issue may to you afford
Which may your foes confound,
And make your joys redound
Upon your bridal day, which is not long:
    Sweet Thames! run softly, till I end my song.'

So ended she; and all the rest around
To her redoubled that her undersong,
Which said their bridal day should not be long:
And gentle Echo from the neighbour ground
Their accents did resound.

So forth those joyous birds did pass along
Adown the Lee that to them murmur'd low,
As he would speak but that he lack'd a tongue;
Yet did by signs his glad affection show,
Making his stream run slow.
And all the fowl which in his flood did dwell
'Gan flock about these twain, that did excel
The rest, so far as Cynthia doth shend
The lesser stars. So they, enrangèd well,
Did on those two attend,
And their best service lend
Against their wedding day, which was not long:
   Sweet Thames! run softly, till I end my song.

At length they all to merry London came,
To merry London, my most kindly nurse,
That to me gave this life's first native source,
Though from another place I take my name,
An house of ancient fame:
There when they came whereas those bricky towers
The which on Thames' broad agèd back do ride,
Where now the studious lawyers have their bowers,
There whilome wont the Templar-knights to bide,
Till they decay'd through pride;
Next whereunto there stands a stately place,
Where oft I gainéd gifts and goodly grace
Of that great lord, which therein wont to dwell,
Whose want too well now feels my friendless case;
But ah! here fits not well
Old woes, but joys to tell
Against the bridal day, which is not long:
   Sweet Thames! run softly, till I end my song.

Yet therein now doth lodge a noble peer,
Great England's glory and the world's wide wonder,
Whose dreadful name late through all Spain did thunder,
And Hercules' two pillars standing near
Did make to quake and fear:
Fair branch of honour, flower of chivalry!
That fillest England with thy triumphs' fame

Joy have thou of thy noble victory,
And endless happiness of thine own name
That promiseth the same;
That through thy prowess and victorious arms
Thy country may be freed from foreign harms,
And great Elisa's glorious name may ring
Through all the world, fill'd with thy wide alarms,
Which some brave Muse may sing
To ages following:
Upon the bridal day, which is not long:
  Sweet Thames! run softly, till I end my song.

From those high towers this noble lord issuing
Like radiant Hesper, when his golden hair
In th' ocean billows he hath bathèd fair,
Descended to the river's open viewing
With a great train ensuing.
Above the rest were goodly to be seen
Two gentle knights of lovely face and feature,
Beseeming well the bower of any queen,
With gifts of wit and ornaments of nature,
Fit for so goodly stature,
That like the twins of Jove they seem'd in sight
Which deck the baldric of the Heavens bright;
They two, forth pacing to the river's side,
Received those two fair brides, their love's delight:
Which, at th' appointed tide,
Each one did make his bride
Against their bridal day, which is not long:
  Sweet Thames! run softly, till I end my song.

ALGERNON CHARLES SWINBURNE

SPRING

WHEN the hounds of spring are on winter's traces,
  The mother of months in meadow or plain
Fills the shadows and windy places
  With lisp of leaves and ripple of rain;

And the brown bright nightingale amorous
Is half assuaged for Itylus,
For the Thracian ships and the foreign faces,
    The tongueless vigil, and all the pain.

Come with bows bent and with emptying of quivers,
    Maiden most perfect, lady of light,
With a noise of winds and many rivers,
    With a clamor of waters, and with might;
Bind on thy sandals, O thou most fleet,
Over the splendor and speed of thy feet!
For the faint east quickens, the wan west shivers,
    Round the feet of the day and the feet of the night.

Where shall we find her, how shall we sing to her,
    Fold our hands round her knees and cling?
O that man's heart were as fire and could spring to her,
    Fire, or the strength of the streams that spring!
For the stars and the winds are unto her
As raiment, as songs of the harp-player;
For the risen stars and the fallen cling to her,
    And the southwest-wind and the west-wind sing.

For winter's rains and ruins are over,
    And all the season of snows and sins;
The days dividing lover and lover,
    The light that loses, the night that wins;
And time remembered is grief forgotten,
And frosts are slain and flowers begotten,
And in green underwood and cover
    Blossom by blossom the spring begins.

The full streams feed on flower of rushes,
    Ripe grasses trammel a traveling foot,
The faint fresh flame of the young year flushes
    From leaf to flower and flower to fruit;
And fruit and leaf are as gold and fire,
And the oat is heard above the lyre,
And the hoofèd heel of a satyr crushes
    The chestnut-husk at the chestnut-root.

And Pan by noon and Bacchus by night,
  Fleeter of foot than the fleet-foot kid,
Follow with dancing and fill with delight
  The Mænad and the Bassarid;
And soft as lips that laugh and hide,
The laughing leaves of the trees divide,
And screen from seeing and leave in sight
  The god pursuing, the maiden hid.

The ivy falls with the Bacchanal's hair
  Over her eyebrows shading her eyes;
The wild vine slipping down leaves bare
  Her bright breast shortening into sighs;
The wild vine slips with the weight of its leaves,
But the berried ivy catches and cleaves
To the limbs that glitter, the feet that scare,
  The wolf that follows, the fawn that flies.

BAYARD TAYLOR

A SONG OF THE CAMP

"Give us a song!" the soldiers cried,
  The outer trenches guarding,
When the heated guns of the camp allied
  Grew weary of bombarding.

The dark Redan, in silent scoff,
  Lay grim and threatening under;
And the tawny mound of the Malakoff
  No longer belched its thunder.

There was a pause. A guardsman said:
  "We storm the forts to-morrow;
Sing while we may, another day
  Will bring enough of sorrow."

They lay along the battery's side,
  Below the smoking cannon;
Brave hearts from Severn and from Clyde,
  And from the banks of Shannon.

They sang of love, and not of fame;
  Forgot was Britain's glory;
Each heart recalled a different name,
  But all sang "Annie Laurie."

Voice after voice caught up the song,
  Until its tender passion
Rose like an anthem, rich and strong,—
  Their battle-eve confession.

Dear girl, her name he dared not speak,
  But, as the song grew louder,
Something upon the soldier's cheek
  Washed off the stains of powder.

Beyond the darkening ocean burned
  The bloody sunset's embers,
While the Crimean valleys learned
  How English love remembers.

And once again a fire of hell
  Rained on the Russian quarters,
With scream of shot and burst of shell,
  And bellowing of the mortars!

And Irish Nora's eyes are dim
  For a singer dumb and gory;
And English Mary mourns for him
  Who sang of "Annie Laurie."

Sleep, soldiers! still in honored rest
  Your truth and valor wearing;
The bravest are the tenderest,—
  The loving are the daring.

ALFRED TENNYSON

LOCKSLEY HALL

COMRADES, leave me here a little, while as yet 'tis early morn:
Leave me here, and when you want me, sound upon the bugle horn.

'Tis the place, and all around it, as of old, the curlews call,
Dreary gleams about the moorland flying over Locksley Hall;

Locksley Hall, that in the distance overlooks the sandy tracts,
And the hollow ocean-ridges roaring into cataracts.

Many a night from yonder ivied casement, ere I went to rest,
Did I look on great Orion sloping slowly to the West.

Many a night I saw the Pleiads, rising through the mellow shade,
Glitter like a swarm of fire-flies tangled in a silver braid.

Here about the beach I wandered, nourishing a youth sublime
With the fairy tales of science, and the long result of time;

When the centuries behind me like a fruitful land reposed;
When I clung to all the present for the promise that it closed:

When I dipt into the future far as human eye could see;
Saw the Vision of the world, and all wonder that would be.——

In the Spring a fuller crimson comes upon the robin's breast;
In the Spring the wanton lapwing gets himself another crest;

In the Spring a livelier iris changes on the burnished dove;
In the Spring a young man's fancy lightly turns to thoughts of love.

Then her cheek was pale and thinner than should be for one so young,
And her eyes on all my motions with a mute observance hung.

And I said, "My cousin Amy, speak, and speak the truth to me;
Trust me, cousin, all the current of my being sets to thee."

On her pallid cheek and forehead came a color and a light,
As I have seen the rosy red flushing in the northern night.

And she turned—her bosom shaken with a sudden storm of sighs—
All the spirit deeply dawning in the dark of hazel eyes—

Saying, "I have hid my feelings, fearing they should do me wrong;"
Saying, "Dost thou love me, cousin?" weeping, "I have loved thee
    long."

Love took up the glass of Time, and turned it in his glowing hands;
Every moment, lightly shaken, ran itself in golden sands.

Love took up the harp of Life, and smote on all the chords with might;
Smote the chord of Self, that, trembling, passed in music out of sight.

Many a morning on the moorland did we hear the copses ring,
And her whisper thronged my pulses with the fullness of the Spring.

Many an evening by the waters did we watch the stately ships,
And our spirits rushed together at the touching of the lips.

O my cousin, shallow-hearted! O my Amy, mine no more!
O the dreary, dreary moorland! O the barren, barren shore!

Falser than all fancy fathoms, falser than all songs have sung,
Puppet to a father's threat, and servile to a shrewish tongue!

Is it well to wish thee happy?—having known me—to decline
On a range of lower feelings and a narrower heart than mine!

Yet it shall be: thou shalt lower to his level day by day,
What is fine within thee growing coarse to sympathize with clay.

As the husband is, the wife is; thou art mated with a clown,
And the grossness of his nature will have weight to drag thee down.

He will hold thee, when his passion shall have spent its novel force,
Something better than his dog, a little dearer than his horse.

What is this? his eyes are heavy—think not they are glazed with wine.
Go to him; it is thy duty—kiss him: take his hand in thine.

It may be my lord is weary, that his brain is overwrought—
Soothe him with thy finer fancies, touch him with thy lighter thought.

He will answer to the purpose, easy things to understand—
Better thou wert dead before me, though I slew thee with my hand!

Better thou and I were lying, hidden from the heart's disgrace,
Rolled in one another's arms, and silent in a last embrace.

Cursed be the social wants that sin against the strength of youth!
Cursed be the social lies that warp us from the living truth!

Cursed be the sickly forms that err from honest Nature's rule!
Cursed be the gold that gilds the straightened forehead of the fool!

Well—'tis well that I should bluster!—Hadst thou less unworthy
     proved—
Would to God—for I had loved thee more than ever wife was loved.

Am I mad, that I should cherish that which bears but bitter fruit?
I will pluck it from my bosom, though my heart be at the root!

Never! though my mortal summers to such length of years should
     come
As the many-wintered crow that leads the clanging rookery home.

Where is comfort? in division of the records of the mind?
Can I part her from herself, and love her, as I knew her, kind?

I remember one that perished; sweetly did she speak and move;
Such a one do I remember, whom to look at was to love.

Can I think of her as dead, and love her for the love she bore?
No—she never loved me truly: love is love for evermore.

Comfort? comfort scorned of devils! this is truth the poet sings,
That a sorrow's crown of sorrow is remembering happier things.

Drug thy memories, lest thou learn it, lest thy heart be put to proof,
In the dead unhappy night, and when the rain is on the roof.

Like a dog he hunts in dreams, and thou art staring at the wall,
Where the dying night-lamp flickers, and the shadows rise and fall.

Then a hand shall pass before thee, pointing to his drunken sleep,
To thy widowed marriage-pillows, to the tears that thou wilt weep.

Thou shalt hear the "Never, never," whispered by the phantom years,
And a song from out the distance in the ringing of thine ears;

And an eye shall vex thee, looking ancient kindness on thy pain,
Turn thee, turn thee on thy pillow: get thee to thy rest again.

Nay, but Nature brings thee solace; for a tender voice will cry.
'Tis a purer life than thine; a lip to drain thy trouble dry.

Baby lips will laugh me down: my latest rival brings thee rest—
Baby fingers, waxen touches, press me from the mother's breast.

O, the child too clothes the father with a dearness not his due:
Half is thine and half is his—it will be worthy of the two.

O, I see thee old and formal, fitted to thy petty part,
With a little hoard of maxims preaching down a daughter's heart.

"They were dangerous guides, the feelings—she herself was not ex-
    empt—
Truly, she herself had suffered"—Perish in thy self-contempt!

Overlive it—lower yet—be happy wherefore should I care?
I must mix myself with action, lest I wither by despair.

What is that which I should turn to, lighting upon days like these?
Every door is barred with gold, and opens but to golden keys.

Every gate is thronged with suitors, all the markets overflow.
I have but an angry fancy: what is that which I should do?

I had been content to perish, falling on the foeman's ground,
When the ranks are rolled in vapor, and the winds are laid with
    sound:—

But the jingling of the guinea helps the hurt that Honor feels,
And the nations do but murmur, snarling at each other's heels.

Can I but relive in sadness? I will turn that earlier page.
Hide me from my deep emotion, O thou wondrous Mother-Age!

Make me feel the wild pulsation that I felt before the strife,
When I heard my days before me, and the tumult of my life;

Yearning for the large excitement that the coming years would yield,
Eager-hearted as a boy when first he leaves his father's field,

And at night along the dusky highway near and nearer drawn;
Sees in heaven the light of London flaring like a dreary dawn;

And his spirit leaps within him to be gone before him then,
Underneath the light he looks at, in among the throngs of men:—

Men, my brothers, men the workers, ever reaping something new;
That which they have done but earnest of the things that they shall do:

For I dipt into the future, far as human eye could see,
Saw the Vision of the world, and all the wonder that would be;

Saw the heavens fill with commerce, argosies of magic sails,
Pilots of the purple twilight, dropping down with costly bales;

Heard the heavens fill with shouting, and there rained a ghastly dew
From the nations' airy navies grappling in the central blue;

Far along the world-wide whisper of the south-wind rushing warm,
With the standards of the peoples plunging through the thunder-
    storm;

Till the war-drum throbbed no longer, and the battle-flags were
    furled
In the Parliament of man, the Federation of the world.

There the common sense of most shall hold a fretful realm in awe,
And the kindly earth shall slumber, lapt in universal law.

So I triumphed, ere my passion sweeping through me left me dry,
Left me with the palsied heart, and left me with the jaundiced eye;

Eye to which all order festers, all things here are out of joint.
Science moves, but slowly, slowly, creeping on from point to point:

Slowly comes a hungry people, as a lion, creeping nigher,
Glares at one that nods and winks behind a slowly-dying fire.

Yet I doubt not through the ages one increasing purpose runs,
And the thoughts of men are widened with the process of the suns.

What is that to him that reaps not harvest of his youthful joys,
Though the deep heart of existence beat forever like a boy's?

Knowledge comes, but wisdom lingers; and I linger on the shore,
And the individual withers, and the world is more and more:

Knowledge comes, but wisdom lingers, and he bears a laden breast,
Full of sad experience, moving toward the stillness of his rest.

Hark! my merry comrades call me, sounding on the bugle-horn,
They to whom my foolish passion were a target for their scorn:

Shall it not be scorn to me to harp on such a mouldered string?
I am shamed through all my nature to have loved so slight a thing.

Weakness to be wroth with weakness! woman's pleasure, woman's
    pain—
Nature made them blinder motions bounded in a shallower brain:

Woman is the lesser man, and all thy passions, matched with mine,
Are as moonlight unto sunlight, and as water unto wine—

Here at least, where nature sickens, nothing. Ah, for some retreat
Deep in yonder shining Orient, where my life began to beat;

Where in wild Mahratta-battle fell my father evil-starred;
I was left a trampled orphan, and a selfish uncle's ward.

Or to burst all links of habit—there to wander far away,
On from island unto island at the gateways of the day.

Larger constellations burning, mellow moons and happy skies,
Breadths of tropic shade and palms in cluster, knots of Paradise.

Never comes the trader, never floats an European flag,
Slides the bird o'er lustrous woodland, droops the trailer from the
    crag;

Droops the heavy-blossomed bower, hangs the heavy-fruited tree—
Summer isles of Eden lying in dark-purple spheres of sea.

There methinks would be enjoyment more than in this march of
    mind,
In the steamship, in the railway, in the thoughts that shake mankind.

There the passions, cramped no longer, shall have scope and breathing-
    space;
I will take some savage woman, she shall rear my dusky race.

Iron-jointed, supple-sinewed, they shall dive, and they shall run,
Catch the wild goat by the hair, and hurl their lances in the sun;

Whistle back the parrot's call, and leap the rainbows of the brooks,
Not with blinded eyesight poring over miserable books.—

Fool, again the dream, the fancy! but I *know* my words are wild,
But I count the gray barbarian lower than the Christian child.

I to herd with narrow foreheads, vacant of our glorious gains,
Like a beast with lower pleasures, like a beast with lower pains!

Mated with a squalid savage—what to me were sun or clime?
I, the heir of all the ages, in the foremost files of time—

I, that rather held it better men should perish one by one,
Than that earth should stand at gaze like Joshua's moon in Ajalon!

Not in vain the distance beacons. Forward, forward let us range;
Let the great world spin forever down the ringing grooves of change.

Through the shadow of the globe we sweep into the younger day:
Better fifty years of Europe than a cycle of Cathay.

Mother-Age (for mine I knew not) help me as when life begun—
Rift the hills, and roll the waters, flash the lightnings, weigh the
    Sun;—

O, I see the crescent promise of my spirit hath not set;
Ancient founts of inspiration well through all my fancy yet.

Howsoever these things be, a long farewell to Locksley Hall!
Now for me the woods may wither, now for me the roof-tree fall.

Comes a vapor from the margin, blackening over heath and holt,
Cramming all the blast before it, in its breast a thunderbolt.

Let it fall on Locksley Hall, with rain or hail, or fire or snow;
For the mighty wind arises, roaring seaward, and I go.

BREAK, BREAK, BREAK

Break, break, break,
    On thy cold gray stones, O sea!
And I would that my tongue could utter
    The thoughts that arise in me.

O well for the fisherman's boy
    That he shouts with his sister at play!
O well for the sailor lad
    That he sings in his boat on the bay!

And the stately ships go on,
    To the haven under the hill;
But O for the touch of a vanished hand,
    And the sound of a voice that is still!

Break, break, break,
    At the foot of thy crags, O sea!
But the tender grace of a day that is dead
    Will never come back to me.

CHARGE OF THE LIGHT BRIGADE

HALF a league, half a league,
Half a league onward,
All in the valley of Death
  Rode the six hundred.
"Forward, the Light Brigade!
Charge for the guns," he said;
Into the valley of Death
  Rode the six hundred.

"Forward, the Light Brigade!"
Was there a man dismayed?
Not though the soldier knew
  Sone one had blundered:
Theirs not to make reply,
Theirs not to reason why,
Theirs but to do and die:
Into the valley of Death
  Rode the six hundred.

Cannon to right of them,
Cannon to left of them,
Cannon in front of them
  Volleyed and thundered;
Stormed at with shot and shell,
Boldly they rode and well;
Into the jaws of Death,
Into the mouth of Hell
  Rode the six hundred.

Flashed all their sabres bare,
Flashed as they turned in air,
Sabering the gunners there,
Charging an army, while
  All the world wondered:
Plunged in the battery-smoke,
Right through the line they broke:
Cossack and Russian
Reeled from the sabre-stroke,
  Shattered and sundered.

Then they rode back, but not,—
Not the six hundred.

Cannon to right of them,
Cannon to left of them,
Cannon behind them
    Volleyed and thundered:
Stormed at with shot and shell,
While horse and hero fell,
They that had fought so well
Came through the jaws of Death
Back from the mouth of Hell,—
All that was left of them,
    Left of six hundred.

When can their glory fade?
O the wild charge they made!
    All the world wondered.
Honor the charge they made!
Honor the Light Brigade,
    Noble six hundred!

FROM IN MEMORIAM

STRONG Son of God, immortal Love,
    Whom we, that have not seen thy face,
    By faith, and faith alone, embrace,
Believing where we cannot prove;

Thine are these orbs of light and shade;
    Thou madest life in man and brute;
    Thou madest Death; and lo, thy foot
Is on the skull which thou hast made.

Thou wilt not leave us in the dust:
    Thou madest man, he knows not why;
    He thinks he was not made to die;
And thou hast made him: thou art just.

Thou seemest human and divine,
  The highest, holiest manhood thou:
  Our wills are ours, we know not how;
Our wills are ours, to make them thine.

Our little systems have their day;
  They have their day and cease to be:
  They are but broken lights of thee,
And thou, O Lord, art more than they.

We have but faith: we cannot know;
  For knowledge is of things we see;
  And yet we trust it comes from thee,
A beam in darkness: let it grow.

Let knowledge grow from more to more,
  But more of reverence in us dwell;
  That mind and soul, according well,
May make one music as before,

But vaster. We are fools and slight;
  We mock thee when we do not fear:
  But help thy foolish ones to bear;
Help thy vain worlds to bear thy light.

Forgive what seemed my sin in me;
  What seemed my worth since I began
  For merit lives from man to man,
And not from man, O Lord, to thee.

Forgive my grief for one removed,
  Thy creature, whom I found so fair,
  I trust he lives in thee, and there
I find him worthier to be loved.

Forgive these wild and wandering cries,
  Confusions of a wasted youth:
  Forgive them where they fail in truth,
And in thy wisdom make me wise.

———

Fair ship, that from the Italian shore
  Sailest the placid ocean-plains
  With my lost Arthur's loved remains,
Spread thy full wings, and waft him o'er.

So draw him home to those that mourn
  In vain; a favorable speed
  Ruffle thy mirrored mast, and lead
Through prosperous floods his holy urn.

All night no ruder air perplex
  Thy sliding keel, till Phosphor, bright
  As our pure love, through early light
Shall glimmer on thy dewy decks.

Sphere all your lights around, above;
  Sleep, gentle heavens, before the prow;
  Sleep, gentle winds, as he sleeps now,
My friend, the brother of my love;

My Arthur, whom I shall not see
  Till all my widowed race be run;
  Dear as the mother to the son,
More than my brothers are to me.

———

I hear the noise about thy keel;
  I hear the bell struck in the night;
  I see the cabin-window bright;
I see the sailor at the wheel.

Thou bring'st the sailor to his wife,
  And travelled men from foreign lands;
  And letters unto trembling hands;
And thy dark freight, a vanished life.

So bring him: we have idle dreams;
  This look of quiet flatters thus
  Our home-bred fancies: O to us,
The fools of habit, sweeter seems

To rest beneath the clover sod,
   That takes the sunshine and the rains,
   Or where the kneeling hamlet drains
The chalice of the grapes of God;

Than if with thee the roaring wells
   Should gulf him fathom-deep in brine;
   And hands so often clasped in mine
Should toss with tangle and with shells.

Calm is the morn, without a sound,
   Calm as to suit a calmer grief,
   And only through the faded leaf
The chestnut pattering to the ground:

Calm and deep peace on this high wold,
   And on these dews that drench the furze,
   And all the silvery gossamers
That twinkle into green and gold:

Calm and still light on yon great plain,
   That sweeps with all its autumn bowers,
   And crowded farms and lessening towers,
To mingle with the bounding main:

Calm and deep peace in this wide air,
   These leaves that redden to the fall;
   And in my heart, if calm at all,
If any calm, a calm despair:

Calm on the seas, and silver sleep,
   And waves that sway themselves in rest,
   And dead calm in that noble breast
Which heaves but with the heaving deep.

Thou comest, much wept for; such a breeze
   Compelled thy canvas, and my prayer
   Was as the whisper of an air
To breathe thee over lonely seas.

For I in spirit saw thee move
  Through circles of the bounding sky,
  Week after week: the days go by:
Come quick, thou bringest all I love.

Henceforth, wherever thou may'st roam,
  My blessing, like a line of light,
  Is on the waters day and night,
And like a beacon guards thee home.

So may whatever tempest mars
  Mid-ocean spare thee, sacred bark;
  And balmy drops in summer dark
Slide from the bosom of the stars.

So kind an office hath been done,
  Such precious relics brought by thee;
  The dust of him I shall not see
Till all my widowed race be run.

———

The path by which we twain did go,
  Which led by tracts that pleased us well,
  Through four sweet years arose and fell,
From flower to flower, from snow to snow:

And we with singing cheered the way,
  And crowned with all the season lent,
  From April on to April went,
And glad at heart from May to May;

But where the path we walked began
  To slant the fifth autumnal slope,
  As we descended, following Hope,
There sat the Shadow feared of man;

Who broke our fair companionship,
  And spread his mantle dark and cold,
  And wrapt thee formless in the fold,
And dulled the murmur on thy lip,

And bore thee where I could not see
  Nor follow, though I walk in haste,
  And think that somewhere in the waste
The Shadow sits and waits for me.

————

Now, sometimes in my sorrow shut,
  Or breaking into song by fits,
  Alone, alone, to where he sits,
The Shadow cloaked from head to foot,

Who keeps the keys of all the creeds,
  I wander, often falling lame,
  And looking back to whence I came,
Or on to where the pathway leads;

And crying, "How changed from where it ran
  Through lands where not a leaf was dumb;
  But all the lavish hills would hum
The murmur of a happy Pan:

"When each by turns was guide to each,
  And Fancy light from Fancy caught,
  And Thought leapt out to wed with Thought
Ere Thought could wed itself with Speech;

"And all we met was fair and good,
  And all was good that Time could bring,
  And all the secret of the Spring
Moved in the chambers of the blood;

"And many an old philosophy
  On Argive heights divinely sang,
  And round us all the thicket rang
To many a flute of Arcady."

————

O yet we trust that somehow good
  Will be the final goal of ill,
  To pangs of nature, sins of will,
Defects of doubt, and taints of blood:

That nothing walks with aimless feet;
   That not one life shall be destroyed,
   Or cast as rubbish to the void,
When God hath made the pile complete;

That not a worm is cloven in vain;
   That not a moth with vain desire
   Is shriveled in a fruitless fire,
Or but subserves another's gain.

Behold, we know not anything;
   I can but trust that good shall fall
   At last—far off—at last, to all,
And every winter change to spring.

So runs my dream: but what am I?
   An infant crying in the night:
   An infant crying for the light:
And with no language but a cry.

———

The wish, that of the living whole
   No life may fail beyond the grave,
   Derives it not from what we have
The likest God within the soul?

Are God and Nature then at strife,
   That Nature lends such evil dreams?
   So careful of the type she seems,
So careless of the single life;

That I, considering everywhere
   Her secret meaning in her deeds,
   And finding that of fifty seeds
She often brings but one to bear,

I falter where I firmly trod,
   And falling with my weight of cares
   Upon the great world's altar-stairs
That slope through darkness up to God,

I stretch lame hands of faith, and grope,
   And gather dust and chaff, and call
   To what I feel is Lord of all,
And faintly trust the larger hope.

———

"So careful of the type?" but no.
   From scarped cliff and quarried stone
   She cries, "A thousand types are gone:
I care for nothing, all shall go.

"Thou makest thine appeal to me:
   I bring to life, I bring to death:
   The spirit does but mean the breath:
I know no more." And he, shall he,

Man, her last work, who seemed so fair,
   Such splendid purpose in his eyes,
   Who rolled the psalm to wintry skies,
Who built him fanes of fruitless prayer,

Who trusted God was love indeed,
   And love Creation's final law,—
   Though Nature, red in tooth and claw
With ravin, shrieked against his creed,—

Who loved, who suffered countless ills,
   Who battled for the True, the Just,
   Be blown about the desert dust,
Or sealed within the iron hills?

No more? A monster then, a dream,
   A discord. Dragons of the prime,
   That tare each other in their slime,
Were mellow music matched with him.

O life as futile, then, as frail!
   O for thy voice to soothe and bless!
   What hope of answer, or redress?
Behind the veil, behind the veil!

———

Dost thou look back on what hath been,
   As some divinely gifted man,
   Whose life in low estate began
And on a simple village green;

Who breaks his birth's invidious bar,
   And grasps the skirts of happy chance,
   And breasts the blows of circumstance,
And grapples with his evil star:

Who makes by force his merit known,
   And lives to clutch the golden keys,
   To mould a mighty state's decrees,
And shape the whisper of the throne;

And moving up from high to higher,
   Becomes on Fortune's crowning slope
   The pillar of a people's hope,
The centre of a world's desire;

Yet feels, as in a pensive dream,
   When all his active powers are still,
   A distant dearness in the hill,
A secret sweetness in the stream,

The limit of his narrower fate,
   While yet beside its vocal springs
   He played at counsellors and kings,
With one that was his earliest mate;

Who ploughs with pain his native lea
   And reaps the labor of his hands,
   Or in the furrow musing stands:
"Does my old friend remember me?"

———

Dip down upon the northern shore,
   O sweet new year, delaying long:
   Thou dost expectant nature wrong;
Delaying long, delay no more.

What stays thee from the clouded noons,
  Thy sweetness from its proper place?
  Can trouble live with April days,
Or sadness in the summer moons?

Bring orchis, bring the foxglove spire,
  The little speedwell's darling blue,
  Deep tulips dashed with fiery dew,
Laburnums, dropping-wells of fire.

O thou, new year, delaying long,
  Delayest the sorrow in my blood,
  That longs to burst a frozen bud,
And flood a fresher throat with song.

———

Who loves not Knowledge? Who shall rail
  Against her beauty? May she mix
  With men and prosper! Who shall fix
Her pillars? Let her work prevail.

But on her forehead sits a fire:
  She sets her forward countenance,
  And leaps into the future chance,
Submitting all things to desire.

Half-grown as yet, a child, and vain,
  She cannot fight the fear of death.
  What is she, cut from love and faith,
But some wild Pallas from the brain

Of Demons? fiery-hot to burst
  All barriers in her onward race
  For power. Let her know her place;
She is the second, not the first.

A higher hand must make her mild,
  If all be not in vain; and guide
  Her footsteps, moving side by side
With Wisdom, like the younger child:

For she is earthly of the mind,
  But Wisdom heavenly of the soul:
  O friend, who camest to thy goal
So early, leaving me behind,

I would the great world grew like thee,
  Who grewest not alone in power
  And knowledge, but by year and hour
In reverence and in charity.

———

Now fades the last long streak of snow,
  Now bourgeons every maze of quick
  About the flowering squares, and thick
By ashen roots the violets blow.

Now rings the woodland loud and long,
  The distance takes a lovelier hue,
  And drowned in yonder living blue
The lark becomes a sightless song.

Now dance the lights on lawn and lea,
  The flocks are whiter down the vale,
  And milkier every milky sail
On winding stream or distant sea;

Where now the sea mew pipes, or dives
  In yonder gleaming green, and fly
  The happy birds, that change their sky
To build and brood; that live their lives

From land to land; and in my breast
  Spring wakens too; and my regret
  Becomes an April violet,
And buds and blossoms like the rest.

———

Contemplate all this work of Time,
  The giant, laboring in his youth;
  Nor dream of human love and truth
As dying Nature's earth and lime;

But trust that those we call the dead
  Are breathers of an ampler day
  For ever nobler ends. They say
The solid earth whereon we tread

In tracts of fluent heat began,
  And grew to seeming random forms,
  The seeming prey of cyclic storms,
Till at the last arose the man—

Who throve and branched from clime to clime,
  The herald of a higher race,
  And of himself in higher place,
If so he types this work of time

Within himself, from more to more;
  And crowned with attributes of woe
  Like glories, move his course, and show
That life is not an idle ore,

But iron dug from central gloom,
  And heated hot with burning fears,
  And dipped in baths of hissing tears,
And battered with the shocks of doom

To shape and use. Arise and fly
  The reeling Faun, the sensual feast!
  Move upward, working out the beast,
And let the ape and tiger die!

COME INTO THE GARDEN, MAUD

COME into the garden, Maud—
  For the black bat, night, has flown!
Come into the garden, Maud,
  I am here at the gate alone;
And the woodbine spices are wafted abroad,
  And the musk of the roses blown.

For a breeze of morning moves,
    And the planet of Love is on high,
Beginning to faint in the light that she loves,
    On a bed of daffodil sky,
To faint in the light of the sun she loves,
    To faint in his light, and to die.

All night have the roses heard
    The flute, violin, bassoon:
All night has the casement jessamine stirred
    To the dancers dancing in tune—
Till a silence fell with the waking bird,
    And a hush with the setting moon.

I said to the lily, "There is but one
    With whom she has heart to be gay.
When will the dancers leave her alone?
    She is weary of dance and play."
Now half to the setting moon are gone,
    And half to the rising day;
Low on the sand and loud on the stone
    The last wheel echoes away.

I said to the rose, "The brief night goes
    In babble and revel and wine.
O young lord-lover, what sighs are those
    For one that will never be thine?
But mine, but mine," so I sware to the rose,
    "Forever and ever, mine!"

And the soul of the rose went into my blood,
    As the music clashed in the hall;
And long by the garden lake I stood,
    For I heard your rivulet fall
From the lake to the meadow and on to the wood—
    Our wood, that is dearer than all;—

From the meadow your walks have left so sweet
    That whenever a March-wind sighs,
He sets the jewel-print of your feet
    In violets blue as your eyes—

To the woody hollows in which we meet,
   And the valleys of Paradise.

The slender acacia would not shake
   One long milk-bloom on the tree;
The white lake-blossom fell into the lake,
   As the pimpernel dozed on the lea;
But the rose was awake all night for your sake,
   Knowing your promise to me;
The lilies and roses were all awake—
   They sighed for the dawn and thee.

Queen rose of the rosebud garden of girls,
   Come hither! the dances are done;
In gloss of satin and glimmer of pearls,
   Queen lily and rose in one;
Shine out, little head, sunning over with curls,
   To the flowers, and be their sun.

There has fallen a splendid tear
   From the passion-flower at the gate.
She is coming, my dove, my dear!
   She is coming, my life, my fate!
The red rose cries, "She is near, she is near!"
   And the white rose weeps, "She is late;"
The larkspur listens, "I hear, I hear;"
   And the lily whispers, "I wait."

She is coming, my own, my sweet!
   Were it ever so airy a tread,
My heart would hear her and beat,
   Were it earth in an earthy bed;
My dust would hear her and beat,
   Had I lain for a century dead—
Would start and tremble under her feet,
   And blossom in purple and red.

THE LADY OF SHALOTT

PART I.

On either side the river lie
Long fields of barley and of rye,
That clothe the wold and meet the sky;
And through the field the road runs by
 To many-tower'd Camelot;
And up and down the people go,
Gazing where the lilies blow
Round an island there below,
 The island of Shalott.

Willows whiten, aspens quiver,
Little breezes dusk and shiver
Through the wave that runs for ever
By the island in the river
 Flowing down to Camelot.
Four gray walls, and four gray towers,
Overlook a space of flowers,
And the silent isle imbowers
 The Lady of Shalott.

By the margin, willow-veil'd,
Slide the heavy barges trail'd
By slow horses; and unhail'd
The shallop flitteth silken-sail'd,
 Skimming down to Camelot:
But who hath seen her wave her hand?
Or at the casement seen her stand?
Or is she known in all the land,
 The Lady of Shalott?

Only reapers, reaping early
In among the bearded barley,
Hear a song that echoes cheerly
From the river winding clearly,
 Down to tower'd Camelot:
And by the moon the reaper weary,
Piling sheaves in uplands airy,
Listening, whispers " 'Tis the fairy
 Lady of Shalott."

PART II.

There she weaves by night and day
A magic web with colours gay.
She has heard a whisper say,
A curse is on her if she stay
 To look down to Camelot.
She knows not what the curse may be,
And so she weaveth steadily,
And little other care hath she,
 The Lady of Shalott.

And moving through a mirror clear
That hangs before her all the year,
Shadows of the world appear.
There she sees the highway near
 Winding down to Camelot:
There the river eddy whirls,
And there the surly village-churls,
And the red cloaks of market-girls,
 Pass onward from Shalott.

Sometimes a troop of damsels glad,
An abbot on an ambling pad,
Sometimes a curly shepherd-lad,
Or long-hair'd page in crimson clad,
 Goes by to tower'd Camelot;
And sometimes through the mirror blue
The knights come riding two and two:
She hath no loyal knight and true,
 The Lady of Shalott.

But in her web she still delights
To weave the mirror's magic sights,
For often through the silent nights
A funeral, with plumes and lights,
 And music, went to Camelot:
Or when the moon was overhead,
Came two young lovers lately wed;
"I am half-sick of shadows," said
 The Lady of Shalott.

PART III.

A bow-shot from her bower-eaves,
He rode between the barley sheaves,
The sun came dazzling through the leaves,
And flamed upon the brazen greaves
　　Of bold Sir Lancelot.
A red-cross knight for ever kneel'd
To a lady in his shield,
That sparkled on the yellow field,
　　Beside remote Shalott.

The gemmy bridle glitter'd free,
Like to some branch of stars we see
Hung in the golden galaxy.
The bridle-bells rang merrily,
　　As he rode down to Camelot;
And from his blazon'd baldric slung
A mighty silver bugle hung,
And as he rode his armour rung,
　　Beside remote Shalott.

All in the blue unclouded weather
Thick-jewell'd shone the saddle-leather,
The helmet and the helmet-feather
Burn'd like one burning flame together,
　　As he rode down to Camelot.
As often through the purple night,
Below the starry clusters bright,
Some bearded meteor, trailing light,
　　Moves over still Shalott.

His broad clear brow in sunlight glow'd;
On burnished hooves his war-horse trode;
From underneath his helmet flow'd
His coal-black curls as on he rode,
　　As he rode down to Camelot.
From the bank and from the river
He flash'd into the crystal mirror,
"Tirra lirra," by the river
　　Sang Sir Lancelot.

She left the web, she left the loom,
She made three paces through the room,
She saw the water-lily bloom,
She saw the helmet and the plume,
　　She looked down to Camelot.
Out flew the web and floated wide;
The mirror crack'd from side to side;
"The curse is come upon me," cried
　　The Lady of Shalott.

PART IV.

In the stormy east-wind straining,
The pale-yellow woods were waning,
The broad stream in his banks complaining,
Heavily the low sky raining
　　Over tower'd Camelot;
Down she came and found a boat
Beneath a willow left afloat,
And round about the prow she wrote
　　The Lady of Shalott.

And down the river's dim expanse—
Like some bold seër in a trance,
Seeing all his own mischance—
With a glassy countenance
　　Did she look to Camelot.
And at the closing of the day
She loosed the chain, and down she lay;
The broad stream bore her far away,
　　The Lady of Shalott.

Lying, robed in snowy white
That loosely flew to left and right—
The leaves upon her falling light—
Through the noises of the night
　　She floated down to Camelot:
And as the boat-head wound along
The willowy hills and fields among,
They heard her singing her last song,
　　The Lady of Shalott.

Heard a carol, mournful, holy,
Chanted loudly, chanted lowly,
Till her blood was frozen slowly,
And her eyes were darken'd wholly,
    Turn'd to tower'd Camelot;
For ere she reach'd upon the tide
The first house by the water-side,
Singing in her song she died,
    The Lady of Shalott.

Under tower and balcony,
By garden-wall and gallery,
A gleaming shape she floated by,
A corse between the houses high,
    Silent into Camelot.
Out upon the wharfs they came,
Knight and burgher, lord and dame,
And round the prow they read her name,
    The Lady of Shalott.

Who is this? and what is here?
And in the lighted palace near
Died the sound of royal cheer;
And they cross'd themselves for fear,
    All the knights at Camelot:
But Lancelot mused a little space;
He said, "She has a lovely face;
God in his mercy lend her grace,
    The Lady of Shalott."

WILLIAM MAKEPEACE THACKERAY

THE AGE OF WISDOM

Ho, pretty page, with the dimpled chin,
    That never has known the barber's shear,
All your wish is woman to win,
This is the way that boys begin,—
    Wait till you come to Forty Year.

Curly gold locks cover foolish brains,
  Billing and cooing is all your cheer;
Sighing and singing of midnight strains,
Under Bonnybell's window panes,—
  Wait till you come to Forty Year!

Forty times over let Michaelmas pass,
  Grizzling hair the brain doth clear—
Then you know a boy is an ass,
Then you know the worth of a lass,
  Once you have come to Forty Year.

Pledge me round; I bid ye declare,
  All good fellows whose beards are gray,
Did not the fairest of the fair
Common grow and wearisome ere
  Ever a month was past away?

The reddest lips that ever have kissed,
  The brightest eyes that ever have shone,
May pray and whisper, and we not list,
Or look away and never be missed,
  Ere yet ever a month is gone.

Gillian's dead, God rest her bier;
  How I loved her twenty years syne!
Marian's married, but I sit here
Alone and merry at Forty Year,
  Dipping my nose in the Gascon wine.

THE END OF THE PLAY

THE play is done; the curtain drops,
  Slow falling to the prompter's bell:
A moment yet the actor stops,
  And looks around, to say farewell.
It is an irksome word and task;
  And, when he's laughed and said his say,
He shows, as he removes the mask,
  A face that's anything but gay.

One word, ere yet the evening ends,
   Let's close it with a parting rhyme,
And pledge a hand to all young friends,
   As fits the merry Christmas time.
On life's wide scene you, too, have parts,
   That Fate ere long shall bid you play;
Good night! with honest, gentle hearts
   A kindly greeting go alway!

Good night!—I'd say, the griefs, the joys,
   Just hinted in this mimic page,
The triumphs and defeats of boys,
   Are but repeated in our age.
I'd say, your woes were not less keen,
   Your hopes more vain than those of men;
Your pangs or pleasures of fifteen
   At forty-five played o'er again.

I'd say, we suffer and we strive,
   Not less nor more as men than boys;
With grizzled beards at forty-five,
   As erst at twelve in corduroys.
And if, in time of sacred youth,
   We learned at home to love and pray,
Pray Heaven that early Love and Truth
   May never wholly pass away.

And in the world, as in the school,
   I'd say, how Fate may change and shift;
The prize be sometimes with the fool,
   The race not always to the swift.
The strong may yield, the good may fall,
   The great man be a vulgar clown,
The knave be lifted over all,
   The kind cast pitilessly down.

Who knows the inscrutable design?
   Blessed be He who took and gave!
Why should your mother, Charles, not mine,
   Be weeping at her darling's grave?

We bow to Heaven that willed it so,
  That darkly rules the fate of all,
That sends the respite or the blow,
  That's free to give, or to recall.

This crowns his feast with wine and wit:
  Who brought him to that mirth and state?
His betters, see, below him sit,
  Or hunger hopeless at the gate.
Who bade the mud from Dives' wheel
  To spurn the rags of Lazarus?
Come, brother, in that dust we'll kneel,
  Confessing Heaven that ruled it thus.

So each shall mourn, in life's advance,
  Dear hopes, dear friends, untimely killed;
Shall grieve for many a forfeit chance,
  And longing passion unfulfilled.
Amen! whatever fate be sent,
  Pray God the heart may kindly glow,
Although the head with cares be bent,
  And whitened with the winter snow.

Come wealth or want, come good or ill,
  Let young and old accept their part,
And bow before the Awful Will,
  And bear it with an honest heart.
Who misses, or who wins the prize
  Go, lose or conquer as you can:
But if you fail, or if you rise,
  Be each, pray God, a gentleman.

A gentleman, or old or young!
  (Bear kindly with my humble lays;)
The sacred chorus first was sung
  Upon the first of Christmas days:
The shepherds heard it overhead—
  The joyful angels raised it then:
Glory to Heaven on high, it said,
  And peace on earth to gentle men.

My song, save this, is little worth;
   I lay the weary pen aside,
And wish you health, and love, and mirth,
   As fits the solemn Christmas-tide.
As fits the holy Christmas birth.
   Be this, good friends, our carol still—
Be peace on earth, be peace on earth,
   To men of gentle will.

HENRY DAVID THOREAU

MIST

Low anchored cloud,
Newfoundland air,
Fountain-head and source of rivers,
Dew-cloth, dream drapery,
And napkins spread by fays;
Drifting meadow of the air,
Where bloom the daisied banks and violets,
And in whose fenny labyrinth
The bittern booms and heron wades;
Spirit of lakes and seas and rivers,—
Bear only perfumes and the scent
Of healing herbs to just men's fields.

THEODORE TILTON

BABY BYE

Baby Bye,
Here's a fly;
Let us watch him, you and I.
   How he crawls
   Up the walls,
   Yet he never falls!
I believe with six such legs
You and I could walk on eggs.
   There he goes
   On his toes,
   Tickling baby's nose.

Spots of red
Dot his head;
Rainbows on his back are spread;
        That small speck
        Is his neck;
        See him nod and beck.
I can show you, if you choose,
Where to look to find his shoes,—
        Three small pairs,
        Made of hairs;
        These he always wears.

Black and brown
Is his gown;
He can wear it upside down;
        It is laced
        Round his waist;
        I admire his taste.
Yet though tight his clothes are made,
He will lose them, I'm afraid,
        If to-night
        He gets sight
        Of the candle-light.

In the sun
Webs are spun;
What if he gets into one?
        When it rains
        He complains
        On the window-panes.
Tongue to talk have you and I;
God has given the little fly
        No such things,
        So he sings
        With his buzzing wings.

He can eat
Bread and meat;
There's his mouth between his feet.
        On his back
        Is a pack
        Like a peddler's sack.

Does the baby understand?
Then the fly shall kiss her hand;
    Put a crumb
    On her thumb,
    Maybe he will come.

Catch him? No,
Let him go,
Never hurt an insect so;
    But no doubt
    He flies out
    Just to gad about.
Now you see his wings of silk
Drabbled in the baby's milk;
    Fie, oh fie,
    Foolish fly!
    How will he get dry?

All wet flies
Twist their thighs;
Thus they wipe their heads and eyes;
    Cats, you know,
    Wash just so,
    Then their whiskers grow.
Flies have hairs too short to comb,
So they fly bareheaded home;
    But the gnat
    Wears a hat.
    Do you believe that?

Flies can see
More than we,
So how bright their eyes must be!
    Little fly,
    Ope your eye;
    Spiders are near by.
For a secret I can tell,—
Spiders never use flies well.
    Then away
    Do not stay.
    Little fly, good day.

JOHN GREENLEAF WHITTIER

BARBARA FRIETCHIE

Up from the meadows rich with corn,
Clear in the cool September morn,

The clustered spires of Frederick stand
Green-walled by the hills of Maryland.

Round about them orchards sweep,
Apple and peach tree fruited deep,

Fair as a garden of the Lord
To the eyes of the famished rebel horde;

On that pleasant morn of the early fall
When Lee marched over the mountain wall,—

Over the mountains winding down,
Horse and foot, into Frederick town.

Forty flags with their silver stars,
Forty flags with their crimson bars,

Flapped in the morning wind: the sun
Of noon looked down, and saw not one.

Up rose old Barbara Frietchie then,
Bowed with her fourscore years and ten;

Bravest of all in Frederick town,
She took up the flag the men hauled down;

In her attic window the staff she set,
To show that one heart was loyal yet.

Up the street came the rebel tread,
Stonewall Jackson riding ahead.

Under his slouched hat left and right
He glanced: the old flag met his sight.

"Halt!"—the dust-brown ranks stood fast;
"Fire!"—out blazed the rifle-blast.

It shivered the window, pane and sash;
It rent the banner with seam and gash.

Quick, as it fell, from the broken staff
Dame Barbara snatched the silken scarf;

She leaned far out on the window-sill,
And shook it forth with a royal will.

"Shoot, if you must, this old gray head,
But spare your country's flag," she said.

A shade of sadness, a blush of shame,
Over the face of the leader came;

The nobler nature within him stirred
To life at that woman's deed and word:

"Who touches a hair of yon gray head
Dies like a dog! March on!" he said.

All day long through Frederick street
Sounded the tread of marching feet:

All day long that free flag tost
Over the heads of the rebel host.

Ever its torn folds rose and fell
On the loyal winds that loved it well;

And through the hill-gaps sunset light
Shone over it with a warm good-night.

Barbara Frietchie's work is o'er,
And the Rebel rides on his raids no more.

Honor to her! and let a tear
Fall, for her sake, on Stonewall's bier.

Over Barbara Frietchie's grave,
Flag of Freedom and Union, wave!

Peace and order and beauty draw
Round thy symbol of light and law;

And ever the stars above look down
On thy stars below in Frederick town!

MAUD MULLER

MAUD MULLER, on a summer's day,
Raked the meadow sweet with hay.

Beneath her torn hat glowed the wealth
Of simple beauty and rustic health.

Singing, she wrought, and her merry glee
The mock-bird echoed from his tree.

But when she glanced to the far-off town,
White from its hill-slope looking down,

The sweet song died, and a vague unrest
And a nameless longing filled her breast—

A wish, that she hardly dared to own,
For something better than she had known.

The Judge rode slowly down the lane,
Smoothing his horse's chestnut mane.

He drew his bridle in the shade
Of the apple-trees, to greet the maid.

And ask a draught from the spring that flowed
Through the meadow, across the road.

She stooped where the cool spring bubbled up,
And filled for him her small tin cup,

And blushed as she gave it, looking down
On her feet so bare, and her tattered gown.

"Thanks!" said the Judge, "a sweeter draught
From a fairer hand was never quaffed."

He spoke of the grass and flowers and trees,
Of the singing-birds and the humming-bees;

Then talked of the haying, and wondered whether
The cloud in the west would bring foul weather:

And Maud forgot her brier-torn gown,
And her graceful ankles, bare and brown.

And listened, while a pleased surprise
Looked from her long-lashed hazel eyes.

At last, like one who for delay
Seeks a vain excuse, he rode away.

Maud Muller looked and sighed: "Ah me!
That I the Judge's bride might be!

"He would dress me up in silks so fine,
And praise and toast me at his wine.

"My father should wear a broadcloth coat;
My brother should sail a painted boat.

"I'd dress my mother so grand and gay,
And the baby should have a new toy each day.

"And I'd feed the hungry and clothe the poor,
And all should bless me who left our door."

The Judge looked back as he climbed the hill,
And saw Maud Muller standing still:

"A form more fair, a face more sweet,
Ne'er hath it been my lot to meet;

"And her modest answer and graceful air
Show her wise and good as she is fair.

"Would she were mine, and I to-day,
Like her, a harvester of hay.

"No doubtful balance of rights and wrongs,
Nor weary lawyers with endless tongues,

"But low of cattle and song of birds,
And health, and quiet, and loving words."

But he thought of his sister, proud and cold,
And his mother, vain of her rank and gold.

So, closing his heart, the Judge rode on,
And Maud was left in the field alone.

But the lawyers smiled that afternoon,
When he hummed in court an old love tune;

And the young girl mused beside the well,
Till the rain on the unraked clover fell.

He wedded a wife of richest dower,
Who lived for fashion, as he for power.

Yet oft, in his marble hearth's bright glow,
He watched a picture come and go;

And sweet Maud Muller's hazel eyes
Looked out in their innocent surprise.

Oft, when the wine in his glass was red,
He longed for the wayside well instead;

And closed his eyes on his garnished rooms,
To dream of meadows and clover blooms;

And the proud man sighed with a secret pain,
"Ah, that I were free again!

"Free as when I rode that day
Where the barefoot maiden raked the hay."

She wedded a man unlearned and poor,
And many children played round her door.

But care and sorrow, and child-birth pain,
Left their traces on heart and brain.

And oft, when the summer sun shone hot
On the new-mown hay in the meadow lot,

And she heard the little spring-brook fall
Over the roadside, through the wall,

In the shade of the apple-tree again
She saw a rider draw his rein,

And gazing down with a timid grace,
She felt his pleased eyes read her face.

Sometimes her narrow kitchen walls
Stretched away into stately halls;

The weary wheel to a spinnet turned,
The tallow candle an astral burned;

And for him who sat by the chimney lug,
Dozing and grumbling o'er pipe and mug,

A manly form at her side she saw,
And joy was duty and love was law.

Then she took up her burden of life again,
Saying only, "It might have been."

Alas for maiden, alas for Judge!
For rich repiner and household drudge!

God pity them both! and pity us all,
Who vainly the dreams of youth recall;

For of all sad words of tongue or pen,
The saddest are these: "It might have been!"

Ah, well! for us all some sweet hope lies
Deeply buried from human eyes;

And, in the hereafter, angels may
Roll the stone from its grave away!

EMMA HART WILLARD

ROCKED IN THE CRADLE OF THE DEEP

Rocked in the cradle of the deep
I lay me down in peace to sleep;
Secure I rest upon the wave,
For Thou, O Lord! hast power to save.
I know Thou wilt not slight my call,
For Thou dost mark the sparrow's fall;
And calm and peaceful shall I sleep,
Rocked in the cradle of the deep.

When in the dead of night I lie
And gaze upon the trackless sky,
The star-bespangled heavenly scroll,
The boundless waters as they roll,—
I feel Thy wondrous power to save
From perils of the stormy wave:
Rocked in the cradle of the deep,
I calmly rest and soundly sleep.

And such the trust that still were mine,
Though stormy winds swept o'er the brine,
Or through the tempest's fiery breath
Roused me from sleep to wreck and death.
In ocean cave, still safe with Thee
The gem of immortality!
And calm and peaceful shall I sleep,
Rocked in the cradle of the deep.

CHARLES WOLFE

BURIAL OF SIR JOHN MOORE

NOT a drum was heard, nor a funeral note,
   As his corse to the rampart we hurried;
Not a soldier discharged his farewell shot
   O'er the grave where our hero we buried.

We buried him darkly, at dead of night,
   The sod with our bayonets turning;
By the struggling moonbeams' misty light,
   And our lantern dimly burning.

No useless coffin inclosed his breast,
   Nor in sheet nor in shroud we wound him;
But he lay like a warrior taking his rest,
   With his martial cloak around him!

Few and short were the prayers we said,
   And we spoke not a word of sorrow;
But we steadfastly gazed on the face of the dead,
   And we bitterly thought of the morrow.

We thought, as we hollowed his narrow bed,
   And smoothed down his lonely pillow,
That the foe and the stranger would tread o'er his head
   And we far away on the billow!

Lightly they'll talk of the spirit that's gone,
   And o'er his cold ashes upbraid him;
But little he'll reck, if they let him sleep on,
   In the grave where a Briton has laid him!

But half of our heavy task was done,
   When the bell tolled the hour for retiring,
And we heard the distant and random gun
   That the foe was sullenly firing.

Slowly and sadly we laid him down,
   From the field of his fame, fresh and gory!
We carved not a line, we raised not a stone—
   But we left him alone with his glory!

SAMUEL WOODWORTH

THE OLD OAKEN BUCKET

How dear to this heart are the scenes of my childhood,
When fond recollection presents them to view!
The orchard, the meadow, the deep-tangled wild wood,
And every loved spot which my infancy knew;
The wide-spreading pond, and the mill which stood by it,
The bridge and the rock where the cataract fell;
The cot of my father, the dairy house nigh it,
And e'en the rude bucket which hung in the well;
The old oaken bucket, the iron-bound bucket,
The moss-cover'd bucket, which hung in the well.

That moss-cover'd vessel I hail as a treasure;
For often, at noon, when return'd from the field,
I found it the source of an exquisite pleasure,
The purest and sweetest that Nature can yield.
How ardent I seized it, with hands that were glowing!
And quick to the white-pebbled bottom it fell;
Then soon, with the emblem of truth overflowing,
And dripping with coolness, it rose from the well;
The old oaken bucket, the iron-bound bucket,
The moss-cover'd bucket arose from the well.

How sweet from the green mossy brim to receive it,
As poised on the curb it inclined to my lips!
Not a full blushing goblet could tempt me to leave it,
Though fill'd with the nectar that Jupiter sips.
And now, far removed from the loved situation,
The tear of regret will intrusively swell,
As fancy reverts to my father's plantation,
And sighs for the bucket which hangs in the well;
The old oaken bucket, the iron-bound bucket,
The moss-cover'd bucket, which hangs in the well

WILLIAM WORDSWORTH

WE ARE SEVEN

——A SIMPLE child,
  That lightly draws its breath,
And feels its life in every limb,
  What should it know of death?

I met a little cottage girl:
  She was eight years old, she said;
Her hair was thick with many a curl
  That clustered round her head.

She had a rustic, woodland air,
  And she was wildly clad:
Her eyes were fair, and very fair,
  —Her beauty made me glad.

"Sisters and brothers, little maid,
  How many may you be?"
"How many? Seven in all," she said,
  And wondering looked at me.

"And who are they? I pray you, tell."
  She answered, "Seven are we;
And two of us at Conway dwell,
  And two are gone to sea.

"Two of us in the churchyard lie,
　My sister and my brother;
And, in the churchyard cottage, I
　Dwell near them with my mother."

"You say that two at Conway dwell,
　And two are gone to sea,
Yet ye are seven!—I pray you tell,
　Sweet maid, how this may be."

Then did the little maid reply,
　"Seven boys and girls are we;
Two of us in the churchyard lie,
　Beneath the churchyard tree."

"You run about, my little maid,
　Your limbs they are alive;
If two are in the churchyard laid,
　Then ye are only five."

"Their graves are green, they may be seen,"
　The little maid replied,
"Twelve steps or more from my mother's door,
　And they are side by side.

"My stockings there I often knit,
　My kerchief there I hem;
And there upon the ground I sit,
　And sing a song to them.

"And often after sunset, sir,
　When it is light and fair,
I take my little porringer,
　And eat my supper there.

"The first that died was sister Jane:
　In bed she moaning lay,
Till God released her of her pain;
　And then she went away.

"So in the churchyard she was laid;
  And, when the grass was dry,
Together round her grave we played,
  My brother John and I.

"And when the ground was white with snow,
  And I could run and slide,
My brother John was forced to go,
  And he lies by her side."

"How many are you, then," said I,
  "If they two are in heaven?"
Quick was the little maid's reply,
  "O master! we are seven."

"But they are dead; those two are dead!
  Their spirits are in heaven!"
'T was throwing words away: for still
The little maid would have her will,
  And said, "Nay, we are seven!"

LUCY GRAY

Oft I had heard of Lucy Gray:
  And when I cross'd the wild,
I chanced to see at break of day
  The solitary child.

No mate, no comrade Lucy knew;
  She dwelt on a wide moor,
The sweetest thing that ever grew
  Beside a human door!

You yet may spy the fawn at play,
  The hare upon the green;
But the sweet face of Lucy Gray
  Will never more be seen.

'To-night will be a stormy night—
You to the town must go;
And take a lantern, Child, to light
Your mother through the snow.'

'That, Father! will I gladly do:
'Tis scarcely afternoon—
The minster-clock has just struck two,
And yonder is the moon!'

At this the father raised his hook,
And snapp'd a faggot-band;
He plied his work;—and Lucy took
The lantern in her hand.

Not blither is the mountain roe:
With many a wanton stroke
Her feet disperse the powdery snow,
That rises up like smoke.

The storm came on before its time:
She wander'd up and down;
And many a hill did Lucy climb:
But never reach'd the town.

The wretched parents all that night
Went shouting far and wide;
But there was neither sound nor sight
To serve them for a guide.

At day-break on a hill they stood
That overlook'd the moor;
And thence they saw the bridge of wood
A furlong from their door.

They wept—and, turning homeward, cried
'In heaven we all shall meet!'
—When in the snow the mother spied
The print of Lucy's feet.

Then downwards from the steep hill's edge
They track'd the footmarks small;
And through the broken hawthorn hedge,
And by the long stone-wall:

And then an open field they cross'd:
The marks were still the same;
They track'd them on, nor ever lost;
And to the bridge they came:

They follow'd from the snowy bank
Those footmarks, one by one,
Into the middle of the plank;
And further there were none!

—Yet some maintain that to this day
She is a living child;
That you may see sweet Lucy Gray
Upon the lonesome wild.

O'er rough and smooth she trips along,
And never looks behind;
And sings a solitary song
That whistles in the wind.

DAFFODILS

I WANDERED lonely as a cloud
  That floats on high o'er vales and hills,
When all at once I saw a crowd,
  A host, of golden daffodils;
Beside the lake, beneath the trees,
Fluttering, dancing in the breeze.

Continuous as the stars that shine
  And twinkle on the Milky Way,
They stretched in never-ending line
  Along the margin of a bay:
Ten thousand saw I at a glance,
Tossing their heads in sprightly dance.

The waves beside them danced, but they
  Outdid the sparkling waves in glee;
A poet could not but be gay
  In such a jocund company;
I gazed, and gazed, but little thought
What wealth the show to me had brought:

For oft, when on my couch I lie,
  In vacant or in pensive mood,
They flash upon that inward eye
  Which is the bliss of solitude;
And then my heart with pleasure fills,
And dances with the daffodils.

TO THE CUCKOO

O blithe new-comer! I have heard,
I hear thee and rejoice:
O Cuckoo! shall I call thee Bird,
Or but a wandering Voice?

While I am lying on the grass
Thy twofold shout I hear;
From hill to hill it seems to pass,
At once far off and near.

Though babbling only to the vale
Of sunshine and of flowers,
Thou bringest unto me a tale
Of visionary hours.

Thrice welcome, darling of the Spring!
Even yet thou art to me
No bird, but an invisible thing,
A voice, a mystery;

The same whom in my school-boy days
I listen'd to; that Cry
Which made me look a thousand ways
In bush, and tree, and sky.

To seek thee did I often rove
Through woods and on the green;
And thou wert still a hope, a love;
Still long'd for, never seen!

And I can listen to thee yet;
Can lie upon the plain
And listen, till I do beget
That golden time again.

O blessèd Bird! the earth we pace
Again appears to be
An unsubstantial, faery place,
That is fit home for Thee!

SHE WAS A PHANTOM OF DELIGHT

SHE was a phantom of delight
When first she gleamed upon my sight;
A lovely apparition, sent
To be a moment's ornament.
Her eyes as stars of twilight fair;
Like twilight's, too, her dusky hair;
But all things else about her drawn
From May-time and the cheerful dawn—
A dancing shape, an image gay,
To haunt, to startle, and waylay.

I saw her upon nearer view,
A spirit, yet a woman too!
Her household motions light and free,
And steps of virgin liberty;
A countenance in which did meet
Sweet records, promises as sweet;
A creature, not too bright or good
For human nature's daily food—
For transient sorrows, simple wiles,
Praise, blame, love, kisses, tears, and smiles.

And now I see with eye serene
The very pulse of the machine;
A being breathing thoughtful breath,
A traveler between life and death;
The reason firm, the temperate will,
Endurance, foresight, strength, and skill;
A perfect woman, nobly planned,
To warn, to comfort, and command;
And yet a spirit still, and bright
With something of an angel-light.

I TRAVELL'D AMONG UNKNOWN MEN

I travell'd among unknown men
    In lands beyond the sea;
Nor, England! did I know till then
    What love I bore to thee.

'Tis past, that melancholy dream!
    Nor will I quit thy shore
A second time; for still I seem
    To love thee more and more.

Among thy mountains did I feel
    The joy of my desire;
And she I cherish'd turn'd her wheel
    Beside an English fire.

Thy mornings show'd, thy nights conceal'd
    The bowers where Lucy play'd;
And thine too is the last green field
    That Lucy's eyes survey'd.

UPON WESTMINSTER BRIDGE

Earth has not anything to show more fair:
Dull would be of soul who could pass by
A sight so touching in its majesty:
This City now doth, like a garment, wear
The beauty of the morning; silent, bare,
Ships, towers, domes, theatres, and temples lie
Open unto the fields, and to the sky;
All bright and glittering in the smokeless air.
Never did sun more beautifully steep
In his first splendor, valley, rock or hill;
Ne'er saw I, never felt, a calm so deep!
The river glideth at his own sweet will:
Dear God! the very houses seem asleep;
And all that mighty heart is lying still!

RESOLUTION AND INDEPENDENCE

There was a roaring in the wind all night;
The rain came heavily and fell in floods;
But now the sun is rising calm and bright;
The birds are singing in the distant woods;
Over his own sweet voice the Stock-dove broods;
The Jay makes answer as the Magpie chatters;
And all the air is filled with pleasant noise of waters.

All things that love the sun are out of doors;
The sky rejoices in the morning's birth;
The grass is bright with rain-drops;—on the moors
The hare is running races in her mirth;
And with her feet she from the plashy earth
Raises a mist, that, glittering in the sun,
Runs with her all the way, wherever she doth run.

POEMS OF TODAY
JOAQUIN MILLER
COLUMBUS

Behind him lay the grey Azores,
  Behind the Gates of Hercules;
Before him not the ghost of shores,
  Before him only shoreless seas.
The good mate said: "Now must we pray,
  For lo! the very stars are gone.
Brave Admiral, speak, what shall I say?"
  "Why, say 'Sail on! sail on! and on!'"

"My men grow mutinous day by day;
  My men grow ghastly wan and weak."
The stout mate thought of home; a spray
  Of salt wave washed his swarthy cheek.
"What shall I say, brave Admiral, say,
  If we sight naught but seas at dawn?"
"Why, you shall say at break of day,
  'Sail on! sail on! sail on! and on!'"

They sailed and sailed, as winds might blow,
  Until at last the blanched mate said,
"Why, now not even God would know
  Should I and all my men fall dead.
These very winds forget their way,
  For God from these dread seas is gone.
Now speak, brave Admiral, speak and say"—
  He said: "Sail on! sail on! and on!"

They sailed. They sailed. Then spake the mate:
  "This mad sea shows his teeth tonight.
He curls his lips, he lies in wait,
  With lifted teeth, as if to bite!
Brave Admiral, say but one good word:
  What shall we do when hope is gone?"
The words leapt like a leaping sword:
  "Sail on! sail on! sail on! and on!"

Then, pale and worn, he kept his deck,
  And peered through darkness. Ah, that night
Of all dark nights! And then a speck—
  A light! a light! a light! a light!
It grew, a starlit flag unfurled!
  It grew to be Time's burst of dawn.
He gained a world; he gave that world
  Its grandest lesson: "On, sail on!"

EMILY DICKINSON

I NEVER SAW A MOOR

I never saw a moor,
I never saw the sea;
Yet know I how the heather looks,
And what a wave must be.

I never spoke with God,
Nor visited in heaven;
Yet certain am I of the spot
As if the chart were given.

WALT WHITMAN

MIRACLES

Why, who makes much of a miracle?
As to me I know of nothing else but miracles,
Whether I walk the streets of Manhattan,
Or dart my sight over the roofs of houses toward the sky,
Or wade with naked feet along the beach just in the edge
  of the water,
Or stand under trees in the woods,
Or talk by day with any one I love, ...
Or watch honey-bees busy around the hive of a summer forenoon,
Or animals feeding in the fields,

Or birds, or the wonderfulness of insects in the air,
Or the wonderfulness of the sundown, or of stars
    shining so quiet and bright,
Or the exquisite delicate thin curve of the new moon
    in spring;
These with the rest, one and all, are to me miracles, ...
To me every hour of the light and dark is a miracle, ...
To me the sea is a continual miracle,
The fishes that swim—the rocks—the motion of the waves—
    the ships with men in them.
What stranger miracles are there?

KATHERINE LEE BATES

AMERICA THE BEAUTIFUL

O beautiful for spacious skies,
    For amber waves of grain,
For purple mountain majesties
Above the fruited plain!
    America! America!
God shed His grace on thee
And crown they good with brotherhood
From sea to shining sea!

O beautiful for patriot dream
    That sees beyond the years
Thine alabaster cities gleam
Undimmed by human tears!
    America! America!
God shed His grace on thee
And crown thy good with brotherhood
From sea to shining sea!

JOHN MASEFIELD

THE WEST WIND

It's a warm wind, the west wind, full of birds' cries;
I never hear the west wind but tears are in my eyes.
For it comes from the west lands, the old brown hills,
And April's in the west wind and daffodils.

It's fine land, the west land, for hearts as tired as mine,
Apple orchards blossom there, and the air's like wine.
There is cool green grass there, where men may lie at rest,
And the thrushes are in song there, fluting from the nest.

"Will you not come home, brother? You have been long away,
It's April, and blossom time, and white is the spray;
And bright is the sun, brother, and warm is the rain,—
Will you not come home, brother, home to us again?

The young corn is green, brother, where the rabbits run;
It's blue sky, and white clouds, and warm rain and sun.
It's song to a man's soul, brother, fire to a man's brain,
To hear the wild bees and see the merry spring again.

Larks are singing in the west, brother, above the green wheat,
So will you not come home, brother, and rest your tired feet?
I've a balm for bruised hearts, brother, sleep for aching eyes,"
Says the warm wind, the west wind, full of birds' cries.

It's the white road westwards is the road I must tread
To the green grass, the cool grass, and rest for heart and head,
To the violets and the brown brooks and the thrushes' song,
In the fine land, the west land, the land where I belong.

ALFRED NOYES

THE BARREL-ORGAN

There's a barrel-organ caroling across a golden street
  In the City as the sun sinks lows;
And the music's not immortal; but the world has made it sweet
  And fulfilled it with the sunset glow;
And it pulses through the pleasures of the City and the pain
  That surround the singing organ like a large eternal light;
And they've given it a glory and a part to play again
  In the Symphony that rules the day and night.
And now it's marching onward through the realms of old romance,
  And trolling out a fond familiar tune,
And now it's roaring cannon down to fight the King of France,
  And now it's prattling softly to the moon.
And all around the organ there's a sea without a shore
  Of human joys and wonders and regrets;
To remember and to recompense the music evermore
  For what the cold machinery forgets . . .
              Yes; as the music changes,
                Like a prismatic glass,
              It takes the light and ranges
                Through all the moods that pass:
              Dissects the common carnival
                Of passions and regrets,
              And gives the world a glimpse of all
                The colors it forgets.
              And there *La Traviata* sighs
                Another sadder song;
              And there *Il Trovatore* cries
                A tale of deeper wrong;
              And bolder knights to battle go
                With sword and shield and lance,
              Than ever here on earth below
                Have whirled into—a dance!—
Go down to Kew in lilac-time, in lilac-time, in lilac-time;
  Go down to Kew in lilac-time (it isn't far from London!)
And you shall wander hand in hand with love in summer's wonderland;
  Go down to Kew in lilac-time (it isn't far from London!)

The cherry-trees are seas of bloom and soft perfume and sweet perfume,
  The cherry-trees are seas of bloom (and oh, so near to London!)
And there they say, when dawn is high and all the world's a blaze
  of sky
  The cuckoo, though he's very shy, will sing a song for London.
The nightingale is rather rare and yet they say you'll hear him there
  At Kew, at Kew in lilac-time (and oh, so near to London!)
The linnet and the throstle, too, and after dark the long halloo
  And golden-eyed *tu-whit, tu-whoo* of owls that ogle London.
For Noah hardly knew a bird of any kind that isn't heard
  At Kew, at Kew in lilac-time (and oh, so near to London!)
And when the rose begins to pout and all the chestnut spires are out
  You'll hear the rest without a doubt, all chorusing for London:—
Come down to Kew in lilac-time, in lilac-time, in lilac-time;
  Come down to Kew in lilac-time (it isn't far from London!)
And you shall wander hand in hand with love in summer's wonderland;
  Come down to Kew in lilac-time (it isn't far from London!)
And then the troubadour begins to thrill the golden street,
  In the City as the sun sinks low;
And in all the gaudy busses there are scores of weary feet
Marking time, sweet time, with a dull mechanic beat,
And a thousand hearts are plunging to a love they'll never meet,
Through the meadows of the sunset, through the poppies and the
  wheat,
  In the land where the dead dreams go.
Verdi, Verdi, when you wrote *Il Trovatore* did you dream
  Of the City where the sun sinks low,
Of the organ and the monkey and the many-colored stream
On the Piccadilly pavement, of the myriad eyes that seem
To be litten for a moment with a wild Italian gleam
As *A che la morte* parodies the world's eternal theme
  And pulses with the sunset-glow?

There's a thief, perhaps, that listens with a face of frozen stone
  In the City as the sun sinks low;
There's a portly man of business with a balance of his own,
There's a clerk and there's a butcher of a soft reposeful tone,
And there all of them returning to the heavens they have known:
They are crammed and jammed in busses and—they're each of
    them alone
  In the land where the dead dreams go.
There's a labourer that listens to the voices of the dead
  In the City as the sun sinks low;
And his hand begins to tremble and his face is rather red
As he sees a loafer watching him and—there he turns his head
And stares into the sunset where his April love is fled,
For he hears her softly singing and his lonely soul is led
  Through the land where the dead dreams go . . .
There's a barrel-organ caroling across a golden street
  In the City as the sun sinks low;
Though the music's only Verdi there's a world to make it sweet
Just as yonder yellow sunset where the earth and heaven meet
Mellows all the sooty City! Hark, a hundred thousand feet
Are marching on to glory through the poppies and the wheat
  In the land where the dead dreams go.
            So it's Jeremiah, Jeremiah,
                What have you to say
            When you meet the garland girls
                Tripping on their way?
            All around my gala hat
                I wear a wreath of roses
            (A long and lonely year it is
                I've waited for the May!)
            If any one should ask you,
                The reason why I wear it is—
            My own love, my true love, is coming
                home today.

And it's buy a bunch of violets for the lady
 (It's lilac-time in London; it's lilac-time in London!)
Buy a bunch of violets for the lady;
 While the sky burns blue above:
On the other side the street you'll find it shady
 (It's lilac-time in London; it's lilac-time in London!)
But buy a bunch of violets for the lady,
 And tell her she's your own true love.
There's a barrel-organ caroling across a golden street
 In the City as the sun sinks glittering and slow;
And the music's not immortal; but the world has made it sweet
And enriched it with the harmonies that make a song complete
In the deeper heavens of music where the night and morning meet,
 As it dies into the sunset glow;
And it pulses through the pleasures of the City and the pain
 That surround the singing organ like a large eternal light,
And they've given it a glory and a part to play again
 In the Symphony that rules the day and night.
                    And there, as the music changes,
                        The song runs round again;
                    Once more it turns and ranges
                        Through all its joy and pain:
                    Dissects the common carnival
                        Of passions and regrets;
                    And the wheeling world remembers all
                        The wheeling song forgets.
                    Once more *La Traviata* sighs
                        Another sadder song:
                    Once more *Il Trovatore* cries
                        A tale of deeper wrong;
                    Once more the knights to battle go
                        With sword and shield and lance
                    Till once, once more, the shattered foe
                        Has whirled into—a dance!
 Come down to Kew in lilac-time, in lilac-time, in lilac-time;
  Come down to Kew in lilac-time (it isn't far from London!)
 And you shall wander hand in hand with Love in summer's wonder-
   land,
  Come down to Kew in lilac-time (it isn't far from London!)

WALTER DE LA MARE

THE LISTENERS

"Is there anybody there?" said the Traveler,
  Knocking on the moonlit door;
And his horse in the silence champed the grasses
  Of the forest's ferny floor.
And a bird flew up out of the turret,
  Above the Traveler's head:
And he smote upon the door again a second time;
  "Is there anybody there?" he said.
But no one descended to the Traveler;
  No head from the leaf-fringed sill
Leaned over and looked into his gray eyes,
  Where he stood perplexed and still.
But only a host of phantom listeners
  That dwelt in the lone house then
Stood listening in the quiet of the moonlight
  To that voice from the world of men:
Stood thronging the faint moonbeams on the dark stair
  That goes down to the empty hall,
Hearkening in an air stirred and shaken
  By the lonely Traveler's call.
And he felt in his heart their strangeness,
  Their stillness answering his cry,
While his horse moved, cropping the dark turf,
  'Neath the starred and leafy sky;
For he suddenly smote on the door, even
  Louder, and lifted his head:—
"Tell them I came, and no one answered,
  That I kept my word," he said.
Never the least stir made the listeners,
  Though every word he spake
Fell echoing through the shadowiness of the still house
  From the one man left awake:
Aye, they heard his foot upon the stirrup,
  And the sound of iron on stone,
And how the silence surged softly backward,
  When the plunging hoofs were gone.

WILLIAM BUTLER YEATS

THE LAKE ISLE OF INNISFREE

I will arise and go now, and go to Innisfree,
And a small cabin build there, of clay and wattles made:
Nine bean rows will I have there, a hive for the honey bee,
And live alone in the bee-loud glade.

And I shall have some peace there, for peace comes dropping slow,
Dropping from the veils of the morning to where the cricket sings;
There midnight's all a glimmer, and noon a purple glow,
And evening full of the linnet's wings.

I will arise and go now, for always night and day
I hear lake water lapping with low sounds by the shore;
While I stand on the roadway, or on the pavements gray,
I hear it in the deep heart's core.

JAKE FALSTAFF

TO A WANDERER

While you have gone around the earth,
   A wanderer and alone,
I have stayed soberly behind,
   A gril's cheek on my own.

When you are sick of foreign lands
   And oceans breaker-pearled,
Come home and I will tell you of
   The wonders of the world.

EDWIN ARLINGTON ROBINSON

THE MASTER
(Lincoln)

A flying word from here and there
Had sown the name at which we sneered,
But soon the name was everywhere,
To be reviled and then revered:
A presence to be loved and feared,
We cannot hide it, or deny
That we, the geneltmen who jeered,
May be forgotten by and by.

He came when days were perilous
And hearts of men were sore beguiled;
And having made his note of us,
He pondered and was reconciled.
Was ever master yet so mild
As he, and so untamable?
We doubted, even when he smiled,
Not knowing what he knew so well.

He knew that undeceiving fate
Would shame us whom he served unsought;
He knew that he must wince and wait—
The jest of those for whom he fought;
He knew devoutly what he thought
Of us and of our ridicule;
He knew that we must all be taught
Like little children in a school.

We gave a glamor to the task
That he encountered and saw through,
But little of us did he ask,
And little did we ever do.
And what appears if we review
The season when we railed and chaffed?
It is the face of one who knew
That we were learning while we laughed.

The face that in our vision feels
Again the venom that we flung,
Transfigured to the world reveals
The vigilance to which we clung.
Shrewd, hallowed, harassed, and among
The mysteries that are untold,
The face we see was never young
Nor could it wholly have been old.

For he, to whom we had applied
Our shopman's test of age and worth,
Was elemental when he died,
As he was ancient at his birth:
The saddest among kings of earth,
Bowed with a galling crown, this man
Met rancour with a cryptic mirth,
Laconic—and Olympian.

The love, the grandeur, and the fame
Are bounded by the world alone;
The calm, the smouldering, and the flame
Of awful patience were his own:
With him they are forever flown
Past all our fond self-shadowings,
Wherewith we cumber the Unknown
As with inept, Icarian wings.

For we were not as other men:
'Twas ours to soar and his to see;
But we are coming down again,
And we shall come down pleasantly;
Nor shall we longer disagree
On what it is to be sublime,
But flourish in our perigee
And have one Titan at a time.

ROBERT FROST

MENDING WALL

Something there is that doesn't love a wall,
That sends the frozen-ground-swell under it,
And spills the upper boulders in the sun;
And makes gaps even two can pass abreast.
The work of hunters is another thing:
I have come after them and made repair
Where they have left not one stone on a stone,
But they would have the rabbit out of hiding,
To please the yelping dogs. The gaps I mean,
No one has seen them made or heard them made,
But at spring mending-time we find them there.
I let my neighbor know beyond the hill;
And on a day we meet to walk the line
And set the wall between us once again.
We keep the wall between us as we go.
To each the boulders that have fallen to each.
And some are loaves and some so nearly balls
We have to use a spell to make them balance:
"Stay where you are until our backs are turned!"
We wear our fingers rough with handling them.
Oh, just another kind of out-door game,
One on a side. It comes to little more:
There where it is we do not need the wall:
He is all pine and I am all apple-orchard.
My apple trees will never get across
And eat the cones under his pines, I tell him.
He only says, "Good fences make good neighbors."
Spring is the mischief in me, and I wonder
If I could put a notion in his head:
"*Why* do they make good neighbors? Isn't it
Where there are cows? But here there are no cows.
Before I built a wall I'd ask to know
What I was walling in or walling out,
And to whom I was like to give offence.
Something there is that doesn't love a wall,
That wants it down!" I could say "elves" to him,

But it's not elves exactly, and I'd rather
He said it for himself. I see him there,
Bringing a stone grasped firmly by the top
In each hand, like an old-stone savage armed.
He moves in darkness, as it seems to me,
Not of woods only and the shade of trees.
He will not go behind his father's saying,
And he likes having thought of it so well
He says again, "Good fences make good neighbors."

CARL SANDBURG

EVENING WATERFALL

What was the name you called me?—
And why did you go so soon?

The crows lift their caw on the wind,
And the wind changed and was lonely.

The warblers cry their sleepy-songs
Across the valley gloaming,
Across the cattle-horns of early stars.

Feathers and people in the crotch of a treetop
Throw an evening waterfall of sleepy-songs.

What was the name you called me?—
And why did you go so soon?

SARA TEASDALE

SPRING NIGHT

The park is filled with night and fog,
  The veils are drawn about the world,
The drowsy lights along the paths
  Are dim and pearled.

Gold and gleaming the empty streets,
  Gold and gleaming the misty lake,
The mirrored lights like sunken swords,
  Glimmer and shake.
Oh, is it not enough to be
Here with this beauty over me?
My throat should ache with praise, and I
Should kneel in joy beneath the sky.
O beauty, are you not enough?
Why am I crying after love
With youth, a singing voice, and eyes
To take earth's wonder with surprise?
Why have I put off my pride,
Why am I unsatisfied,—
I, for whom the pensive night
Binds her cloudy hair with light,—
I, for whom all beauty burns
Like incense in a million urns?
O beauty, are you not enough?
Why am I crying after love?

A. E. HOUSMAN

LOVELIEST OF TREES

Loveliest of trees, the cherry now
Is hung with bloom along the bough,
And stands about the woodland ride
Wearing white for Eastertide.

Now, of my threescore years and ten,
Twenty will not come again,
And take from seventy springs a score,
It only leaves me fifty more.

And since to look at things in bloom
Fifty springs are little room,
About the woodlands I will go
To see the cherry hung with snow.

EDNA ST. VINCENT MILLAY

GOD'S WORLD

O world, I cannot hold thee close enough!
   Thy winds, thy wide gray skies!
   Thy mists, that roll and rise!
Thy woods, this autumn day, that ache and sag
And all but cry with color! That gaunt crag
To crush! To lift the lean of that black bluff!
World, world, I cannot get thee close enough!

Long have I known a glory in it all,
   But never knew I this,
   Here such a passion is
As stretcheth me apart. Lord, I do fear
Thou'st made the world too beautiful this year.
My soul is all but out of me—let fall
No burning leaf; prithee, let no bird call.